Proceedings of the *Académie Internationale de Philosophie des Sciences*

Comptes Rendus de l'Académie Internationale de Philosophie des Sciences

Tome III

Models and Representations in Science

Tome I
Science's Voice of Reflection
Gerhard Heinzmann and Benedikt Löwe, Éditeurs

Tome II
Justification, Creativity, and Discoverability in Science
Lorenzo Magnani, Éditeur

Tome III
Models and Representations in Science
Hans-Peter Grosshans, Éditeur

Models and Representations in Science

Éditeur

Hans-Peter Grosshans

© Individual author and College Publications 2025
All rights reserved.

ISBN 978-1-84890-480-4

College Publications, London
Scientific Director: Dov Gabbay
Managing Director: Jane Spurr

http://www.collegepublications.co.uk

Original cover design by Laraine Welch

All rights reserved. No part of this publication may be reproduced, stored in a retrieval system or transmitted in any form, or by any means, electronic, mechanical, photocopying, recording or otherwise without prior permission, in writing, from the publisher.

Table of Contents

Preface
Hans-Peter Grosshans   vii–x

Thought experiments, computer simulations, and real world
experiments in scientific knowledge: a comparison
Marco Buzzoni   1–17

Models and representation in functional realism
Alberto Cordero   19–38

Non-standard realistic models of quantum phenomena
and new forms of complementarity
Niccolò Covoni, Giovanni Macchia, Davide Pietrini, and Gino Tarozzi   39–54

Science and scientific realism: challenges from quantum physics
Dennis Dieks   55–72

Models or theories: what is the real representation in science?
Jan Faye   73–89

The structural view of representation: a defence
Michel Ghins   91–116

Model and normativity
On the relation of nature—technology—ethics
Elisabeth Gräb-Schmidt   117–127

What do models in theology represent?
Hans-Peter Grosshans   129–138

Scientific cognition based on models as epistemic warfare
Do scientific models serve as epistemic weapons or fictions?
Lorenzo Magnani   139–156

Models and representation in science:
for a new image of the objectivity of knowledge
Fabio Minazzi   157–197

Scientific worldviews and models in Hermann von Helmholtz
and Werner Heisenberg
Gregor Schiemann   199–208

The requirement of total evidence:
epistemic optimality and political relevance
Gerhard Schurz   209–225

What logic represents
Johan van Benthem   227–241

Models, representation, and idealization
Revisiting the inferentialism debate
Jesús Zamora Bonilla   243–259

Preface

Models have recently become increasingly important in academia and the public sphere, particularly given the Covid-19 pandemic and discourses on climate change. How can we describe their relationship to what they represent and make conceivable? The essays in this volume discuss this fundamental question in the philosophy of science and engage with the understanding, function and use of models in various academic disciplines. In all sciences—whether natural, technical or life sciences, social sciences or humanities—models are important for understanding, conceiving and explaining complex relations within the realm of knowledge and reality. All sciences work with models, which are then taken as a given, although every scientist knows that the model may not produce conclusive knowledge about something. One must then necessarily reflect on the difference between the model and the reality the model depicts.

The *Académie Internationale de Philosophie des Sciences* (AIPS) discussed these and many other questions at its annual conference from 26 to 29 September 2023 at the University of Münster (Germany). This third volume of the *Comptes Rendus de l'Académie Internationale de Philosophie des Sciences* contains a selection of the papers presented at the conference.

In order to document the full programme of the conference and the work of the AIPS, all the papers presented at the conference should be listed here in the preface:

Tuesday, 26 September 2023. Fürstenberghaus, Room F2, Domplatz 20–22, 48143 Münster.

9.00–9.30. Welcome of Participants. Chair: Hans-Peter Grosshans. Speakers: Michael Quante, Vice-Rector of the University of Münster & Jure Zovko, President of the AIPS.

9.30–10.15. Johan van Benthem (Amsterdam, Netherlands): *The importance of representation in enabling logical reasoning.*

10.15–11.00. Itala Loffredo d'Ottaviano (São Paulo, Brazil): *Partial-structures and partial-truth in science.*

11.00–11.15. Coffee Break.

11.15–12.00. Chen Bo (Wuhan, China): *Does logic represent this world and our mind? Yes!*

12.00–12.45. Hannes Leitgeb (München, Germany): *On non-representational parts of models.*

13.00–15.30. Lunch Break.

15.30–16.15. Demetris Portides (Nicosia, Cyprus): *Idealization and abstraction in scientific models.*

16.15–17.00. Michel Ghins (Louvain, Belgium): *A defence of the structural view of scientific representation.*

- **17.00–17.45.** Jean-Guy Meunier (Montréal, Canada): *Modeling computer assisted conceptual analysis from philosophical texts.*
- **17.45–18.00.** Coffee Break.
- **18.00–18.45.** Pablo Lorenzano (Buenos Aires, Argentina): *Models and theory construction: structuralist and models in scientific practice programs.*
- **18.45–19.30.** Bernard Feltz (Louvain, Belgium): *Modelling and simulating in biology: a comparative approach.*
- **20.00.** Dinner Restaurant Mimigernaford (Bült 23).

Wednesday, 27 September 2023. Fürstenberghaus, Room F2, Domplatz 20–22, 48143 Münster.

- **9.00–9.45.** Atocha Aliseda Llera (Mexico City, Mexico): *Models of change.*
- **9.45–10.30.** Jure Zovko & Jörn Witt (Zadar, Croatia & Düsseldorf, Germany): *Diagnosis as an explanatory model of reality: Philosophical-medical approaches.*
- **10.30–11.15.** Lorenzo Magnani (Pavia, Italy): *Model-based scientific cognition as epistemic warfare.*
- **11.15–11.30.** Coffee Break.
- **11.30–12.15.** Hans-Jörg Rheinberger (Berlin, Germany): *Modelling in experimentation.*
- **12.15–13.00.** John Symons (Kansas, United States of America): *What is the scientific value of machine learning models?*
- **13:00–15:30.** Lunch Break.
- **15.30–16.15.** Gerhard Schurz (Düsseldorf, Germany): *The Principle of total evidence: Justification and political significance.*
- **16.15–17.00.** Gino Tarozzi (Urbino, Italy): *Non-standard realistic models of quantum phenomena and new forms of complementarity.*
- **17.00–17.15.** Coffee Break.
- **17.15–18.00.** Jesus Pedro Zamora Bonilla (Madrid, Spain): *Models and representations in an inferential-deflationary view of scientific knowledge.*
- **18.00–18.45.** Marco Buzzoni (Macerata, Italy): *Thought experiments and computer simulations: a comparison.*
- **20.00.** Dinner Restaurant Mocca d'or (Rothenburg 14).

Thursday, 28 September 2023. Fürstenberghaus, Room F2, Domplatz 20–22, 48143 Münster.

- **9.00–9.45.** Alberto Cordero (New York, United States of America): *Models and representation in functional realism.*

- **9.45–10.30.** Anjan Chakravartty (Miami, United States of America): *Models of science education and representations of science.*
- **10.30–11.15.** Martin Carrier (Bielefeld, Germany): *Model-building in practice-driven research.*
- **11.15–11.30.** Coffee Break.
- **11.30–12.15.** Gregor Schiemann (Wuppertal, Germany): *Scientific worldviews and models in Hermann von Helmholtz and Werner Heisenberg.*
- **12.15–13.00.** Jan Faye (Copenhagen, Denmark): *Models or theories: what is the real representation in science?*
- **13:00–15:00.** Lunch Break.
- **15.00–15.45.** Hans-Peter Grosshans (Münster, Germany): *What do models in theology represent?*
- **15.45–16.30.** Elisabeth Gräb-Schmidt (Tübingen, Germany): *Model and normativity: On the relation of nature—technology—ethics.*
- **16.30–19.30.** *Assemblée Générale de l'Académie Internationale de Philosophie des Sciences.*
- **20.15.** Gala dinner Mövenpick Restaurant (Kardinal-von-Galen-Ring 65).

- **Friday, 29 September 2023.** Fürstenberghaus, Room F2, Domplatz 20–22, 48143 Münster.
- **9.00–9.45.** Harvey Brown (Oxford, England): *Do symmetry principles explain conservation laws in physics? Lessons from the modern (first) Noether theorem.*
- **9.45–10.30.** Dennis Dieks (Utrecht, Netherlands): *Factivity of representation in science.*
- **10.30–11.15.** Otavio Bueno (Miami, United States of America): *Empiricism and microscopy.*
- **11.15–11.30.** Coffee Break.
- **11.30–12.15.** James McAllister (Leiden, Netherlands): *Are empirical data representations?*
- **12.15–13.00.** Reinhard Kahle (Tübingen, Germany): *Hilbert on sciences.*
- **13:00–15:30.** Lunch Break.
- **15.30.** City tour & visit to the museums in Münster.
- **19.30.** Dinner Restaurant A2 am See (Annette-Allee 3).

As editor of this volume and organiser of the conference, I am very grateful to all those who made the conference and the publication possible. I would like to thank those who presented papers at the conference and those who made their contributions available for this publication. I would like to thank Benedikt Löwe for the editorial work and Ivana Nicolić, the secretary of AIPS, for her coordination. With the great support of my research assistants Lena Mausbach, Daniel Scheuermann and Jan Turck, and my student assistants Jantje Bartels, Marcel Ide and Ephraim Schäfer, the conference became a well-organised and enjoyable event, for which I am very grateful. Finally, I would like to thank the Alfred Kärcher GmbH & Co. KG and its CEO, Hartmut Jenner, for their generous financial support of the conference, as well as the University of Münster and my own Chair of Systematic Theology for their substantial financial contributions.

Münster, Westfalen H.-P.G.
November 2024

Thought experiments, computer simulations, and real world experiments in scientific knowledge: a comparison

Marco Buzzoni

Sezione di Filosofia e Science Umane, Università di Macerata, via Garibaldi 20, 62110 Macerata, Italy

Abstract. The purpose of this paper is to restate, in a more concise form and taking into account some articles subsequently appeared in the literature, the main point of a previous article regarding the relationship between real world experiments, computer simulations and (empirical) thought experiments. After distinguishing four main families of accounts which have emerged in the literature, it is argued that they, although each contains an element of truth, have failed to distinguish between real experiment, computer simulation and thought experiment. In fact, concerning the empirical intension of the respective concepts, it is a hopeless task to find a qualitative difference which applies exclusively to thought experiments, computer simulations, or real experiments. For every particular characteristic of one of these notions there is a corresponding characteristic in the two others. However, from another point of view, there is between thought experiment and computer simulation on the one hand, and real experiment (or empirical knowledge) on the other, an epistemological-reflective difference which we must not overlook. Unlike computer simulations and thought experiments, real experiments always involve an 'external' or impersonal realisation, namely that of what I propose to call an 'experimental-technical machine', always in causal-real interaction with the experimenter's body.

1 Introduction

The purpose of this paper is to restate, in a more concise form and taking into account some articles subsequently appeared in the literature, a point made elsewhere (cf. Buzzoni 2016) regarding the relationship between real world experiments (hereafter REs), computer simulations (hereafter CSs) and (empirical) thought experiments (hereafter TEs). After distinguishing four main families of accounts which have emerged in the literature, it is argued that they, although each contains an element of truth, have failed to distinguish between RE, CS and TE (Section 2). In the second part of the paper, I shall briefly outline my own account on this topic. To avoid comparisons that are insignificant or of little importance for the philosophy of science, it will be convenient to compare TEs and CSs with real world experiments (hereafter REs). To take the notion of RE as the basis of comparison between CS and TE will enable us not only to better understand the methodological similarities between CS, TE and RE, but also to find a subtle but important distinction between CS and TE. I shall maintain that—from the perspective of the analysis of the empirical-methodological intensions of the respective concepts—it is a hopeless task to find a particular methodological trait which applies exclusively to TE, CS, or RE. However, from another point of view, there is between TE and CS on the one hand, and RE on the other an epistemological (or transcendental) difference which we must not overlook. An aspect of the difference between CSs and REs reverberates in the relationship between TE and CS: CSs involve an 'external' realisation, which explains some differences in degree between TEs and CS (for example, the usually greater methodological complexity of the latter).

2 Four families of accounts on the relationship between TE and CS

Two preliminary remarks are in order before we plunge *in medias res*:

1) In first approximation, I shall presuppose the broad sense of CS defined by Winsberg 2013 in its authoritative entry for the Stanford Encyclopedia of Philosophy (now confirmed in the 2019 updated version):

> we can think of computer simulation as a comprehensive method for studying systems. In this broader sense of the term, it refers to an entire process. This process includes choosing a model; finding a way of implementing that model in a form that can be run on a computer; calculating the output of the algorithm; and visualizing and studying the resultant data. The method includes this entire process—used to make inferences about the target system that one tries to model—as well as the procedures used to sanction those inferences. (Winsberg 2013/2019)

2) Here, however, I am interested above all in empirical TEs and CSs, that is, TEs and CSs whose results are liable to correction by new experimental findings. TEs and CSs in formal disciplines deserve a separate treatment, and a fortiori the same applies to philosophical TEs (on these distinct kinds of TE, see Buzzoni 2011, 2022 and 2021).

With this in mind, I propose to distinguish four main families of accounts of the relationship between TE and CS. According to the first view, there is close similarity, or even an identity, of TEs and CSs because "thought experimenting is a form of 'simulative model-based reasoning'" (Nersessian 1992, p. 291; see also Miščević 1992 and 2007, Palmieri 2003, Gendler 2004, Misselhorn 2005, Cooper 2005, Morrison 2009, and Chandrasekharan, Nersessian, and Subramanian 2013). In TEs we manipulate mental models instead of physical models, and we gain knowledge through TEs only to the extent that they contain a manipulation of some mental model.

As far as TEs are concerned (but, *mutatis mutandis*, this also holds true of CSs), the main difficulty with this approach consists in the fact that it seems to assume mental mediators in order to explain how words relate semantically to the world. In both cases, "something must be said about how they acquire their semantical properties." (Häggqvist 1996, p. 81) The upholders of this view have attempted to overcome this problem with the introduction of some "engineering" (Nersessian 2006) or manipulative (cf. Miščević 2007) constraints in their theorizing. But it is only a metaphorical and loose way of speaking: we cannot manipulate mental models in the same way in which we manipulate objects and processes of everyday life.

Moreover, this view has led to treat TEs as a sort of mere provisional means that someday will be abandoned in favour of CSs. The complexity of the natural systems that scientists and engineers are modelling today would be such that the relationship between the different elements of natural systems cannot be captured through TEs, but only by the new computational visualization tools that are being developed in computer science: "computational modeling is largely replacing thought experimenting, and the latter will play only a limited role in future practices of science, especially in the sciences of complex nonlinear, dynamical phenomena." (Chandrasekharan, Nersessian, and Subramanian 2013, p. 239)

As we shall see later, it is true that, generally speaking, there is a difference in degree between CSs and TEs, but, taken as it stands, this claim is a prediction about human knowledge, and therefore it may be considered as a kind of "promissory eliminativism" (in Popper's sense) concerning TEs. As such, it is undermined by Popper's argument according to which, "if there is such a thing as growing human knowledge, then we cannot anticipate to-day what we shall know only tomorrow." (Popper 1957 [1961], italics in original).

The second view to be examined is defended by authors who follow Norton's theory that TEs can be reconstructed as arguments based on both tacit and explicit assumptions (cf., e.g., Norton 1996, pp. 336; see also Norton 1991 and 2004). Following Norton's account, they have drawn a detailed comparison between TE and CS (Stäudner 1998; Stöckler 2000; Velasco 2002; Beisbart 2012, Beisbart and Norton 2012). According to Beisbart, for example, to the crucial question how scientists gain new knowledge, "[t]he argument view answers this question by saying that computer simulations are arguments." (Beisbart 2012, p. 429) Stäudner 1998 made the most detailed comparison between TEs and CSs. As he sums up his results:

> The initial equations that we are striving to solve, together with the relevant boundary values, form a set of 'premises'. The numerical procedure by means of which we calculate the solutions we are looking for corresponds to a 'logical type of inference', that is to a determinate form of argument. The result of the calculation is the 'conclusion'. As in valid arguments true conclusions follow from true premises, we may consider the result of the calculation of a simulation as an adequate

description of nature if the 'premises' contain adequate descriptions of nature, in the sense that they are empirically confirmed and therefore belong to the well-established 'theoretical patrimony' of the natural sciences. (Stäudner 1998, p. 157; see also p. 8)

The difficulties of this approach are the same as those of Norton's view. For Norton, TEs "are arguments which (i) posit hypothetical or counterfactual states of affairs, and (ii) invoke particulars irrelevant to the generality of the conclusion" (Norton 1991, p. 129; see also Norton 1996, 2004a and 2004b). For Norton, TEs can always be reconstructed as deductive or inductive arguments ("reconstruction thesis") and, more importantly, they must always be evaluated as such:

> The outcome is reliable only insofar as our assumptions are true and the inference valid [...] [W]hen we evaluate thought experiments as epistemological devices, the point is that we should evaluate them as arguments. A good thought experiment is a good argument; a bad thought experiment is a bad argument. (Norton 1996, p. 336)

Many methodological objections can be and have been raised in the literature against Norton's account, but for our purposes the main weakness is that it tends to undermine any distinction between empirical and formal knowledge. Even though in a TE this or that particular empirical element may be "irrelevant to the generality of the conclusion" (for example, in Einstein's lift experiment it is irrelevant whether the observer is or is not a physicist), it is not irrelevant that TEs are generally performed by constructing particular cases, which need concrete elements that are in principle reproducible in specific spatio-temporally individuated situations. TEs, stripped of any reference to concrete experimental situations, are confined to a domain of purely theoretical statements and demonstrative connections. As a result, empirical TEs are reduced to logico-mathematical arguments (on this point, see especially Buzzoni 2008, pp. 67–68 and Stuart 2016).

Now, this same difficulty applies to Beisbart's claim of important features common to CSs and arguments. Given the equation of CS with argument, the same difficulty comes to light that has been noticed in Norton's view about TEs, that is, of reducing empirical TEs to logical arguments. In order to remove this difficulty, in his first papers on CSs Beisbart adopted two strategies. First, he suggested that "running a computer simulation may be thought of as the execution of an argument" (Beisbart 2012, p. 423; this point is interpreted by Beisbart in the light of the extended mind hypothesis of Clark and Chalmers (1998); on this point, as far as CS is concerned, see also Charbonneau 2010). However, this is in contradiction with Beisbart's explicit rejection of the idea that CSs produce new knowledge because they are real world experiments (Beisbart 2012, pp. 425), a thesis which indeed would have undermined his whole argument view. According to the extended mind thesis, cognitive systems may extend beyond a human being. But if the construction of what might be called an 'experimental machine', which extends the original operativity of our organic body, is treated as a part of the mind, there can be no difference in principle between TE and CS on the one hand and RE on the other.

Moreover, Beisbart 2012 accepts the idea that CSs, unlike TEs, are "opaque" and must be explored. This, however, is an autonomous third line of interpretation of the relationships between TE and CS, which we have now to examine separately. As Di Paolo et al. 2000 write:

> A thought experiment has a conclusion that follows logically and clearly, so that the experiment constitutes in itself an *explanation* of its own conclusion and its implications. [...] In contrast, a simulation can be much more powerful and versatile, but at a price. This price is one of *explanatory opacity*: the behaviour of a simulation is not understandable by simple inspection. (Di Paolo et al. 2000, p. 502; cf. also Bedau 1999, Buschlinger 1993, Lenhard & Winsberg 2010).

At least two objections may be raised against this position, and all support the conclusion that opacity must be relativized to a background context and cannot be treated as an absolute concept. First, 'opacity' is no hallmark of CSs (or REs) in contrast with TEs. Indeed, in this regard there is only a difference of degree between CSs and TEs, that is, a difference that may be turned upside down in particular cases: a very simple CS may be less opaque than many TEs (such as Einstein's black body radiation TE: cf. Norton 1991). Moreover, this thesis presupposes that TEs have a kind of almost Cartesian clearness, which, at least apparently, like that of Descartes' *cogito*, would be static and without a history. This presupposition has been probably inspired by Hacking's claim that, while REs "have a life of their own", TEs "are rather fixed, largely immutable". But this thesis is untenable. To see this, it is sufficient to recall the history of the interpretations of the most important TEs (such as Maxwell's Demon or Galileo's falling bodies).

The second objection is even more serious, since it concerns a fundamental trait of scientific thinking. A particular truth-claim resulting from a CS may be considered as scientific only under the condition that it is in principle intersubjectively testable. CSs must consist in concrete methodical procedures which we may, at least in principle, reconstruct, re-appropriate and evaluate in the first person. No matter how complicated the 'modellization' or even 'mechanization' of cognitive performances may be, if we accept the results of a CS, we presuppose that any change concerning the hardware/software may be in principle reconstructed and reappropriated in the first person (this is also true of a random number generation) (for this objection, Buzzoni 2008 and 2016).

According to the fourth view, CSs are considered as intimately connected with real experiments. Recently, the relationship between CS and traditional experimentation has attracted more and more attention (cf. Galison 1996; Keller 2003; Parker 2010; Morrison 2009; Chandrasekharan, Nersessian, and Subramanian 2013; Guala 2002, 2005; Morgan 2002, 2005; Norton and Suppe 2001; Winsberg 2003 [2010]; Küppers and Lenhard 2005a; and 2005b, Lenhard 2007). Among these authors, the thesis most frequently recurring is that a CS is, as Winsberg has called it, a "hybrid of experiment and theory" (Winsberg 2003 [2010], p. 220. For a similar view, see Norton and Suppe 2001; Guala 2002, 2005; Morgan 2002, 2005; Küppers and Lenhard 2005a—who speak of a "quasi-empirical character" of CSs—and 2005b; Lenhard 2007). Other authors have emphasized the experimental aspects of CSs to such an extent that the latter are considered as falling under the more general concept of experiment (cf. esp. Morrison 2009 and Norton and Suppe 2001). As Norton and Suppe 2001 write:

> Simulations often are alleged to be only heuristic or ersatz substitutes for real experimentation and observation. This will be shown false. Properly deployed simulation models are scientific instruments that can be used to probe real-world systems. Thus, simulation models are just another source of empirical data. (Norton and Suppe 2001, p. 87)

We can, of course, undertake no minute discussion of the many varieties of this approach. I shall confine myself to criticising the claim that CSs provide knowledge in the same way as that in which experiments do. It was rightly noted that a computer simulation may give us information about the actual world, only because "we have independent evidence of the model's significance": "we will know whether or not the theory of cosmic defects is adequate, not via computer experiments, but through the use of satellite-based instruments." (Hughes 1999, p. 142; a similar objection has been made, among others, by Muldoon 2007, p. 882; Frigg & Reiss 2009; Beisbart 2012, p. 245).

But this objection should be formulated in a more radical form, by saying that in a RE the construction of an experimental setup that extends the original operativity of our organic body is connected not only to the "method of variation"—as emphasized by Mach—, but also to the causal interaction between our organic body and the 'experimental machine' that actually makes up a scientific experiment. On the contrary, in the case of CS, our 'contact' with reality is always mediated by models, to which real objects may or may not correspond (Buzzoni 2008).

One might try to elude this difficulty, as Lusk 2016 did, by maintaining that "insofar as certain common forms of measurement interact with their target and return new knowledge of their target system, simulations, under certain conditions, can as well." (p. 145) But this is not the point: the point is that in the case of CSs we cannot causally interact with the intended target in the same causal sense in which we interact with real word objects by experimenting, that is, by means of our organic body.

This point applies as much to the account of Lusk (2016) as it does to those of Johannes Lenhard and Claus Beisbart. According to Johannes Lenhard, the process of simulation modelling

> takes the form of an explorative cooperation between experimenting and modeling and that it is this characteristic mode of modeling that turns simulations into autonomous mediators in a specific way; namely, it makes it possible for the phenomena and the data to exert a direct influence on the model. (Lenhard 2007, pp. 176–177)

Although not citing Lenhard, this is also the view that Beisbart, clearly changing his mind, has developed since 2018. Now Beisbart argues that CSs, while not essentially arguments (as previously argued), bear many similarities to real-world experiments, while not identifying with them. This is possible because, although they are not REs, they "can model possible experiments and do often do so. Using this suggestion, we can account for the similarities between experiments and CSs without unduly assimilating the two methods." (Beisbart 2018, p. 173)

In this way the author rightly distinguishes CSs and REs, but he is no longer able to distinguish CSs and empirical TEs. He might reply that, even though he admits that intervention and observation can be modeled in a CS *study*, this happens in a different way:

> In a CS study, the simulationalist can set the initial conditions and the values of important parameters, and this is in fact what is often done. This is similar to manipulation and activities of control on the part of the experimenter in an experiment. [...] In some cases, the simulationalist may even consciously imitate the activities typical of an experimenter. We can thus say that simulation scientists can make quasi-interventions that reflect possible interventions in experiments. (Beisbart 2018, p. 194)

However, this is by no means sufficient to distinguish empirical CSs not only, as already mentioned, from REs, but also from empirical TEs, which are empirical only insofar as they contain explicit or implicit reference to a set-up that is in principle, first, realizable and, second, capable of entering into causal interaction with our body. Thus, when he speaks of "quasi-intervention" in a simulation in order to express with greater accuracy his point of view, he reveals de facto his difficulty in distinguishing between CSs and TEs of the empirical type. And the same applies to the claim that the model targeted in a CS is "an imagined experiment," an expression by which Beisbart would like to distinguish the conceptual content of CSs from that of TEs, but which, by a singular irony, was used many times in the past precisely as a synonym for "thought experiment."

It is therefore no accident that many statements by Beisbart are reminiscent of similar statements made by this or that author about empirical TEs: "Other simulations assume that the laws of nature are different from those in this world. [...] Setting the initial conditions and tinkering around with several parameters can nevertheless be conceptualized as a surrogate for an intervention, if only one that is not physically possible to us, but which would be of interest." (Beisbart 2018, pp. 196–197)

In sum, Beisbart is able to distinguish CSs and real world experiments only at the cost of confusing CSs and TEs. This is not only contrary to his explicit intent to distinguish CSs from both TEs and REs, but more importantly it fails to take into account the essential epistemological difference between CSs and REs that we have already pointed out and that also undermines Lenhard's sophisticated analyses: in every CS the real interaction between the experimenter's body and empirical reality is lost, at least in its operational sense.

I shall return to the importance of this point later in order to consistently conceive of a relationship of unity and distinction between CSs and REs on the one hand and CS and TE on the other.

3 Computer simulations and thought experiments vs. real world experiments

In the second part of this paper, I shall briefly outline an account of CSs as compared with TEs that manages to avoid at least some of the difficulties we have just considered.

According to Mach, the principle of economy is not only the source of science as such—and hence of REs—, but also of thought experimentation: We experiment with thought, so to say, at a low price because our own ideas are more easily and readily at our disposal than physical facts (Mach 1905a, p. 183–184, Engl. Transl., pp. 136–137). Moreover, both real world experiments and TEs are based on the "method of variation" (*Methode der Variation*): while in REs it is natural circumstances, in TEs it is representations that are made to vary in order to see the consequences of those variations (cf. Mach 1905a, 1905b, 1905c, 1883).

Now such similarities between TEs and REs may be easily extended to include CSs: on the one hand, historically speaking, CSs also aroused out 'economical' reasons in the broad sense in which the term was used by Mach (cf. Keller 2003); on the other hand, it is difficult to deny that CSs are also based on the "method of variation".

But it is very easy to find many other similarities. For instance: 1) TEs, CSs and REs are constituted by a theory and a particular, well-specified experimental situation (Buzzoni 2013, pp. 97–98); 2) all of them ask questions about nature and its laws in a theory-laden and idealized way, so that the meaning of all of them must always be interpreted; 3) in all cases visualisation, perspicuity, intuitive appeal, and clarity are important because TEs, CSs and REs apply general hypotheses to particular cases that are relevant for testing their truth or falsity (for the importance of visualisation in CSs, see for example Winsberg 2003 [2010] and Beisbart 2012).

For this reason, there is a prima facie ground for maintaining a much more radical thesis. We shall argue that it is no coincidence that we find so many similarities between REs, TEs, and CSs in the literature, since these similarities can in principle be multiplied without limit. From the perspective of the analysis of the empirical intensions of the respective concepts, REs, TEs, and CSs show only differences in degree, not in kind.

In order not only to justify, but also to restrict the meaning of this thesis, it will be best to discuss a point of contact between TE and CS that I have already mentioned. As Mach pointed out, when faced with the slightest doubt about the conclusions of a TE, we have to resort to REs:

> The outcome of a thought experiment [...] can be so definite and decisive that any further test by means of a physical experiment, whether rightly or wrongly, may seem unnecessary to the author. [...] The more uncertain and more indefinite the outcome is, however, the more the thought experiment pushes towards the *physical experiment* as its natural continuation, which must now intervene to complete and determine it. (Mach 1905a, pp. 185, Engl. Transl., pp. 137–138; italics restored and translation modified)

It is true that TEs and CSs have a certain autonomy as regards experience in the sense that both anticipate an answer to a theoretical problem without resorting directly to REs. Empirical TEs and CSs anticipate, at the linguistic-theoretical or representational level, a hypothetical experimental situation so that, on the basis of previous knowledge, we are confident that certain interventions on some variables will modify some other variables, with such a degree of probability that the actual execution of a corresponding real world experiment becomes superfluous.

But Mach was right, since this autonomy is only a relative one. If someone puts two coins, and then two more coins into an empty money box, I know that there are now four coins in that money box, and I will persist in that knowledge even if, say, the money box immediately afterwards falls into a deep lake so that I will never again be able to count how many coins it contains. But this knowledge can never outstrip our initial knowledge as to its certainty or degree of justification: for example, if the person that put the coins into the money box was a conjurer, this might cause doubts about the box's content that could be dispelled only by resorting to experience.

Similarly, if in the simulation of a hurricane there appeared objects that my background knowledge told me should not appear, I might be faced by a difficulty that only a real test, in the last analysis, could solve in the most reliable way.

The just mentioned difference between TEs and CSs on the one hand and REs on the other, is a very important exception to the rule that, from the perspective of the analysis of the empirical-methodological intensions of the respective concepts, REs, TEs, and CSs do not essentially differ. But strictly speaking this is no exception because it expresses not an empirical, but an epistemological or reflective-transcendental difference between TE and CS on the one hand, and REs on the other.

More precisely, this epistemological-transcendental difference has two distinct, but related, sides or senses, one subjective and one objective. The subjective side consists in the capacity of the mind to anticipate a hypothetical or counterfactual experimental situation. From this point of view, what TEs and CSs have over and above real ones is only the fact that they exist in a purely hypothetical sphere. But this transcendental difference has also an objective counterpart: what REs have over and above TEs and CSs is only the fact that they are the expression of causal-operational interactions between our bodies and the surrounding reality.

In this connection, Kant's example of a hundred dollars is very instructive. On the one hand, "the real contains no more than the merely possible. A hundred real thalers do not contain the least coin more than a hundred possible thalers." On the other hand, "My financial position is, however, affected very differently by a hundred real thalers than it is by the mere concept of them (that is, of their possibility). For the object, as it actually exists, is not analytically contained in my concept, but is added to my concept (which is a determination of my state) synthetically" (KrV B 627, AA III 401).

It is interesting to note that the epistemological-transcendental difference between TE and CS on the one hand and RE on the other is the true reason of the fact that the intensions of the concepts of TEs, CSs, and REs coincide, as do the hundred real dollars and the hundred merely thought ones. Every (empirical) TE or CS corresponds to a real one that satisfies the same conceptual characteristics, and vice versa. *All REs may also be thought of as realisations of TEs or CSs; conversely, all empirical TEs and CSs must be conceivable as preparing and anticipating RE: They must, that is, anticipate a connection between objects which, when thought of as realised, makes TE and CS coincide completely with the corresponding RE.*

As we shall see now, an aspect of this last difference reverberates in the relationship between TE and CS. Briefly stated: any simulation, even a computer one, involves a kind of *real* execution, one that is not merely psychological or conceptual. In TEs the subject uses in the first person concepts, inferences, etc.; in contrast, REs and CSs involve, in a very particular sense, an 'external' realisation, so that we can reconstruct them only *ex post* (reconstructed *ex ante*, they are TEs again!). In a CS, the striking of certain keys is followed by a sequence of actual physical steps, i.e., the operations carried out by the hardware and the software, with the appearance of certain signs on the screen or in the print-out. As in REs (though in a distinct sense), this execution depends on us for its realisation only in the initial moment when we set off its 'mechanism'. The initial action is followed by a real process that occurs independently of a perceiving mind and ends, for example, with a pointer moving on a dial.

Thus, CS has two distinct aspects: on the one hand, as TE does, it anticipates an answer to a theoretical problem without resorting directly to experience. On the other hand, the similarities between the two should not obscure the distinction between the *hypothetical-counterfactual* context where the test of a hypothesis is planned, and the *real* context where this plan is actually carried out. CSs share the first aspect with TEs, and the second with real ones. A plan for testing the relevant hypothesis must have been devised before CSs get under way (this holds also for "experimental simulations", such as that of a car prototype in a wind tunnel). But CSs involve an application of logics and mathematics to reality which is, in the last analysis, a technical-practical execution.

From this point of view, we may recognize certain elements of truth in Di Paolo et al. 2000's opacity thesis, in Fritz Rohrlich's claim that CS provides a new and different methodology for the physical sciences (Rohrlich 1990), and finally in Lenhard's thesis that "while thought experiments are a cognitive process that employs intuition, simulation experiments rest on automated iterations of formal algorithms." (Lenhard 2018, p. 484; cf. also Roman Frigg and Julian Reiss 2009). The realisation involved in a CS is different in meaning from the causal interactions occurring in REs: as Hughes aptly says, when physicists talk of 'running experiments on the computer', they presumably do not mean that CSs are performed to learn something about computers. But this suggests at least one of the reasons for the *de facto* greater methodological complexity of CSs in comparison with TEs. Accuracy, error analysis, calibration, and in general the management of uncertainty, though not peculiar to CSs, are *de facto* concepts that we encounter more frequently in discussing CSs than TEs (cp. above all Winsberg 2003 [2010], and Muldoon 2007).

4 Conclusion

The main conclusions, at which we have arrived so far, may be briefly summed up as follows:

1) The attempts to find a distinction in logical kind between TEs, CSs and REs from an empirical-operational or methodological sense break down: for every particular characteristic of one of these notions there is a corresponding characteristic in the others.

2) There is a difference in kind (an epistemological-reflective difference) between TEs and CSs on the one hand and REs on the other (which, on reflection, is the deepest reason of their similarities!).

3) An aspect of this last difference reverberates in the relationship between TE and CS. CSs involve an 'external' realisation, which must be carefully distinguished from that involved in REs, since CSs are not performed to learn something about computers.

References

Bedau M. 1999. Can unrealistic computer models illuminate theoretical biology? In: Wu A.S. (ed.), *Proceedings of the 1999 Genetic and Evolutionary Computation Conference Workshop Program*, pp. 20–23. Morgan Kaufmann, San Francisco.

Beisbart C. 2012. How can computer simulations produce new knowledge? *European Journal for Philosophy of Science*, 2, pp. 395–434.

Beisbart C 2018. Are computer simulations experiments? And if not, how are they related to each other? *European Journal for Philosophy of Science*, 8, pp.171–204.

Beisbart C. and J. D. Norton 2012. Why Monte Carlo Simulations Are Inferences and Not Experiments. *International Studies in the Philosophy of Sciences*, 26, pp. 403–422.

Buschlinger W. 1993. *Denk-Kapriolen? Gedankenexperimente in Naturwissenschaften, Ethik und Philosophy of Mind*. Königshausen & Neumann, Würzburg.

Buzzoni M. 2008. *Thought Experiment in the Natural Sciences*. Königshausen & Neumann, Würzburg.

Buzzoni M. 2011. On Mathematical Thought Experiments. *Epistemologia. An Italian Journal for Philosophy of Science*, 34, pp. 5–32.

Buzzoni M. 2013. Thought Experiments from a Kantian Point of View. In: J. R. Brown, M. Frappier, L. Meynell (eds.), *Thought Experiments in Philosophy, Science, and the Arts*, pp. 90–106. Routledge, London/New York.

Buzzoni M 2016. Thought Experiments and Computer Simulations, in: L. Magnani and C. Casadio (eds.), *Model-Based Reasoning in Science and Technology. Logical, Epistemological, and Cognitive Issues*. Springer, Heidelberg-New York 2016, pp. 57–78.

Buzzoni M 2019. Thought Experiments in Philosophy: A Neo-Kantian and Experimentalist Point of View, *Topoi*, 38, pp. 771–779.

Buzzoni M 2021. A Neglected Chapter in the History of Philosophy of Mathematical Thought Experiments: Insights from Jean Piaget's Reception of Edmond Goblot, in *HOPOS*, 2021, 11(1), pp. 282–304.

Buzzoni M 2022. Are there Mathematical Thought Experiments? *Axiomathes* 2022, 32, pp. 1–16.

Chandrasekharan S., Nersessian N.J, and Subramanian Vrishali V. 2013. Computational Modeling. Is This the End of Thought Experiments in Science? In: M. Frappier, L. Meynell, and J. R. Brown (eds.), *Thought Experiments in Philosophy, Science, and the Arts*, pp. 239–260. Routledge, London.

Charbonneau M. 2010. Extended Thing Knowledge. *Spontaneous Generations*, 4, pp. 116–128.

Clark A., and Chalmers D. J. 1998. The Extended Mind. *Analysis*, 541, 7–19.

Cooper R. 2005. Thought experiments. *Metaphilosophy*, 3, pp. 328–347.

Di Paolo E. A., Noble J. and Bullock S. 2000. Simulation Models as Opaque Thought Experiments. In: M. Bedau (ed.), *Artificial Life VII. Proceedings of the Seventh International Conference on Artificial Life*, pp. 497–506. MIT Press, Cambridge MA.

Frigg R. and Reiss J. 2009. The Philosophy of Simulation: Hot New Issues or Same Old Stew? *Synthese*, 169, pp. 593–613.

Galison P. 1996. Computer Simulations and the Trading Zone. In: P. Galison and D. Stump (eds.), *The Disunity of Science: Boundaries, Contexts, and Power*, pp. 118–157. Stanford University Press, Stanford.

Gendler T. 2004. Thought Experiments Rethought—and Reperceived. *Philosophy of Science*, 71, pp. 1152–1164.

Guala F. 2002. Models, Simulations, and Experiments. In: L. Magnani and N. Nersessian (eds.), *Model-Based Reasoning: Science, Technology, Values*, pp. 59–74. Kluwer, New York.

Guala F. 2005. *The Methodology of Experimental Economics.* Cambridge University Press, Cambridge.

Hacking I. 1993. Do Thought Experiments have a Life of Their Own?, *Proceedings of the Philosophy of Science Association*, 2, pp. 302–308.

Häggqvist S. 1996. *Thought Experiments in Philosophy.* Almqvist & Wiksell International, Stockholm.

Hughes R. I. G. 1999. The Ising Model, Computer Simulation, and Universal Physics. In: M. S. Morgan and M. Morrison (eds.), *Models as Mediators*, pp. 97–146. Cambridge University Press, Cambridge.

Keller E. F. 2003. Models, Simulation, and 'Computer Experiments. In: Hans Radder (ed.), *The Philosophy of Scientific Experimentation*, pp. 198–215. University of Pittsburgh Press, Pittsburgh.

Küppers G., & Lenhard J. 2005a. Computersimulationen: Modellierungen 2. Ordnung. *Journal for General Philosophy of Science*, 36, pp. 305–329.

Küppers G., & Lenhard J. 2005b. Validation of Simulation: Patterns in the Social and Natural Sciences. *Journal of Artificial Societies and Social Simulation*, 8, 4.

Lenhard J. 2007. Computer simulation: The cooperation between experimenting and modeling. *Philosophy of Science*, 74, 1, pp. 76–194.

Lenhard J. 2018. Thought Experiments and Simulation Experiments. Exploring Hypothetical Worlds. In: M. Stuart, Y. Fehige, and J. R. Brown(eds.), *The Routledge Companion to Thought Experiments*, pp. 484–497. Routledge, London/New York.

Lenhard J., & Winsberg E. 2010. Holism, entrenchment, and the future of climate model pluralism. *Studies in History and Philosophy of Science Part B*, 41, 253–262.

Lusk G. 2016. Computer simulation and the features of novel empirical data. *Studies in History and Philosophy of Science, Part A*, 56, pp. 145–152.

Mach E. 1883 [1933]. *Die Mechanik in ihrer Entwickelung. Historisch-kritisch dargestellt*, Brockhaus, Leipzig (9th ed., Leipzig 1933). Engl. Transl. T. J. McCormack, *The Science of Mechanics. A Critical and Historical Account of its Development.* Kegan Paul and Open Court, Chicago and London, 1919 (fourth edition).

Mach E. 1905a. Über Gedankenexperimente, in: *Erkenntnis und Irrtum*, Leipzig, Barth, 1905 (5th ed. 1926), pp. 183–200 (ch. xi). Engl. Transl. T. J. McCormack (chapters xxi and xxii) and P. Foulkes (all other material), On Thought Experiments. In E. Mach, *Knowledge and Error*, Reidel, Dordrecht (Holland) and Boston (U.S.A.), 1976, pp. 134–147.

Mach E. 1905b, Das physische Experiment und dessen Leitmotive, in: *Erkenntnis und Irrtum*, Leipzig, Barth (5th ed. 1926), 201–219 (ch. xii). Engl. Transl. T. J. McCormack (chapters xxi and xxii) and P. Foulkes (all other material), Physical Experiment and its Leading Features, in E. Mach, *Knowledge and Error*, Reidel, Dordrecht (Holland) and Boston (U.S.A.), 1976, pp. 148–161.

Mach E. 1905c. Die Hypothese, in: *Erkenntnis und Irrtum*, Barth, Leipzig, 1905, 5th ed. 1926, pp. 232–250 (ch. xiv). Engl. Transl. T. J. McCormack (chapters xxi and xxii) and P. Foulkes (all other material), Hypothesis, in E. Mach, *Knowledge and Error*, transl. T. J. McCormack, Reidel, Dordrecht (Holland) and Boston (U.S.A.), 1976, pp. 171–184.

Miščević N. 1992. Mental Models and Thought Experiments. *International Studies in the Philosophy of Science*, 6, pp. 215–226.

Miščević N. 2007, Modelling Intuitions and Thought Experiments. *Croatian Journal of Philosophy*, 7, pp. 181–214.

Misselhorn C. 2005. *Wirkliche Möglichkeiten – Mögliche Wirklichkeiten*. Mentis, Paderborn.

Morgan M. S. 2002. Model Experiments and Models in Experiments. In: L. Magnani and N. Nersessian (eds.), *Model-Based Reasoning: Science, Technology, Values*, pp. 41–58. Kluwer, New York.

Morgan M. S. 2005. Experiments versus models: New phenomena, inference and surprise. *Journal of Economic Methodology*, 12:2, pp. 317–329.

Morrison M. 2009. Models, measurement and computer simulation: The changing face of experimentation. *Philosophical Studies*, 143, pp. 33–57.

Muldoon R. 2007. Robust Simulations. *Philosophy of Science*, 74, pp. 873–883.

Nersessian N. 1992. How Do Scientists Think? Capturing the Dynamics of Conceptual Change in Science. In: R. Giere (ed.), *Cognitive Models of Science*, pp. 3–44. University of Minnesota Press, Minneapolis.

Nersessian N. 1993. In the Theoretician's Laboratory: Thought Experimenting as Mental Modeling. In: D. Hull, M. Forbes, and K. Okruhlik (eds), *PSA 1992*, vol. 2, pp. 291–301, Philosophy of Science Association, East Lansing, MI.

Nersessian N. 2006. Model-Based Reasoning in Distributed Cognitive Systems. *Philosophy of Science*, 73, pp. 699–709.

Norton J. D. 1991. Thought experiments in Einstein's work. In: T. Horowitz & G. J. Massey (eds.), *Thought Experiments in Science and Philosophy*, pp. 129–144. Rowman and Littlefield, Savage, MD.

Norton J. D. 1996. Are thought experiments just what you thought? *Canadian Journal of Philosophy*, 26, pp. 333–366.

Norton J. 2004a. Why thought experiments do not transcend empiricism. In: C. Hitchcock (ed.), *Contemporary Debates in the Philosophy of Science*, pp. 44–66. Blackwell, Oxford.

Norton J. 2004b. On Thought Experiments: Is There More to the Argument? *Philosophy of Science*, 71, pp. 1139–1151 (Proceedings of the Biennial Meeting of the Philosophy of Science Association, Milwaukee, Wisconsin).

Norton S. and Suppe F. 2001. Why Atmospheric Modeling is Good Science. In: C. A. Miller and P. Edwards (eds.), *Changing the Atmosphere: Expert Knowledge and Environmental Governance*, pp. 67–106. MIT Press, Cambridge, MA.

Palmieri P. 2003. Mental models in Galileo's early mathematization of nature. *Studies in History and Philosophy of Science*, 34, pp. 229–264.

Parker W. S. 2010. An Instrument for What? Digital Computers, Simulation and Scientific Practice. *Spontaneous Generations: A Journal for the History and Philosophy of Science*, 4, pp. 39–44.

Popper K. 1957 [1961]. *The Poverty of Historicism*. Routledge, London and New York (quotations are from the 3th edition, 1961).

Rohrlich F. 1991. Computer Simulation in the Physical Sciences. *PSA 1990*, Vol. 2, pp. 507–518 (East Lansing, MI, The Philosophy of Science Association).

Stäudner F. 1998. *Virtuelle Erfahrung. Eine Untersuchung über den Erkenntniswert von Gedankenexperimenten und Computersimulationen in den Naturwissenschaften*. Diss. Friedrich-Schiller-Universität, Erlangen.

Stöckler M. 2000. On modeling and simulations as instruments for the study of complex systems. In: M. Carrier, G. J. Massey, & L. Ruetsche (eds.), *Science at the Century's End: Philosophical Questions on the Progress and Limits of Science*, pp. 355–373. University of Pittsburgh Press, Pittsburgh, PA.

Stuart M. 2016. Norton and the Logic of Thought Experiments. *Axiomathes* 26, pp. 451–466.

Velasco M. 2002. The use of computational simulations in experimentation. *Theoria* (new series), 17, pp. 317–331.

Winsberg E. 2003 [2010]. Simulated Experiments: Methodology for a Virtual World. Philosophy of Science, 70, pp. 105–125, reprinted in E. Winsberg. *Science in the Age of Computer Simulation*. University of Chicago Press, Chicago, 2010.

Winsberg E. 2013/2019. Computer Simulations in Science. In: E. N. Zalta (ed.), *Stanford Encyclopedia of Philosophy*. Summer 2013 edition/Winter 2019 edition.

Models and representation in functional realism

Alberto Cordero

CUNY Graduate Center, 365 Fifth Avenue, New York NY 10016, United States of America & Philosophy Department, Queens College, City University of New York, 65–30 Kissena Blvd, Flushing NY 11367, United States of America

> **Abstract.** Selective realists confine ontological commitment to the scientifically established content of theories, but critics complain that the selection criteria used let in regrettable choices. Part of the trouble is that the selection requirements leave the ontology approved for commitment unclear. This paper provides clarifications that shift the realist stance toward functional and effective theoretical content in successful theories—i.e., content focused on what the entities and processes posited do rather than what they ultimately are. Historical anticipations of the proposed turn are traced, and their contemporary relevance is considered, followed by a discussion of some reservations about approaching scientific realism in functionalist terms.

1 Background

This is how Ernan McMullin saw the link between scientific practice and realism at the start of the current debate between realists antirealists:

> The near-invincible belief of scientists is that we come to discover more and more of the entities of which the world is composed through the constructs around which scientific theory is built. (McMullin, 1984).

He was reacting to antirealist complaints that had gained purchase in philosophy over the previous decades. Critics claimed that science yields exceedingly little (if any) legitimate substantive retention of theoretical description and no referential stability beyond the observable level in theory change. In their view, it is generally false that well-confirmed scientific theories are approximately true—the entities they postulate often turn out to be non-existent, and we lack good reason to believe their central tenets.

By contrast, to scientific realists like McMullin, theories making successful novel predictions do so because what they say about the world is *approximately* true. However, one problem with this thesis is that history suggests that, in the long run, theories generally turn out to be "false" as total constructs—a claim raised influentially by Larry Laudan's skeptical reading of the history of science (1981). According to Laudan, so many past successful scientific theories have turned out to be false that there is no reason to believe that currently successful theories are approximately true, let alone that there is a realist link between success and truth. History, his followers urge, is littered with evidence unfavorable to realism. For example, at the peak of its heyday, the ether theory of light was declared to be established beyond a reasonable doubt—such was its perceived success and good sense, as numerous physics reports at the dawn of the 20th century show. Here are two distinguished appraisals:

> [Regarding the ether] its discovery may well be looked upon as the most important feat of our century (Williams 1901/ 2007, p. 230).

> [It is] a fact deduced by reasoning from experiment and observation .... There is abundant proof that it is not merely a convenient scientific fiction, but is as much an actuality as ordinary gross, tangible, and ponderable substances. It is, so to speak, matter of a higher order, and occupies a rank in the hierarchy of created things which places it above the materials we can see and touch" (Fleming 1902, p. 192; quoted in Swenson 1972, p. 138).

Only a few years later, however, Einstein regarded the ether of light as an optional posit. As the 20th century advanced, physicists widely agreed that no ether of light had to be postulated. This case suggests a radical failure of reference, reaching into the central terms and fabric of the deposed theory. To critics, the overoptimistic realist interpretation of the pre-Einsteinian optical theory of light proved not just wrong but wrong at the level of its central ontology. Furthermore, the episode is typical of successful science, as attested not only by theories from comparatively underdeveloped sciences like those of phlogiston and caloric but also from discernibly mature disciplines like electromagnetism. One more recent example is the alternative theory presented by Feynman and Wheeler, according to which Maxwell's equations do not describe an undulating, self-subsisting electromagnetic field but describe just how the movements of charges are deterministically coordinated over spacetime. The complaint is that realists assert that there are transversal microscopic undulations where simply nothing might exist. (More about this in Section 5C).

Seminal Selective-realist responses from the late 1980s and 1990s include John Worrall (1989), Philip Kitcher (1993), Jarrett Leplin (1997), and Stathis Psillos (1999). Selectivists see in the history of science a past littered with epistemic failures (as Laudan claims) but also enduring successes, especially from theories that emphasize the epistemological importance of initially implausible novel predictions (a trend that grew strong in the physical sciences in the early 19th century), exemplified by the part of Fresnel's wave that remains accepted to this day. The whole theory got many parts of its intended domain wrong. Notably, Fresnel's original account of reflection and diffraction was embedded in a conceptual framework that metaphysically required the existence of the ether of light. That explanatory part of the theory is now widely recognized as wrong. Yet, selectivists stress that a substantial part of Fresnel's theoretical claims remains hard to question—for instance, that "light is made of microscopic transversal physical waves that (to a very high approximation) obey Fresnel's laws for reflection, refraction, and polarization," without any claims about light's material substratum. Let us call this part "Fresnel's Core" ([FC] for short). It constitutes a nucleus of theoretical descriptions that light phenomena satisfy at a level that, in the non-purged theory, is "non-fundamental." (A "fundamental" physical theory is one expected to provide accurate descriptions without restrictions (i.e., in all regimes). It is an open question whether there "must" be a fundamental theory of physics in that sense).

From the selectivist perspective, discarded theories that, like Fresnel's, yield successful predictions contain substantive parts that correctly describe (at the very least) local law-like structures, processes, and entities. On the other hand, identifying those parts has proven difficult, resulting in enduring controversy (for an outline of the disputes, see, e.g., Cordero 2024)

As said, selective realists focus on theory parts that enjoy high empirical corroboration rather than complete theories. From their perspective, theory parts with posits systematically deployed in corroborated novel predictions are, with high probability, descriptively true or contain a proper part that is. Unlike traditional realists, selectivists admit the following claims:

(i) Radical conceptual change is a recurring scientific phenomenon, and

(ii) Empirical theories have poor reliability records at the most profound ontological level.

At the same time, selectivists point out the existence of significant descriptive continuities at *intermediate* theoretical levels between successful theories and their successors, as illustrated by [FC]. If so, a false theory can (and often does) contain parts that succeed as correct descriptions. Selectivists seek to identify those parts, and their approaches confine ontological commitment exclusively to highly confirmed theoretical descriptions. Unfortunately, the selection criteria they use allow for regrettable choices (see, e.g., Saatsi and Vickers 2011). One source of trouble is that selectivists leave the ontology described by the parts picked for commitment unclear. Historical cases and scientific practice gesture toward a functional resolution of this difficulty, but the clues are unclear and need elaboration.

From the selectivist perspective, theories that make corroborated predictions contain correct parts worthy of realist commitment. As noted, Fresnel's Theory Core [FC] is one such component in Fresnel's and Maxwell's theories. [FC] describes a domain of interest at an abstract level that filters out the portion that deals with the material substrate of light (the ether). This abstract core explains how undulations of microscopic wavelengths give rise to light's reflection, refraction, and polarization—phenomena that [FC] inferentially predicts in detail, even though the explanation leaves out the deeper ontological underpinnings.

The debate continues. Criticism has led to changes to the selectivist approach, and some have improved it, but it still faces some problems. In particular, it most acutely needs a non-ad hoc criterion for selecting the correct parts in theories. And selectivists must clarify their ontological commitment to the theory parts thus selected. Advances are on view in both these regards, but controversies remain. Here, I will assume that the noted problems have solutions and explore the character and promise of the project.

(1A) Theory cores

Fresnel's Core is not an isolated case. Comparably substantive theory parts are widespread in contemporary science. One conspicuous example from physics is the Standard Model of Elementary Particles, an abstract framework that harmonizes quantum field theory (QFT) and Special Relativity. Frank Wilczek (2015) calls it the "Core Theory" and presents it as an "intermediary" account that delivers already an accurate representation of physical reality, which any future, hypothetical "real thing" must take into account.

Wilczek hails the Core Theory as one that works "for all practical purposes." Most mainstream physicists agree. Importantly, Wilczek's Core gestures towards *functional explications* of the entities and descriptions involved, as do [FC] and numerous theory hubs of intermediate theoretical content in science. But his proposal contains a whiff of instrumentalism that needs philosophical attention to improve its appeal to realists. I will suggest (Section 3) that, once purged of optional instrumentalist concessions, Wilczek's and numerous other cores in science invite realist interpretation. However, the clues need clarification, elaboration, and precise labeling. But first, a word about giving selective realism a functional turn.

(1B) Focus on what things do

"Functional Realism" is a perspective multiply revived in recent literature; see, e.g., Cordero (2011, 2016, 2017, 2019)), Egg (2017, 2021), and Alai (2017, 2021). Nods toward the perspective are also discernible among some "agnostic sympathizers" (e.g., Saatsi 2019). This approach reacts to the antirealist challenge of successful theories marred by false or dubious content, empirical underdetermination, or conceptual problems. It does so by trying to thin down content without eliminating it (as radical empiricists strive to do). In the functionalist approach, theoretical entities and regularities are identified by *what they do at an abstract level rather than by what they "ultimately are" or are made of*. In Cordero (2017, 2024) the prospectively correct theory parts focus on effective (as opposed to exact) regularities and descriptions and involve functional (instead of "fundamental") entities. In the noted references, the parts selected as prospectively correct:

(a) Show empirical success.

(b) Have remained free of compelling specific doubts.

(c) In addition, many have gained elucidation from sources initially external to them.

The basic functional strategy at play has a tradition in modern natural philosophy. It has precedents in, e.g., Galileo's method and Newton's take on incomplete theorizing.

2 A bit of history

Selective and functional modeling has a presence in the transition from holistic categories to mechanistic concepts in the discussion of Copernicus' theory. Among numerous other places, functional explanations show up in Galileo's letter to the Grand Duchess Christina (1615), where he points to a way of separating the wheat from the chaff in successful theories. Only some parts of the biblical story, he argues, should receive literal interpretation—the parts about the Sun moving around the Earth are not crucial to the Bible's intended outcome, which is *salvation*. Natural philosophers after Galileo expanded this strategy, most daringly in Newton's dictum "hypothesis non fingo." Indeed, functional turns appear at many levels in Galileo's and Newton's piecemeal approach to describing natural objects instead of the traditional holistic approach to theorizing (see, e.g., Dudley Shapere 1975, 1984, 1986). In analytic philosophy of science, realist interpretations focused on *what things do rather than by what they "ultimately are" (i.e., functional interpretations)* gained traction in the 1970s as part of the critique of attempts to explain theoretical progress by logical-deductive reduction of discarded theories to their successors. One critical line recognizes the coarse-grained and restricted character of laws and regularities that survive theory change, as emphasized by, e.g., Toraldo di Francia (1975/1981). A complementary reaction focuses on inter-theory relations and accumulation of coarse-grained descriptions across conceptual change in many cases, from planetary orbits in Kepler's and Newton's theories—a topic developed in, e.g., Erhard Scheibe (1983) and others. Recognition of the epistemic import of coarse-grained description has become prominent in recent decades, notably in studies of the emergence of classical behavior in Everettian quantum mechanical worlds (see, e.g., David Wallace 2012).

(2A) Realist-friendly readings of history

Interpretations akin to the suggested functionalist turn have played a role in realist-friendly readings of the history of successful science from the early responses to Kuhnian antirealism (e.g., Mary Hesse 1961, Dudley Shapere 1984, and Ernan McMullin 1984). Regarding the new method by which Galileo rethought the project of natural philosophy, these and other thinkers underline Galileo's appeal to abstraction and his mathematization of scientific description, his piecemeal theorizing, and his defense of experimentation (as opposed to mere observation). Each of those Galilean moves required great imagination to meet challenges from reasonable worries. For example, even in the ideal state of a vacuum, the phenomenon of free fall could depend on an indefinitely large number of factors—the body's composition, shape, temperature, and color(s), to mention some candidates. In a decisive modern turn, Galileo took as relevant factors only time, the uniform acceleration of gravity, and the body's position (its center of mass). To Shapere (1975) and di Francia (1976/1981), Galileo showed how, by filtering out information, one could achieve precision and objectivity. This strategy proved a crucial modern resource.

Newtonian extensions of the approach soon fulfilled Galileo's goals against the expectations of his Aristotelian and Cartesian rivals (who achieved little meanwhile). A central factor here was the role played in the new science by abstraction, mathematical precision, the focus on experimentation, and the piecemeal approach to theoretical description.

Galileo was shunning the traditional holistic project of explaining everything at once. This move involved laying out boundaries of separable areas of investigation, which produced a standard against which theories could be assessed. Whatever else might be required to explain a particular body of information (domain), an explanation could be successful only to the extent that it considers the characteristics of the items of the domain (Shapere 1975). Galileo reasoned that it is possible to develop and test theories by actively interacting with nature (as opposed to passively observing it). *De Motu* (1590) sketches illustrative descriptions of experiments with falling bodies using an inclined plane to slow down the rate of descent.

A significant point in the story is Galileo's (and other early scientists') emphasis on what natural objects do rather than what they ultimately ("fundamentally") are. These scientists investigated natural entities only as far as it was possible to measure their properties rather than with the impossible goal of discovering their ultimate essence (di Francia 1976/1981). For this shift, the approach they developed was snubbed by many as epistemically second class because the resulting findings do not bring us nearer the intimate reason of things.

So, many of their contemporaries accused Newton and Galileo of betraying the enterprise of natural philosophy. Some thinkers still disparage the functionalist twist those early scientists encouraged. Nevertheless, their new modern approach has yielded much knowledge about nature. As di Francia stresses, after Galileo, no sensible person who has taken an unbiased look at the experiments will affirm that (within limits) a freely falling body does not cover distance proportional to the square of time. The same goes for the *theoretical* (not directly observable) content of models that get at least part of their intended domains partially correct.

Admittedly, the "Galilean" approach's success is a contingent development, not something guaranteed by logical necessity or the "nature of science." Nonetheless, although limited, the achievements of the modern scientific approach are manifestly outstanding in the magnitude, degree of articulation, subtlety, systematic integration, explanatory power, and predictive power of the contemporary disciplines that embrace the approach.

(2B) The contemporary stage

A closer example of functional entities is the light waves in electromagnetic theory after Einstein, free of reference to light's material substratum (like the waves in Fresnel's Core in Section 1. These waves are characterized by what they *do* rather than what they *ultimately are*, their "deep nature" left opaque (but not their "intermediate" nature). Einstein's waves contrast with the waves Fresnel and Maxwell had endorsed, which were conceptually embedded in a metaphysis of modes of being that required the existence of a luminiferous medium (Cordero 2011, 2012).

Like its selective predecessor, functional realism seeks to free successful theories of problematic parts, but now with a functional emphasis on restricted domains (regimes). The purge involved is not directed at "metaphysical" content, only at explicitly problematic posits. Entities and processes accepted as physically real are assessed to be free of specific doubts and indispensable for the theory's empirical success within a "physical regime."

For each empirical phenomenon, natural scientists associate some measurable parameters that determine the "regime" in which the phenomenon occurs. A regime is thus a domain of measurable aspects, entities, regularities, range of application, and degree of descriptive resolution or coarse-graining, marked by the energy, mass, and size of interest. The values of these parameters determine in which physical regime the phenomenon occurs. For example, the mass, size, and velocity of an ordinary apple falling from a tree place it in a physical regime in which classical mechanics provides extremely accurate descriptions.

The theory parts selected for realist commitment are generally "functional" rather than fundamental, emergent within regimes of an empirical domain, and the descriptions associated with them are "effective" rather than exact.

The effective descriptions derived from selected parts purport to be correct only within certain margins of relevant representation.

Truth content may lay at any theoretical level, including levels intermediate between the 'phenomenological' and the 'fundamental (more details in Section 3F).

This selective approach concentrates the realist position on claims established beyond reasonable doubt. Important arrays of such claims occur at intermediate theoretical levels of abstraction, generalization, and domain restriction (of lesser ontological height than the "fundamental" level of description sought by traditional philosophy and early science).

> **Functional-Realist Thesis:** Theory parts selected using the realist criterion for identifying epistemically promising components are either true or contain a sub-part that is. These will generally gain retention *as functional/effective parts* within specifiable descriptive regimes in successor theories.

One advantage of the above thesis is its refutability. It will fail if, more than rarely, theory parts selected from an empirically successful theory fail to gain substantive retention in successor theories. Here is another plus: The proposed approach abandons the emphasis on the fundamental ontological level, which leads standard realism to overlook that theories' most apparent epistemic achievements occur at intermediate theoretical levels.

3 Some needed clarifications

The realist strategy outlined in the previous section contains implicit features and distinctions that need spelling out.

(3A) The task of purging content

As Galileo did with the law of free fall and (at a higher theoretical level) Einstein did with light waves, selective-functional realists analyze successful theories that contain problematic parts. They remove the troublesome parts and then consider the remaining contents, focusing on intermediate theoretical levels with corroborated empirical success. The purge proceeds with the help of three resources:

(i) abstraction

(ii) coarse graining, and

(iii) domain restriction.

(3B) Theoretical representation

Practicing physicists have an established way of describing the regularities found in nature, displayed, for example, by the mature version of the Galilean representation of the law of free fall. It takes the form $\langle \Lambda, O, L, \delta, \Delta \rangle$, where the symbols stand for the following aspects:

The set Λ is the set of aspects/quantities considered relevant, $\Lambda = \{\lambda_i\}$. In the present case, Λ includes time, position, instantaneous velocity, and acceleration of the falling body. The set O consists of entities populating the domain, in this case material bodies. The set L is the set of laws and regularities holding over the targeted domain. Typically, these are justified as coarse-grained regularities rather than exact laws, their general form being (to first approximation):

$$L(x_i) = f(x_i) \pm \delta(x_i).$$

By δ_i, we denote the amount of coarse graining tolerated on values for each of the λ_i quantities listed in Λ, and by Δ, we mean the restricted domain over which the representation is expected to hold.

Consider Fresnel's Core and its revision in the 20th century as a second example. Tellingly, the level of generality it was initially granted contracted in response to subsequent information about the dependence of the optical indices on various factors, most dramatically, light intensity, non-linear features, and quantum effects (e.g., creation and destruction of photons). A theory part's theoretical level typically changes when it lands in a successor theory, usually moving to a lesser relative depth than in the initial theory.

(3C) Focus on functional entities and effective descriptions

As used here, the label "functional posit" applies to entities characterized by what they *do* rather than what they *are* according to the theory's fundamental level. A "functional" entity or property is individuated by its effective causal role in the intended domain. Like Einstein's light waves, functional entities have their *"deep nature" left opaque*. Contemporary science has a mainstream approach to conjecturing effective theories and functional ontologies. QFT is a choice example, as mentioned before.

"Effective" descriptions are expected to apply only within certain precision margins. Still, effective descriptions and functional entities have more than mere instrumental interest. In scientific usage, the term "effective" often refers not only to theories that agree with data but to physical interactions and entities that emerge under the conditions of a domain. The resulting descriptions are usually partial and incomplete compared to those provided by the base (fundamental) theory. *They are intended to represent behaviors within a specific regime, outside which the functional/effective theory may not apply.* Common examples include continuous matter, "classical" systems, and [FC].

(3D) Face-value ontology

A theory's "face value ontology" (FVO) is its literal, undiluted ontology. For example, Newtonian gravitational theory's FVO includes massive objects existing in space and time (bodies), their position and momentum, and forces acting at a distance. In Maxwell's theory, FVO includes light waves with ether as the medium for transmission.

By contrast, a "functional" ontology typically has restricted universality and limited Λ (applying to a particular physical regime of the theory). The FVO of one theory (e.g., continuous matter) can have functional status in another (e.g., molecular theory).

(3E) Modal statements

Claims about what is possible, impossible, essential, necessary, and contingent have nuances in functional realism:

(A) The modal structure of a proposed functional entity will be generally more modest (thinner) than that of its counterpart in a fundamental (base) theory.

(B) Multiple realizations: At some more profound ontological level, an entity might differ from what a scientifically well-established functional theory proposes at face value.

(C) The existence of more profound descriptions does not render incorrect functional-effective descriptions within the intended regime, which are more abstract (shallower).

(D) Correct description is possible without reference to any "fundamental ontological level." The classical mechanical description of an ordinary falling apple is correct to a high degree of approximation within the standards of the ordinary regime.

Items (A) to (D) above add precision to the suggested ideas of selective-functional purge, functional entities and effective descriptions, multiple realizations, and the non-fundamentality of face-value ontology. Functional realism concentrates on theories at intermediate levels between the 'phenomenological' and the 'fundamental.'

Next on the list is the topic of levels of description, closely related to the idea of "regime".

(3F) Descriptive levels

The term "descriptive level" (DL) generalizes the idea of "regimes" in physics, as summarized in Section 1. Taking guidance from the analysis of Galileo's Law in (3B), a set of five "regime parameters" will characterize a DL in what follows, presented in a structure $\langle \Lambda, O, L, \delta, \Delta \rangle$ where the abstract level of the representation is specified by the list Λ of physical aspects considered relevant; by O, we denote for the level's face value ontology; by L, we denote the set of laws and regularities over the targeted domain. Typically, these are asserted only as coarse-grained relations, their general form given (to a first approximation) by $L(x_i) = f(x_i) \pm \delta(x_i)$. The parameters ($\delta$) specify the amount of coarse-graining tolerated and Δ gives the domain where the descriptions are expected to hold effectively.

For example, the ontology of classical thermodynamics comprises entities that have thermodynamical properties, conspicuously (1) rate properties (e.g., energy flow rate, entropy flow rate); (2) state properties (e.g., energy amount, entropy amount); and (3) constitutive properties (e.g., thermal capacity, thermal conductivity).

Some clarification comments are helpful here:

1. Crucially, in functional realism, the features listed in Λ are considered as real as any other considered "real."

2. Descriptive levels can have considerable autonomy. For instance, within a given regime, we can describe and understand something as a liquid without knowing about its molecular composition, even if a description of microscopic components is available.

3. The parameter Δ registers that empirically successful theories typically have a limited scope of accurate applicability.

4. The above focus on DLs discloses the pluralist character of the proposed selective realism.

(3G) Incompleteness and opacity

Functional entities and accurate descriptions under a regime $\langle \Lambda, O, L, \delta, \Delta \rangle$ are typically "incompletely" specified *relative to counterparts in fuller theories or more profound levels of description*. In what follows, functional-effective versions of a theory T will be represented by putting T in brackets followed by the corresponding parameters: $[T]_{\Lambda,O,L,\delta,\Delta}$ (the indexes will be generally omitted for easiness, and the functional version of T will be written $[T]$).

(3H) Ontological significance

Taking a realist stance towards a selected $[T]$ amounts to asserting that the kinds of entities and regularities explicit in it are *real*. So, the claim is that those entities and regularities are physically at play (i.e., act and react) in the intended domain, even if they stand as incompletely described non-fundamental beings relative to a base theory in the background.

As in the days of Galileo and Newton, the above suggestions offend those who think that a physical theory is not scientific if it is not fundamental and exact. Today, functional realists accept substantive theories of "intermediate" fundamentality, about which—they argue—we can adopt a realist stance. These theories include some with outstanding scope and fecundity. For example, the functional interpretation of QFT as an effective theory has proven admirably reliable in low-energy interactions.

The following section uses the above precisions to argue for shifting the realist emphasis toward functional and effective theoretical content.

4 Functional/effective content

"Standard" realism concentrates on unrestricted theories and theoretical claims. Although, in principle, unrestricted theoretical descriptions may be true, history places them among the least epistemically reliable in science due to the poor record of their ambitious content. On the other hand, functional realism focuses on epistemically more secure claims—e.g., limited claims about functional entities. Functional attention focuses on how entities and processes behave effectively within a particular descriptive regime of interest.

We thus reach the following suggestion: Taking an explicitly functional turn clarifies the notion of realist gain in selective realism and helps overcome some objections to the project. Accordingly, a deflationary approach is proposed here, in which realist commitment goes primarily to entities and processes corroborated as objectively active in the domain in question (as described by the relevant "functional" theories or parts of them).

In the functional realist approach proposed, the criterion for realist commitment focuses on theory parts free from specific doubts, backed by corroborated novel predictions, even better if they also have external support (Cordero 2019). Admittedly, the selection criterion of the theoretical parts remains controversial. Suppose, however, the sought criterion will settle around the choice just suggested.

Which theories satisfy the realist test? There is a vast and robust population of functional entities, processes, and accounts that satisfy the conditions of being free from specific doubts, backed by corroborated novel predictions, and having some external support. It comprises *a highly textured tapestry of clustered behaviors beyond the reach of unaided perception*. The resulting picture is not a haphazard quilt of dubious significance but a corpus of abstract, finite-range, coarse-grained assertions that, nevertheless, display astonishing (and growing) levels of integration into a detailed and textured picture of the world.

As a further bonus, the noted functional-effective theories are immune to arguments from unconceived alternatives in the following sense. Suppose a functional core $[T]$ merits selective realist commitment. In that case, the existence of alternative theories will not compromise its realist status if those alternatives contain $[T]$, as they must on pain of empirical inadequacy. An illustration of the latter feature is provided by the plurality of ontic theories of quantum mechanics—ontic in that they interpret the quantum state as a physically real thing (Cordero, 2001, 2024). The case involves three leading offers, which provide different ontologies with different laws of nature. Bohmian Mechanics postulates an ontology of particle(s) whose motion follows a new equation hooked up to a wave equation—a guidance law. Everettian "many worlds" theories present decohered superposition as indicators of effective ontological multiplicity in physical reality. Collapse theorists modify the linear dynamical evolution of the wavefunction, changing the state equation to produce a unified story of the macro and micro realms. These ontic approaches portray radically different worlds from top to bottom but make no diverging predictions accessible by present technology. They are effectively empirically equivalent, agreeing on little more than what is observable. It is thus hard to find a theoretical core shared by the above proposals such that we can regard them all as different interpretations of that core. Hard—but not impossible. Cordero (2001, 2024) points to two complementary statements selective realists can make in the case at hand:

(a) Disagreement between the three noted camps is confined to certain parts of the theories—parts that, being empirically underdetermined, realists cannot take as veridical.

(b) On the other hand, realists can point to substantive theoretical content shared by the competing proposals. If this is correct, the key claim is that we can trust theory parts that are empirically successful, free of specific doubts, and shared by all three theories (i.e., not marred by underdetermination).

Which parts are thus shared by the three competing theories? In all three, the quantum state expresses the system's ability to exert causal influence (cause something) at spatial locations where it is non-zero. A system's ability to produce effects—its efficacy in doing something over a spatiotemporal region—is structured by its quantum state.

Nevertheless, some thinkers claim that the quantum state is just a tool for making predictions, not something representing a physical entity. In response, realists like Harvey Brown (2019) explain how the quantum state contains enough information about physical systems to satisfy realist selection criteria like the one outlined earlier. Quantum state-based information about physical systems that meets the selection criterion includes, for example, details of their energy structure, energy exchange channels between its parts and other systems, quantum amplitudes and probabilities, interference between material systems, entanglement, and quantum nonlocality, quantum limits to the principle of energy conservation, intrinsic quantum spin and spin-based interactions; the stability of matter, its scope and limits; the effective dynamics of quantum-probabilities (at all levels). In more concrete situations, the quantum state consistently accounts for numerous properties of material systems. Examples include the color of things, the detailed geometric structure and effective properties of molecules, the probabilistic structure of superconductivity, electrons in molecular bonds (wavefunction shapes and their effects, e.g., in graphene and diamond); it even grounds the notion of "world."

A crucial question is whether the suggested functional/effective turn helps the selectivist project, and if so, how much. The last section explores some plausible suspicions invited by the proposed approach.

5 Some concerns

(5A)

Some traditional realists deny that functional entities and structures are either "real"—or "as real"—as "full theoretical" ones.

Turning this concern into an objection requires argumentation that is seemingly impossible to provide without begging the question. We have at play at least two different notions of what makes something physically real:

Notion (a): The "physically real" is just the most fundamental material basis of the physical world.

Notion (b): The physically "real" are the entities and dynamical patterns that effectively emerge at various physical regimes and function accordingly. On this second notion (favored by the functional-realist stance), to "exist" physically is to have causal efficacy in agreement with the physical laws within the regime at hand.

Traditional realists may also insist that, from a theory's perspective, the only existing objects are the ones the theory includes in its central principles. I.e., all others should either be reduced to the central objects or recognized as convenient constructs. However, while objects placed at the most central theoretical level are of great interest, the functional-realist concern is what shows activity (exists) in the intended part of the world. Antirealist skeptical inductions are correct about the epistemic weakness of the highest theoretical levels but err about the epistemic stability of intermediate theoretical contents. The reductionist objection (5A) lacks warrant.

(5B)

Many critics reject the realist optimism of the previous sections. One source of suspicion is skeptical inductions of the following sort: Like today's scientists, past ones, too, thought highly of their epistemic success, inferring wrongly that their leading theories were highly correct. (e.g., Brad Wray 2013). In Wray's view, the case for today's theories is no better.

Several relevant differences between past and present theories come to mind, particularly regarding: (a) scientific methodology; (b) The character of theories in basic science today; (c) the realist stances available now; (d) while full theories are epistemically unstable, theory cores ($[T]$) are generally robust.

(a) Scientific methodology has become more demanding in the last two centuries. Past scientists did not emphasize successful *novel prediction* as we do now. Today's scientists are more open to revising their theories at the deepest conceptual levels.

(b) The *character* of theorizing has changed, too. There is now a better appreciation of the robustness of explanations at intermediate levels (between phenomenological and fundamental description).

(c, d) Also, the notion of *realism* has changed. Two developments are worth stressing. First, there is a greater metaphysical modesty. Scientific theories were embedded in conceptual networks that entangled theory parts in ways that blocked attempts to break many of them into separate components. An example of conceptual entanglement is that of 'being a wave' (W) and 'having a material substratum' (S) in classical electromagnetism (Cordero 2011). To 'emancipate' concept (W) one had to cut the metaphysically tied (entangled) cluster [W-S] by turning it into a conjunctive (separable) one [W·S], as it is now. Secondly, being approximately correct does not require being error-free. Unlike traditional realists, selectivists are not troubled by the suggestion that scientific proposals are generally false as *complete, unrestricted theories*. Nobody claims that successful theories (past or present) are true as whole proposals in the current dispute. The issue is whether successful theories *have identifiable functional/effective cores with substantive positive truth content* that will generally gain retention in successor theories.

(5C)

Worries about ending up committed to physically non-existent posits: According to some critics[1], if selective realists followed the characterization of Fresnel's Core proposed in Section 1, they would over-commit ontologically. Specifically, they would *end up accepting that there is something where nothing exists*. This worry is fuelled, for example, by the Feynman-Wheeler alternative view of electromagnetism (FW). According to FW, Maxwell's equations do not describe an undulating self-subsisting electromagnetic field but how the movements of charges are deterministically coordinated over spacetime. The objection is thus that selectivists conclude that there are transversal microscopic undulations where simply nothing exists (in a way

---

[1] I thank Juha Saatsi for pressing this objection on me.

analogous to someone who commits to there being something in the center of a donut).

I suggest it is false that, on FW, *nothing* exists where the transversal undulations associated with light play out. As noted, something "exists physically" if it has causal efficacy in agreement with the physics principles for the regime at hand. One example is the local interaction between electromagnetic waves and charges. The waves do not exist because they figure at the fundamental level of a successful theory (say, post-electromagnetism after Einstein). They are granted existence because of their multiply attested independent interactions with numerous physical systems. The functional reality of microscopic undulations does not amount to their being classical undulations in a fundamental sense—just like the reality of a macroscopic table does not amount to its being continuous at all descriptive levels; they are continuous only at macroscopic levels.

(5D)

A FAPP Approach? In several of his last papers and presentations, John Bell admonished against solving interpretative problems in ways that work merely "for all practical purposes" (FAPP). He was reacting against the way theorists responded to the measurement problem in quantum mechanics by claiming that, as the reduced density matrix arising from decoherence cannot be locally distinguished from that of an ensemble, that solves the issue for all practical purposes. In Bell's view, the natural philosopher's duty is to understand the quantum world, not to ignore aspects of it or to take only a schematic (FAPP) account of (say) the interaction across the split between pre- and post-measurement situations in quantum mechanics (see, e.g., Bell 1990). Some critics might worry that the functionalist realist turn proposed in this paper works merely "for all practical purposes"[2].

The functional-realist turn advocated in this paper admits that content not selected for realist commitment may correctly represent reality. Commitment goes to a thinned-down (but still theoretical) version of the best current theories. The parts selected for realist interpretation may come from any theory level if they show predictive power and are free from specific doubts (especially if, in addition, they enjoy independent attestation). The proposed turn acknowledges the possible existence of entities and interactions underpinning the relatively abstract functional accounts selected, and in this way, it agrees with Bell's demand. The approach welcomes pursuing explanatory accounts beyond the restricted domains/regimes under consideration. Whether the ensuing explorations result in new theory parts worthy of realist interpretation depends on how things play out in each case. It discourages

---

[2] I thank Dennis Dieks for raising this point and making many other valuable suggestions.

"bad" FAPP. Its goal is to identify models that correctly describe the *local ontology and nomology at work under each regime without prejudice against further ontological inquiry.*

For example, in the functional terms of ordinary discourse, a billiard ball is a system of continuous matter within the appropriate energy regime and spatial coarse-graining of (e.g.) 10^{-5} m). Outside this regime, the system diverges radically from the ordinary description. Here is another example that is closer to Bell's worries. As noted in Section 4, in the 1980s, several approaches to the measurement problem in quantum mechanics identified the onset of decoherence in linear evolution with the "collapse of the wave function." Some leading theorists declared the ontological issue "solved." But, as Bell objected, after decoherence, in the standard theory, the initial quantum superpositions remain "alive" indefinitely along multiple wavefronts. Their relative phases become blurred, rendering the fronts "effectively independent," but the superposed components continue. So, we have a FAPP resolution of the measurement problem that gives up the realist interpretation of the quantum state. That is antirealist FAPP. By contrast, the functional turn suggested in this paper follows scientific-realist lines all the way through. From its perspective, the emergence of classical entities does not make quantum entities disappear. Nor does the deeper fundamentality of quantum mechanics deny classical entities' existence. Classical entities exist as natural systems that objectively arise in a quantum mechanical world *within* the confines of specific regimes. Classical entities are not presumed to be *fundamentally classical*—they are *functionally* classical. "Ultimately," they may be quantum many-worlds systems, Bohmian systems, spontaneous collapse systems, or something else[3]—we cannot tell yet.

6 Concluding remarks

This paper's functional/effective version of selective realism shifts realist commitment. In particular, it drops the traditional emphasis on fundamental theoretical entities and focuses instead on causal efficacy at specific descriptive levels. The realism proposed is deflationist and pluralist. The proposed reformulation helps the project of selective realism in two ways. First, it clarifies the structure and character of a realist stance toward just part of a theory. Secondly, it highlights relevant differences with the standard realist stance, particularly regarding the accumulation of scientific knowledge across theory change.

---

[3]Approaching quantum physics in functional terms has gained welcome elucidation in recent years thanks to the second generation of theorists of Everett's many worlds, notably David Wallace's work on the coherence of the idea of an emerging multiverse entirely within the framework of quantum mechanics (2014), a topic of philosophical interest independently of the credibility of the many worlds proposal.

References

Alai, Mario (2021): "The Historical Challenge to Realism and Essential Deployment In: Contemporary Scientific Realism." In: *Contemporary Realism*. Edited by: Timothy D. Lyons and Peter Vickers, Oxford University Press. Oxford University Press 2021: 184–215.

Alai, Mario (2017): "Resisting the Historical Objections to Realism: Is Doppelt's a Viable Solution?" *Synthese* (194): 3267–3290.

Bell, John S. (1990): Against "measurement." *Physics World* 3, 8: 33–40.

Brown, Harvey R. (2019): "The Reality of the Wavefunctions: Old Arguments and New. In: Cordero, A, (ed.) *Philosophers Look at Quantum Mechanics*. Springer: 63–86.

Cordero, Alberto (2024): "Mario Alai and the Quest for a Realist Scientific Realism." Forthcoming in *Realism vs Antirealism in Metaphysics Science and Language*.

Cordero, Alberto (2019): "Introduction." In *Philosophers Look at Quantum Mechanics*. Springer: 1–17.

Cordero, Alberto (2017): "Retention, Truth-Content and Selective Realism. In Evandro Agazzi (ed.), *Scientific Realism: Objectivity and Truth in Science*. Cham: Springer Nature (2017): 245–256.

Cordero, Alberto (2016): "Eight Myths about Scientific Realism," Biennial Meeting, Philosophy of Science, Atlanta, Ga., November 2016. PhilSci Archive E-print 12533.

Cordero, Alberto (2011): "Scientific Realism and the *Divide et Impera* Strategy: The Ether Saga Revisited. *Philosophy of Science* (Vol. 78, 2011): 1120–1130.

Cordero, Alberto (2001): "Realism and Underdetermination: Some Clues from the Practices-Up." *Philosophy of Science* 68S: 301–12.

Egg, Matthias (2021): "Quantum Ontology without Speculation", *European Journal for Philosophy of Science* 11 (2021): 32.

Egg, Matthias (2017): The Physical Salience of Non-Fundamental Local Beables." *Studies in History and Philosophy of Modern Physics* 57 (2017): 104–110.

Hesse, Mary B. (1961): *Forces and Fields*. Edinburgh: Thomas Nelson and Sons, Ltd.

Kitcher, Philip (1993): *The Advancement of Science: Science Without Legend, Objectivity Without Illusions.* Oxford University Press.

Laudan, Larry. 1981. "A Confutation of Convergent Realism". *Philosophy of Science* 48: 19–49.

Leplin, Jarrett (1997): *Novel Defense of Scientific Realism.* New York: Oxford University Press.

McMullin, Ernan (1984): "A Case for Scientific Realism." In J. Leplin (ed.), *Scientific Realism.* University of California Press.

Psillos, Stathis (1999): *Scientific Realism: How Science Tracks Truth.* New York: Routledge.

Saatsi, Juha and Peter Vickers (2011): "Miraculous Success? Inconsistency and Untruth in Kirchhoff's Diffraction Theory." *British Journal for the Philosophy of Science* (62): 29–46.

Saatsi, Juha (2019): "Scientific Realism Meets Metaphysics of Quantum Mechanics." In: Cordero, A, (ed.) *Philosophers Look at Quantum Mechanics.* Springer: 141–142.

Saatsi, Juha (2016). What is theoretical progress of science. *Synthese*, 196, 611–631.

Scheibe, Erhard (1983): "Two Types of Successor Relations between Theories." *Journal for General Philosophy of Science*, (Vol. 14): 68–80.

Shapere, Dudley (1986): "External amd Internal Factors in the Development of Science." *Science & Technology Studies* (Vol. 4): 1–9.

Shapere, Dudley (1984): "The Concept of Observation in Science and Philosophy," in Dudley Shapere: *Reason and the Search for Knowledge.* Dordrecht: Reidel Publishing Company: 342–351.

Shapere, Dudley (1975): *Galileo: A Philosophical Analysis.* University of Chicago Press.

Swenson, Loyd S., Jr. (1972): *The Aetherial Ether.* Austin: University of Texas Press.

Toraldo di Francia, Giuliano (1981/1976): *The Investigation of the Physical World.* Cambridge, U.K.: Cambridge University Press.

Wallace, David (2014): *The Emergent Multiverse: Quantum Theory according to the Everett Interpretation.* Oxford University Press.

Wilczek, Frank (2015): *A Beautiful Question: Finding Nature's Deep Design*. New York: Penguin Press.

Williams, Henry Smith. 1901/2007. *The Story of Nineteenth-Century Science*. Whitefish, MT: Kessinger.

Worrall, John (1989): "Structural realism: The best of both worlds?" Dialectica, 43: 99–124. Reprinted in D. Papineau (ed.), *The Philosophy of Science*, Oxford: Oxford University Press, pp. 139–165.

Wray, K. Brad (2013): "The Pessimistic Induction and the Exponential Growth of Science Reassessed." *Synthese* 190, 4321–4330.

Non-standard realistic models of quantum phenomena and new forms of complementarity

Niccolò Covoni, Giovanni Macchia, Davide Pietrini, and Gino Tarozzi

Dipartimento di Scienze Pure e Applicate, Università Urbino Carlo Bo, Via Valerio 9, 61029 Urbino, Italy

Abstract. This paper addresses the problem of different complementary interpretations of atomic phenomena. We take complementarity seriously as a meaningful philosophical principle, in the same way that the same principles to which complementarity limits simultaneous recourse, such as realism and causality, are endowed with meaning.

We will then discuss the attempts to overcome the complementary relation between waves and particles in a realistic sense by attributing an independent physical reality to both wave-like and particle-like entities, showing the negative results of such attempts, which instead reveal the validity of another formulation of the principle of complementarity: the so-called *smooth complementarity*, according to which wave and corpuscular representations can mix without a rigid distinction, although one continues to manifest itself at the expense of the other.

We will emphasize how a particularly weak realist interpretation of the quantum mechanical wave function conflicts with a (strong) formulation of the causal principle, and show the emergence of another form of classical complementarity between the realist and causal interpretations, which may assume a new smooth form even in this case. Complementarity confirms, in this way, its central role in the foundations of quantum mechanics and indicates at the same time how the philosophical interpretation of this theory, from the point of view of both realism and causality, remains a meaningful open question.

1 Bohr's (non-)famous proposal at the Lake Como congress

Niels Bohr's principle of complementarity, which posits that specific pairs of complementary properties cannot be observed or measured simultaneously, is one of the most debated principles in quantum mechanics. This principle has been criticized both by proponents of non-standard interpretations and by advocates of the orthodox interpretation of quantum mechanics, who have often attempted to reduce it to a synonym for Heisenberg's uncertainty principle. The latter, as is well known, asserts a fundamental limit to the precision with which certain pairs of classical physical properties—such as position and momentum, or time and energy—can be simultaneously known.

In 1927, a pivotal year for quantum physics, Heisenberg introduced the uncertainty principle, and two fundamental physics congresses were organised: the *International Congress of Physicists* in Como and the *Fifth*

Congress Solvay in Brussels. During the Como congress, Bohr exposed the famous complementarity principle that, together with Heisenberg's uncertainty principle, would give rise to modern quantum mechanics.

The Como Congress was organised by the *Italian Physical Society* (SIF) and the *Italian Electrotechnical Association* (AEI) in honour of the first centenary of Alessandro Volta's death.

For the first time, the discussions were broadcast via radio, allowing the public to follow the proceedings and hear the voices of the distinguished scientists in attendance. This technical achievement was made possible by the *International Standard Electric Corporation* carried out this task so that anybody could follow the proceedings and hear the voices of the eminent personalities convened in Como (Auctores varii 1928, p. xii).

The Congress was attended by the most influential physicists of the time. Remarkable was the absence of Albert Einstein, who rejected the invitation due to opposition to the Mussolini fascist government.

The Congress opened on September 11, 1927, in Como and closed on September 20, 1927, in Rome on the Campidoglio. On September 17, Bohr, at the same Pavia University where Alessandro Volta taught, presented his lecture on the principle of complementarity titled "The quantum postulate and the recent development of atomic theory". His lecture was shorter than he had prepared for the Congress. A few weeks before the Congress, the congress committee had informed the Danish physicist that the lecture should have lasted only twenty minutes. Comparing his lecture with the article for the proceedings published in 1928, we can observe that Bohr cut his lecture. The published article contains a more complete presentation than the one held at the Congress and includes some observations made during the next Solvay congress in October 1927. It should also be noted that Bohr used the neologism "complementarity" for the first time in the proceedings. The reviewer also underlined the originality of this term.

Bohr's talk at the Como congress was not warmly received. The lecture during the Congress probably did not clarify the core of his thought on complementarity.

In the days following the conference, the reception of the principle of complementarity was not jointly accepted, above all in the Italian academic community. The spirit of the time can be summarised by one of the most influential physicists in Italy, the President of the Pontifical Academy of Science, Giuseppe Gianfranceschi, who was well known for translating Minkowski's paper on space-time into Italian. Over the years, Gianfranceschi tried to reinterpret modern physics according to Aristotelian physics (Maiocchi 1991, pp. 194–198; Fano 1991; Pietrini 2019). Gianfranceschi also participated in the Como Congress by giving a lecture, just before Bohr's, entitled "The Physical Significance of Quantum Theory". This was followed by a discussion with Maurice de Broglie on the measurement of individual electronic quantities.

Gianfranceschi's lecture summarized the main doubts and criticisms of quantum mechanics. According to him, quantum mechanics could not be interpreted as a physical theory because a physical theory should be "a model capable of accounting for what we find in phenomena and bodies, and must precisely serve as a guide in the search for the true nature of things" (Gianfranceschi 1928, pp. 559–564). Finally, Gianfranceschi, after recalling the importance of quantum formulas in the solution of many problems, said that "the criteria of statistical distribution [...] are those that are best suited to transport problems from a discontinuous process to a process of continuity". He asserted that it was not necessary to exclude other ways of investigation. Gianfranceschi's reservations were partly shared by many Italian physicists of the "older generation" who, because of their certainties and scientific background, were not inclined to fully accept the characteristics of young modern physics. Behind their criticism lay the problem of causality. Physicists are worried about rejecting the principle of causality, one of the main pillars of science.

Born's comment after Bohr's lecture answered this problem:

> Quantum theory abandons the determinism that has dominated all-natural research. However, in the strict sense, the abandonment of causality is only an apparent distortion. The mechanistic view of nature, as it was in force before, in order to predict future events, had to assume that the state of the world was completely known in every detail at all times. However, this assumption is an illusion. The real insight of quantum theory is that the very laws of nature forbid completely fixing the state of a closed system. The more precisely one measures a coordinate, the less precisely one determines the associated momentum (Bohr 1928, pp. 589–591).

Concerning the problem of causality, Bohr will explain his position in his memory: "This recognition, however, in no way points to any limitation of the scope of the quantum-mechanical description, and the trend of the whole argumentation presented in the Como lecture was to show that the viewpoint of complementarity may be regarded as a rational generalisation of the very idea of causality" (Schilpp 1970, p. 211).

2 The irrelevance of complementarity in the treatises of quantum mechanics

Complementarity has played only a minor role in the orthodox interpretation of quantum mechanics, as evidenced by its limited presence in the two foundational texts of the field: Dirac's *Principles of Quantum Mechanics* and von Neumann's *Mathematical Foundations of Quantum Mechanics*. In both books Bohr's principle is rarely mentioned, while a great space is given to the exposition and discussion of Heisenberg's uncertainty principle. In particular, Dirac underlined how the two founding principles of the new theory were the uncertainty principle and the superposition principle. He characterized the former as a negative principle because it imposes restrictions on classical notions, such as the simultaneous attribution of position and momentum to a physical system. Conversely, he described the superposition principle as a positive principle because it allows phenomena impossible in classical physics, such as describing a system's state as a combination of multiple possible values before measurement.

Non-orthodox quantum theorists have also criticized the role and relevance of complementarity. They viewed it as a term rooted in dubious philosophical premises, introduced to compensate for the inability to develop new concepts that could adequately explain quantum phenomena. For instance, Louis de Broglie referred to Bohr as a "master of chiaroscuro," while Einstein remarked on the incomprehensibility of complementarity, finding it resistant to any attempt at understanding.

In the case of Göttingen theorists, two interpretations of complementarity were identified, the first related to the limitation of two classically compatible concepts or descriptions such as position or momentum, or causal and spacetime coordination. The importance of the latter was underlined above all by Pauli. The second interpretation, peculiar of Bohr's view, extended complementary relation to incompatible classical concepts like waves and particles. Such a dual nature of atomic objects represented for Bohr the fruitful experimental evidence on which the quantum theory was born and developed, whereas for Göttingen theorists saw it as a metaphysical assumption linked to the old ontology of classical physics.

On the ground of Dirac's distinction between the negative and positive nature of the principles of quantum mechanics, Bohr's complementarity, according to its original formulation, should have had the double status of a negative and, at the same time, positive principle: negative for restricting the use of compatible classical concepts, and positive for enabling the simultaneous consideration of incompatible classical representations. However, the restrictive interpretation of the Göttingen school reduced complementarity to a purely negative principle, synonymous with indeterminacy relations, adding no substantial insights. This is probably the reason why Dirac did not include complementarity among the basic principles of quantum mechanics. Complementarity was accepted, therefore, only as a negative principle by the Göttingen school, but was rejected as a positive principle, allowing the recourse to classically incompatible concepts such as particles and waves, thus denying one of the peculiarities and conceptual novelty of quantum theory.

A further restrictive version of complementarity was proposed more than thirty years later by the Soviet physicist Vladimir Fock (Fock 1957) in the form of the principle of relativity to our means or instruments of observation. Based on this principle, which Fock considered an extension of the principle of relativity to our reference frame, the wave or corpuscular properties of atomic objects would have manifested themselves depending on the instruments used to investigate them. According to this point of view, some instruments or classes of instruments would have only detected waves. In contrast, other ones would have detected only particles but never the properties of these objects simultaneously. As Karl Popper would have rightly pointed out in his criticism of the restricted interpretations of complementarity, the classic and well-known double-slit experiment already contradicts this kind of merely "negative" interpretations since, on the detector screen, we reveal both localised impacts of particles and the classic wave-like interference pattern of their distribution.

3 Arguments against and for the wave-particle duality

Three main arguments have been proposed to reject the wave-particle duality as conceptualized by Bohr.

The first stems from the interpretation of "beables"[1] in ontological analyses. In the complementarity framework, both waves and particles are considered to exist. However, some argue that neither truly exists, suggesting instead that their apparent dual behavior is a pseudo-problem tied to the outdated ontology of classical physics. This view is supported by figures like Heisenberg and Jordan, who advocated a radical anti-realist stance that emphasized the necessity of "withdrawing" into mathematical formalism.

The second and third arguments involve asserting the exclusive existence of either particles or waves. One possibility is that only particles exist

The first possibility is that particles exist without waves. This is the case of Born's famous interpretation of the Schrödinger equation, in which the wave function is regarded as a mere mathematical tool that allows one to calculate, through its square modulus, the probability density of finding a given particle in a given region of space.

The alternative argument posits that only waves exist. Schrödinger's view supports this proposal. He advocated a purely wave-like ontology, interpreting his wave function as a real physical wave and denying any corpuscular aspect to atomic phenomena.

There are also three reasons to endorse a form of wave-particle duality. According to Bohr's principle of complementarity, either waves or particles (in a mutually exclusive sense) exist. In his view, the necessity of resorting to

---

[1] The term "beable" refers to items that exist according to the theory, things that are "just there." The beables of a theory just are the ontology of the theory (Maudlin 2019).

both representations (wave and corpuscular) is assumed with the impossibility of fully reconciling them in one unitary image of physical reality. In addition, without accepting the complementarity principle, it is possible to advocate for a duality of both waves and particles. De Broglie—who firmly believed, having extended the duality from radiation to matter in the dual nature of atomic objects—rejected the limitation of complementarity, asserting the possibility of coexistence between an extended wave phenomenon and a localised particle.

Another possibility is represented by particles driven by ghost waves, as sustained by Einstein, who, despite having reintroduced through his famous hypothesis of light quanta a corpuscular theory of radiation, believed that the phenomena of interference and diffraction were not explainable on the grounds of a purely corpuscular conception, but also required the presence of a wave, accompanying and guiding the quanta in their movement. However, the fact that all the energy was concentrated in the quantum and that the wave associated with it was consequently devoid of this fundamental property led Einstein to introduce the term *Gespensterfelder*[2] for such "waves".

4 Alternatives to complementarity with an ontological commitment to the reality of the wave function

To bypass the notion of complementarity, one possibility is to make some ontological commitments about the reality of the wave function. In this section, we will briefly introduce three non-standard realistic interpretations of the wave function, on which one of us (G. T.) has focused our research on the foundations of quantum mechanics for some time.

These realistic interpretations of quantum mechanics are the following:

1. de Broglie pilot waves (de Broglie, 1957), according to which the fundamental ontology of the quantum world consists of particles guided by pilot waves, which are understood as real physical entities;

2. Selleri empty (or quantum) wave (Selleri, 1971) defined by Renninger and Selleri as *zero energy wave-like (undulatory) phenomenon*;

3. the approach of the reality of the "no-photon" state (Albert 1996, 2023, Ney 2023), replacing traditional superposition with an *entanglement* between a particle and a *no-particle* in the case of a single particle.

These three realist interpretations seem apparently different but are actually conceptually very close. They reject the antirealist perspective of the Göttingen School and attempt to eliminate the complementary and exclusive nature of the wave-particle duality. As we shall show, however, they each lead to new forms of complementarity.

---

[2]The term introduced by Einstein can be translated as ghost waves.

On the one hand, the reality of de Broglie's pilot waves and Selleri's empty waves imply smooth complementarity, which we will explain in the following paragraphs, between wave-like and particle-like behaviour. On the other hand, the reality of the no-thing, in the sense of the attribution of a physical state to the no-photon, conflicts, as we will see, with a non-metaphysical formulation of Cartesian causality, highlighting how even the complementarity between two philosophical principles, such as realism and causality, highlighted by Bohr since the Como congress in the case of space-time coordination and Kantian causality, can have a smooth nature.

Let us briefly introduce each of these interpretations in the following paragraphs.

4.1 Pilot wave interpretation

The first realistic interpretation of the wave function that tries to avoid complementarity is the theory of the pilot wave proposed by de Broglie.[3] This interpretation posits that the quantum world comprises two distinct entities, both endowed with physical reality: the wave and the particle.

In this interpretation, the wave ψ is understood as a classical field that moves wave-likely in space and that 'pilots' a classical particle embedded in the field. The particle is, therefore, sensible to any wave-like superposition of the field. In the example of a two-slit experiment, the particle, factually, though both slits are open, always passes only through one slit, and the diffraction pattern is entirely due to the strange and wave-like trajectory impressed by the field. From this perspective, there is no complementarity between wave and particle and no 'indeterminacy'.

Einstein's point of view constituted a sort of weakening of de Broglie's pilot wave interpretation and, at the same time, rejected the incomprehensibility of Bohr's complementary interpretation.

Nonetheless, this approach raises an essential question: how can we accept the existence of an entity, such as the guiding wave, that lacks directly observable physical properties?

De Broglie's interpretation was unsatisfactory because the physical quantities were mainly associated with particles. However, an infinitesimally small fraction of them, so small that it escaped all possible observations, was associated with the wave in contrast with Planck's fundamental postulate of unity and indivisibility of the quantum of action.

---

[3]He proposed this interpretation in several articles and presented his theory at the Fifth Physical Conference of the Solvay Institute in Brussels (October 1927). However, the various essential criticisms of his proposal led de Broglie to abandon the theory. He did so in a public lecture at the University of Hamburg in early 1928, but later (1955–1956), he returned to his old proposal.

4.2 Selleri empty wave

De Broglie's interpretation was revived in the 1960s by Renninger in his paradox of negative measurement and by Selleri, who developed an original alternative interpretation of the wave function. This interpretation, like that of de Broglie, assumed the reality of waves and corpuscular particles, but with an ontological priority of the latter over the former, insofar as quantum waves were identified as a "zero energy undulatory phenomenon".

Selleri proposed a new hypothesis according to which the wave function, even without any physical quantity associated with it, could give rise to physically observable phenomena. Indeed, in quantum mechanics, "we do not only measure energies, momenta, and so on. We also measure probabilities, e.g. the lifetime of an unstable system" (Selleri 1969, p. 910). The wave function could, therefore, have acquired physical reality, independently of the associated particles, if it can give rise to changes in the transition probabilities of the system with which it interacts.

Starting from this original intuition, Selleri presented the first version of his experiment to reveal the properties of quantum (empty) waves, considering a piece of matter composed of unstable entities, such as nuclei, atoms or excited molecules crossed by a continuous flow of neutrinos. He, therefore, proposed to measure the average life of these nuclei and then compare it with the average life of the same entities in the absence of any flow: if a difference is observed, the only logical explanation is that "it is due to the action of the wave function since the neutrinos are extremely weakly interacting particles and only a few of them, at most, can have interacted in the piece of matter with presently available neutrino intensities" (Selleri 1969, p. 910).[4]

4.2.1 De Broglie's endorsement and the revival of the pilot wave

Selleri's hypothesis was greatly appreciated by de Broglie, who identified that idea as "an important attempt aimed at obtaining an interpretation of wave mechanics more satisfactory than the one currently adopted and a confirmation of the ideas that had guided me when I proposed the basic conceptions of wave mechanics in 1923–24" (L. de Broglie, letter to F. Selleri, 11–IV 1969).

This endorsement also led to a revival of de Broglie's pilot wave by the main exponent of the de Broglie school, Jean-Pierre Vigier, who was strongly motivated in the search for a realistic and causal interpretation of quantum mechanics, on which he had already worked with David Bohm, proposing their nonlocal theories of hidden variables.

The experiments proposed by Vigier and others were aimed at revealing the wave-like interference properties by finding the persistence of the inter-

---

[4]Selleri's original idea was perfected in the proposal of an experiment: see Selleri (1971).

ference pattern, even in physical situations where, in a Mach-Zender device (such as the double slit), one can distinguish the path followed by the wave without the particle and the path followed by the wave with the particle.

In these cases, however, we are not simply dealing with an alternative philosophical interpretation of the wave function, but with experiments that also test the validity of the reduction postulate, according to which the interference disappears every time one is able to know which path the particle has followed.

The most advanced of these experiments, designed by Vigier, Garuccio, Rapisarda, and in a later version by these three authors together with Karl Popper, was based on the possibility of being realised only if the hypothesis of the detection of the Selleri wave's property of producing stimulated emission in a laser gain tube was verified.

However, G. T. has shown that the possibility of detecting the interference while determining the path followed by the particle without producing the reduction of the wave function did not necessarily require the denial of Selleri's hypothesis, and therefore, it was possible to do a single experiment to detect either de Broglie–Vigier waves or Selleri waves.

4.3 The failure to reveal empty waves and the emergence of *smooth* complementarity

Two types of experiments were done to detect quantum waves.

The first type was to find the empty wave, that is, to see if it produced stimulated emission or had properties separate from the particle; in this case, it did not contradict the formalism of quantum mechanics but only Born's interpretation of the wave function. The results were negative both in the Mandel and co-worker experiment and of Hardy[5], which could arrive at no conclusive results because the effect could also be explained by ordinary quantum mechanics without empty waves.

Therefore, Selleri's hypothesis was not confirmed by experiments.

The second type of experiment—which we have already mentioned in the previous paragraph—consisted, instead, of searching for the path of a photon or electron inside an interferometer without destroying the interference pattern in order, therefore, to have both the path and the interference, thus violating complementarity. This proposal by Vigier and co-authors would have undermined a postulate of the wave function collapse. Therefore, it would have been a much more crucial experiment concerning the validity of the formalism of quantum mechanics.

These experiments seemed at first to favour Vigier's interpretation, in the sense of the possibility of both determining the path and finding the interference; in reality, it was later discovered, thanks to Mittelstaedt, Prieur,

---

[5] For both experiments, see Auletta and Tarozzi (2004b).

and Schieder (1987), that these two aspects were not fully determined. They were only partially determined (neither was precise). Therefore, an experiment that initially had to contradict complementarity by letting waves and particles coexist was transformed into an experiment that contradicted complementarity only in the restrictive form of Heisenberg and, more generally, of Göttingen (i.e., the one that stated that there are classical properties that are mutually exclusive)[6]. Mittelstaedt, Prieur, and Schieder reinterpreted these experiments as a confirmation of a new version of complementarity, called *smooth*, according to which one can have partly the path, partly the interference, that is, a form of complementarity no longer sharp between waves and particles, but between a partly wave image and a partly corpuscular image, which can coexist but only partially. They showed that complementarity is a smooth variation between wave-like and particle-like behaviours. Therefore, there are infinite intermediate possibilities between the two extreme alternatives. What emerged, therefore, was a confirmation of Bohr's complementarity, indeed, in some ways even beyond Bohr, towards a somewhat more realistic perspective.

The previous examinations seem to lead to no conclusive result: any attempt to prove the reality of quantum waves seems to fail. However, we underline the positive result of the smooth complementarity, which runs against the idea that complementarity is a sharp relation in which we have either the wave or the particle: the smooth version shows that there is no reason to assign reality only to the particle since there is a continuous link between something like the particle—that we do not hesitate to judge physical and real because it is provided with energy and momentum—and a wave which seems devoid of these detectable properties.

In the spirit of Heisenberg's interpretation, one could also reject the reality of the particle and limit oneself to admitting the reality of detection events only. However, there are reasons to think that a measurement can never completely purify a system from the interference effects that are present. In fact, interference effects have been shown to exist also at the mesoscopic level and probably still exist in the macroscopic world.

4.4 The reality of the state of the no-photon

This section explores a weaker realist interpretation of the wave function, grounded in the recognition of physical reality as "nothingness"—specifically, the absence of a particle (such as a photon or electron). This approach reframes the wave function collapse as a consequence not of an interaction between an empty wave and the measuring device, but of detecting the particle's absence.

---

[6] Note that Mittelstaedt et al.'s results were anticipated by Wootters and Zurek, and confirmed by Greenberger and Yasin, and by Englert (see the references in Auletta and Tarozzi 2004b).

Our argument is based on the idea of describing a single photon that can be found at one or another of two distant places, here and there. Let us suppose, for instance, Bologna and Münster, through an entanglement replacing the standard superposition state.

The photon is indivisible and cannot appear partly here and partly there. It will not be there if it is found here, and vice versa. We will use $|1\rangle$ to denote the presence of the photon, $|0\rangle$ to denote its absence; the product $|0\rangle \otimes |1\rangle$, which we can write $|01\rangle$, will accordingly indicate that there is a photon there and nothing (no photon) here. Similarly, $|10\rangle$ indicates a photon here and no photon there. If we consider the physical situation similar to de Broglie's paradox, here and there would correspond to Bologna and Münster.

The two possibilities $|01\rangle$ and $|10\rangle$ can be combined in the superposition:

$$|\psi\rangle = \frac{1}{\sqrt{2}}(|01\rangle - |10\rangle),$$

whose fundamental aspect stays in its coherence, expressed by the minus sign between the two terms, which means the two products are physically related and communicate. This coherence means that both possibilities, $|01\rangle$ and $|10\rangle$, are present before an observation or a measurement operation produces the collapse to either one or the other.

Note that the state of entanglement that we will use is a formal complication intentionally adopted to do the detection. This state is a sort of formal stratagem precisely chosen, as we will see shortly, to give a physical state to the non-being of the photon (no-photon) and, therefore, make an overlap between being (here or there) and non-being (there or here, respectively) of the photon. So without entanglement, one does not have the detection of the no-photon that causes the collapse, as the one of the empty wave in Selleri's interpretation.

Let us make an observation or a measuring operation on the photon *here* in Bologna and not find the photon. Its absence will produce a collapse of the superposition to its second term $|01\rangle$, while the expectation of the photon *there* in Münster jumps from 0 to 1.

The jump takes place once we have found out that the photon is not here in Bologna, where we have detected or registered nothing. However, what does the discovery of the absence of the photon involve?

Our no-thing does not correspond to an absolute no-being or nothingness, but simply to a relative no-photon. In this way, one attributes the collapse of the wave function, and the corresponding modification of the physical situation, to the registration process of the absence of the photon, namely, in our formalism, $|01\rangle$, *no-photon* here and photon there, or in other terms to the photon registration failure here and consequent registration there.

So that, if there is no photon, one can explain the collapse of the wave function and the corresponding modification of the physical situation by appealing to the physical properties of nothing, here understood as the absence of the photon (*no-photon*).

Does this attempt allow us to get rid of complementarity and also of Born's interpretation, according to which the wave function is only a mathematical tool for calculating the probability of particle detection, through a new form of wave function realism, assuming the reality of the particle and of the no-particle (wave function without the particle)?

We will try to show that if this may be true for the complementary interpretation of the wave-particle duality, this conclusion cannot be maintained for the complementary principle in general. To do this, we must briefly introduce Descartes' concept of causality.

5 Cartesian causality and the consequences of its violation

Descartes' causality is based on his so-called principle of "non-inferiority of causes" as outlined in his *Third Meditation*:

> But Now, it is evident by the *Light of Nature* that there must be *as much* at least in the *Total efficient Cause*, as there is in the *Effect* of *that Cause*; For from Whence can the *effect* have its *Reality*, but from the *Cause*? and how can the *Cause* give it that *Reality*, unless *it self have* it?
>
> And from hence it follows, that neither a *Thing* can be made out of *Nothing*, Neither a *Thing* which is *more Perfect* (that is, Which has in it self *more Reallity*) *proceed* from *That* Which is *Less Perfect*. (in Gaukroger, 2006, pp. 216–217).

According to this fundamental conception, the Cause can never be "inferior" to its effect: a "more real" thing cannot come from a "less real" thing. Hence, it follows that a thing whatsoever cannot be made out of nothing since nothing is the "least real" of all things. This view is similar to the principles already expressed by Parmenides and Lucretius.

It is important to note that Cartesian causality's concept of "nothing" is a form of metaphysically absolute nothingness, namely the complete absence of any property or determination of being. This is even more explicit in the fourth meditation in which Descartes stresses that nothing is a *negative idea* and an absolute *no-being* (an antipode to the perfect and absolute being, which is God):

> ... when I return to the *Contemplation* of *my self*, I find my self liable to *Innumerable Errors*. Enquiring into the *cause* of which, I find in my self an *Idea*, not only a *real* and *positive one* of a *God*, that is, of a

Being infinitely perfect, but also (as I may so speak) a *Negative Idea* of *Nothing*; that is to say, I am so constituted between God and Nothing or between a perfect *Being* and *No-being*, that as I am *Created* by the *Highest Being*, I have nothing in Me by which I may be *deceived* or drawn into *Error*; but as I pertake in a manner of *Nothing*, or of a *No-Being*, that is, as I my self am *not* the *Highest Being*, and as I *want* many *perfections*, 'tis no Wonder that I should be *Deceived*. (*ibid.*, p. 223)

Cartesian causality is violated in the realistic interpretations of QM seen before, both in attributing a weak level of physical reality to the wave function and in recognising some kind of reality as nothing. The reason for the former interpretations is evident: the lower causes embodied in empty waves would give rise to more "real", in a sense more manifest, effects embodied in interferences and stimulated emissions of particles so that a weaker level of reality would produce a detectable stronger one, contrary to Cartesian' principle of the inferiority of causes over effects.

Regarding the latter interpretation, in order to comprehend the kind of nothing implied by our previous argument—a nothing as negation—is useful to recall Henri Bergson's concept of void as introduced in his *Creative Evolution*: "The void of which I speak [...] is, at bottom, only *the absence of some definite object, which was here at first, is now elsewhere* and, in so far it is no longer in its former place, leaves behind it, so to speak, the void of itself" (1922, pp. 296–7). Therefore, Bergson's relative void adheres perfectly to our partial/relative nothing regarded as the no-photon: it is a nothing understood not as the absence of a metaphysical being but of a physical object that could be identified by the measurement process, before which QM attributes a sort of potential reality through the wave function.

In this way, the attribution of some sort of reality—we could paradoxically say of presence—to the absence of the photon, which implies the reality of a relative nothing, entails a significant violation of Cartesian causality, in its more general form corresponding to the principle of the non-inferiority of causes: the no-photon state, being fundamentally a relative nothing devoid of all the physical characteristics of normal things, has a weaker degree of reality than the consequences it originates.

Therefore, the increasingly weaker realistic interpretations seen so far conflict with Cartesian causality. This implies that overcoming the complementarity between waves and particles effectively means reintroducing the classical complementarity between realism and causality, which was the original one of the Como Congress. However, unlike the one that emerged in that Congress, the complementarity between realism and causality is *smooth*, just as Mittelstaedt, Prieur, and Schieder had shown for waves and particles. Thus, in QM, there are other forms of incompatibility between causality and realism (in addition to that of Bohr, where realism is identified with space-time coordination and causality with conformity to law, according to Kant). It turns out that Mittelstaedt's smooth complementarity is not limited only to ontology, namely to the wave-particle pair, but can also be extended to philosophical conceptions (or categories): in our case, to the "pair" realism-causality.

6 Conclusions

Based on the preceding analysis, we conclude that adopting a minimal ontological commitment to the foundational concepts of quantum mechanics ultimately reaffirms the principle of complementarity, albeit in the weaker and smoother forms discussed. Simultaneously, this analysis rejects restrictive interpretations of complementarity that oversimplify its scope.

All the tentative attempts to eliminate complementarity made by the wave function realists (like Albert, de Broglie, Selleri) have led to the reintroduction of complementarity between two philosophical concepts: weak realism and strong Cartesian causality.

On the other hand, it must be stressed that Bohr's position was never closed with regard to the recognition of the reality of the wave-like phenomena.

First of all, it must be remembered that in 1924 Bohr tried to develop his theory of the virtual wave (which was soon abandoned because it was contradicted by experimental evidence).

Finally, it should not be forgotten that less than a year after Born interpreted the Schrödinger wave function as a mathematical tool to calculate the probability density of finding a particle, Bohr formulated his complementarity principle, which implied the wave-particle dualism instead.

The complementarity principle survives independently of the various interpretations of quantum mechanics and the beables that they assert.

We are persuaded that the dualism claimed by complementarity, despite repeated criticism and attempts to eliminate it by both orthodox and non-standard interpretations, is destined to persist, taking on different forms and modalities from time to time, as a fundamental character of quantum phenomena, at least until a more satisfactory theory is found.

References

Auctores varii (1928), *Atti del Congresso Internazionale dei fisici, 11–20 settembre 1927, V, Como – Pavia – Roma*, Pubblicati a cura del Comitato, Vol. I, Zanichelli, Bologna, p. xii.

Albert, D. Z. (1996), "Elementary quantum metaphysics", in J. T. Cushing, A. Fine, & S. Goldstein (eds.), *Bohmian mechanics and quantum theory: An appraisal*, Kluwer Academic Publishers, pp. 277–284.

Albert, D. Z. (2023), *A Guess at the Riddle: Essays on the Physical Underpinnings of Quantum Mechanics*, Harvard University Press, Harvard.

Auletta, G., Tarozzi, G. (2004a), "Wavelike Correlations Versus Path Detection: Another Form of Complementarity", *Foundations of Physics Letters*, Vol. 17, No. 1, pp. 89–95.

Auletta, G., Tarozzi, G. (2004b), "On the Physical Reality of Quantum Waves", *Foundations of Physics*, Vol. 34, No. 11, pp. 1675–1694.

Bergson, H. (1922), *Creative Evolution*, Macmillan, London.

Bohm, D. (1957), *Causality and Chance in Modern Physics*, Routledge & Kegan, London.

Bohr, N. (1928), "The quantum postulate and the recent development of atomic theory", in Auctores varii, *Atti del Congresso Internazionale dei fisici, 11–20 settembre 1927, V, Como – Pavia – Roma*, Pubblicati a cura del Comitato, Vol. I, Zanichelli, Bologna, pp. 589–591.

de Broglie, L. (1957), "Foreword", in D. Bohm, *Causality and Chance in Modern Physics*, Routledge and Kegan.

Fano, V. (1991), "La riflessione degli scienziati sulla meccanica quantistica in Italia fra le due guerre", in G. Cattaneo & A. Rossi (eds.), *I fondamenti della meccanica quantistica. Analisi storica e problemi aperti*, Commenda di Rende.

Fock, V. (1957), "On the interpretation of Quantum Mechanics", *Czechoslovak Journal of Physics*, Vol. 7, No. 6, pp. 643–656.

Gaukroger, S. (ed.)(2006), *The Blackwell Guide to Descartes' Meditations*, Blackwell P., Malden, USA.

Gianfranceschi, G. (1928), "Il significato fisico della teoria dei quanti", in Auctores varii, *Atti del Congresso Internazionale dei fisici, 11–20 settembre 1927, V, Como – Pavia – Roma*, Pubblicati a cura del Comitato, Vol. I, Zanichelli, Bologna, pp. 559–564.

Heidegger, M. (1998), "What is Metaphysics?", in W. McNeill (ed.), *Pathmatks*, Cambridge University Press, Cambridge.

Lewis, P. (2004), "Life in configuration space", *British Journal for the Philosophy of Science*, Vol. 55, pp. 713–729.

Maiocchi, R. (1991), *Non solo fermi. I fondamenti della meccanica quantistica nella cultura italiana tra le due guerre*, Le Lettere, Firenze, pp. 194–198.

Maudlin, T. (2019), *Philosophy of Physics: Quantum Theory*, Princeton University Press, Princeton.

Mittelstaedt, P., Prieur, A., Schieder, R. (1987), "Unsharp particle-wave duality in a photon split-beam experiment", *Foundations of Physics*, Vol. 17, pp. 891–903.

Ney, A. (2021), *The world in the wave function: A metaphysics for quantum physics*, Oxford University Press, Oxford.

Pietrini, D. (2019), "Gianfranceschi e la divulgazione della relatività in Italia. Storia di una conferenza manoscritta e della corrispondenza inedita con Tullio Levi-Civita", in *Isonomia, Rivista online di Filosofia – Epistemologica*.

Schilpp, P. A. (ed.) (1970), *Albert Einstein: Philosopher-Scientist*, in *The Library of Living Philosophers*, Vol. VII, Evanston, Illinois, pp. 201–241.

Selleri, F. (1969), "On the Wave Function of Quantum Mechanics", *Lettere al Nuovo Cimento*, Vol. 1, No. 17, pp. 908–10.

Selleri, F. (1971), "Realism and the Wave-function of Quantum Mechanics", in B. D'Espagnat (ed.), *Foundations of Quantum Mechanics*, Academic Press, New York.

Science and scientific realism: challenges from quantum physics

Dennis Dieks

History and Philosophy of Science, Utrecht University, Princetonplein 5, 3584 CC Utrecht, The Netherlands

1 Introduction

The current predominant philosophical view of scientific progress is a form of scientific realism that holds that science provides increasingly accurate representations of reality (see Alai 2017 and references therein). According to this "accumulative realist" view, scientific theories should be seen not only as tools for predicting observable phenomena, but also as accurate descriptions of real, albeit largely unobservable, processes and entities. Terms such as electron or quark, for example, should be understood as referring to submicroscopic objects that exist in the same way as the observable things around us. Many philosophers of science take this perspective almost for granted. They argue that the predictive success of theories, consistently verified by experiments, is convincing evidence for their truth. Indeed, they say, it would be miraculous if our theories could be so predictively successful without tapping into the unobservable processes responsible for what we see happening in the world; the best explanation for predictive success is undoubtedly truth.

It is widely recognized, nevertheless, that all scientific theories, even the most successful, are provisional. Every theory contains unresolved questions and areas where predictions fail. The history of science shows that even seemingly untouchable theories are eventually replaced by new ones. Yet proponents of accumulative scientific realism argue that the provisional nature of scientific theories and their replacement by newer theories does not indicate that current theories are fundamentally flawed. Rather, they argue that the consistent empirical success of a theory in a given domain demonstrates that the theory contains parts that are true or at least close to the truth. Scientific progress then consists in selecting, preserving and refining these accurate aspects, while abandoning or revising those parts of the theory that turn out to be incorrect and unnecessary for empirical success. Through this process, they argue, science gets closer and closer to the truth. Thus, the evolution of atomic theory from the idea of indivisible particles in 19th-century physics to the contemporary picture of atoms built up from subatomic particles such as quarks illustrates the gradual refinement of our understanding of atoms.

In this article, we will challenge this notion of continuous and accumulative growth of our scientific knowledge of physical reality. Much of the philosophy of science literature on the subject focuses on 18th and 19th century physical theories and tends to overlook the important new problems posed by 20th and 21st century physics (see, however, Dieks 2017, Callender 2020, and Egg and Saatsi 2021, as examples of exceptions). To compensate for this bias, we will here concentrate on the relationship between quantum mechanics and classical physics. We will argue that accumulative realism in this case underestimates the drastic conceptual differences between the classical and quantum frameworks.

As we will explain, the fact that new theories are able to reproduce the empirical success of their predecessors does not entail that parts of the old ontology are (approximately) retained in the new theories. Instead, features of older theories often *emerge* from the predictions of newer theories, in limiting scenarios that represent only a small part of the broader scope of those newer theories. The ontologies that fit this broader range of the new theories may differ radically from what was assumed previously. Moreover, the huge gap between direct observation and the abstract formalisms of modern physics turns out to leave room for multiple conflicting ontological interpretations. Modern physics thus tangibly exacerbates concerns about both discontinuity and theoretical underdetermination.

2 Quantum mechanics

Understanding the argument of this article requires knowledge of only a small number of basic principles of quantum mechanics. Quantum mechanics has replaced classical mechanics because the latter fails to correctly predict the results of experiments involving submicroscopic matter. But quantum mechanics also introduces fundamental changes in the general conceptual framework of physics.

In classical mechanics, matter is depicted as composed of small particles possessing definite values of mass, position, and velocity, possibly also of additional properties like electric charge. The mathematical representation of classical particles therefore involves specifying the values of these quantities, typically focusing on position and velocity, or equivalently, position and momentum (denoted as (x, p), where $p = mv$, mass times velocity). Classical mechanics formulates laws of motion that dictate how these quantities change over time under the influence of forces.

Quantum mechanics replaces this intuitively clear and plausible picture with a considerably more abstract one. Instead of the classical particle representation (x, p), quantum mechanics introduces wave functions denoted as $\psi(x)$. Here, x still represents position, but not as a particle property as in classical mechanics. The precise physical interpretation of the mathematical symbols in quantum mechanics is a subject of debate, with various interpretations proposing different perspectives (this multiplicity of interpretations and its significance for our theme will be addressed later in this article). However, it is universally agreed-upon that in a *measurement* of position, the value x has a probability $|\psi(x)|^2$ of being observed as the outcome. This interpretative rule forms the core of what may be termed the standard or textbook interpretation of quantum mechanics.

The wave function $\psi(x)$ evolves over time according to a deterministic equation known as the Schrödinger equation, which serves as the quantum analogue of the classical Newtonian equation of motion. Just as the classical equation of motion determines a particle's unique position and velocity at an instant t given its initial properties and all forces acting upon it, the Schrödinger equation determines a unique wave function $\psi(x,t)$ given the initial wave function $\psi(x,0)$ and all interactions and potentials.

This ultra-short summary of the difference between classical and quantum mechanics will form the basis for our argument that the very notion of a particle, and indeed the concept of a material object more broadly, becomes problematic within the framework of quantum mechanics. The core innovation on which we will focus is that quantum mechanics does not characterize its subject matter with the help of combinations of *properties*, like (x, p), but instead uses wave functions $\psi(x)$ whose meaning is given in terms of measurement outcomes and their probabilities, without reference to preexisting particle properties.

3 Modeling a macroscopic object in quantum mechanics

The mathematical formalism used by quantum mechanics diverges significantly from its classical counterpart. As we have seen, an important aspect is that the quantum formalism does not rely on the existence of objects with definite positions and velocities. This striking fact prompts questions about how quantum mechanics can accommodate the behavior of objects as we perceive them in our everyday experience. If quantum "entities" lack well-defined positions and velocities, the notion of following definite trajectories becomes dubious as well, which raises questions even about the identity of systems over time.

These concerns can be given a more rigorous, mathematical form. Consider the following scenario described classically: a box divided into two compartments by a threshold (represented mathematically by a potential barrier), with a small yet macroscopic ball placed in one compartment. For quantum mechanics to be empirically adequate in this situation, it must be capable of describing and predicting the behavior of the ball. Representing a localized ball with a wave function must involve assuming a very narrow $\psi(x)$;

indeed, a measurement of the ball's position should yield results confined to a narrowly defined region. On the basis of our classical experience we expect the ball, and therefore the narrow wave function assigned by quantum mechanics, to remain stationary in the absence of external forces; perhaps with some kind of quantum fluctuations.

As noted by Leggett and Garg (1985) in a paper discussing a very similar scenario, even physicists often tend to conceptualize such situations in broadly classical terms, despite years of exposure to quantum mechanics. However, applying the Schrödinger equation to the initial wave function, while considering the repulsive potential barrier representing the threshold, yields a result that defies classical expectations. Calculating $\psi(x,t)$ reveals a non-zero probability emerging over time for finding the ball in the other compartment, across the threshold. The wave function transforms into a "superposition" encompassing parts located in both compartments, implying that upon measurement, the ball may be found in either compartment.

Although the wave function extends across both compartments, quantum mechanics dictates that a measurement will always yield the ball in either the left or right compartment—never both simultaneously. This prediction of quantum mechanics aligns with our classical expectations and invites an interpretation in terms of a classical object. We could accordingly suppose that an at all times localized ball exhibits quantum fluctuations, occasionally traversing the threshold to end up in the alternate compartment.

However, Leggett and Garg demonstrated that if we assume that in such scenarios objects are always localized either in the left or the right compartment, and that this could be verified, in principle, by means of measurements that disturb the object only insignificantly, an inequality analogous to Bell's inequality must be satisfied. This inequality involves correlations between the results of position measurements conducted at various times.

The two assumptions needed for the argument—always definite localization of objects and the possibility in principle of non-invasive measurements revealing these locations--are typical of classical physics. Leggett and Garg take these assumptions to define what they call "macroscopic realism". Indeed, it is essential for the classical worldview that there are objects with always definite positions, and the predictions made for these positions by classical physics are always assumed to correspond to what is found in observation. However, in well-chosen quantum versions of the scenario (with the right forms for the potential barrier and the ball's interaction with it) the quantum mechanical predictions violate the Leggett-Garg inequalities. This violation establishes that it is possible to experimentally disprove the classical picture of an always localized object moving between compartments.

Several such experiments have been conducted since 1985. The results accord with the quantum mechanical predictions, and conflict with "macro realism".

This result may be interpreted as simply another piece of evidence for the universal validity of the non-classical ontology provided by quantum mechanics, even at the macroscopic level, and as such it may be deemed unsurprising (Bacciagaluppi 2016). Indeed, there are good reasons anyway to believe that quantum mechanics does not stop to be valid at some border line between what is microscopic and what is macroscopic. If this universal validity is accepted, then the non-existence of classical objects with always definite and non-invasively measurable dynamical quantities is only to be expected, since this is the rule in the microscopic quantum realm (more on this in the next section).

If quantum theory is universally valid, the question arises of why the concept of a classical object with well-defined properties works so well in our ordinary dealings with the physical world. The answer, from the point of view of quantum mechanics, is that in everyday circumstances factors are present, in particular "decoherence" mechanisms, that mask typical quantum effects like dissipation of the wave function and the occurrence of superpositions. As a result, classical patterns *emerge* in observational results: although everything happens in accordance with the quantum rules, and although precise measurements can reveal the inapplicability of a classical particle picture, a coarse-grained description exhibits patterns that look like classical particle behavior. In other words, the (approximate) applicability of a classical particle picture is an *emergent phenomenon*—a point whose relevance for the scientific realism debate will be discussed later in this article.

4 Quantum objects

Experimental evidence supporting the validity of quantum mechanics even at near-macroscopic scales has accumulated in many forms over recent decades. This evidence suggests that macroscopic entities exhibit the same fundamental characteristics as submicroscopic entities. Thus, the existence of classical objects is challenged in a general and coherent way, which reinforces the conclusions drawn from specific tests like the Leggett-Garg experiments.

That our classical intuitions about objects fail in the submicroscopic world has for long been common knowledge. A standard illustration is the double slit experiment. Suppose an electron is made to traverse a screen with two slits, and we attempt to discover through which slit the electron passes. Quantum mechanics predicts, and we actually find in experiments, that on traversal the electron is always found in exactly one single slit. This is analogous to what we explained for the ball in the box scenario: the ball will always be found in exactly one single compartment. But, returning to the case of the electron, we know that the assumption that the electron goes through exactly one slit leads to trouble if we consider other possible experiments. In particular, when we measure where the electron lands on a second screen (after having traversed the double-slit screen without experiments taking place there) we will be confronted with the effects of interference, whose explanation needs the assumption of contributions from *both* slits. According to standard quantum mechanics this implies that the electron was *not* localized in one of the slits when it traversed the screen (the Bohm interpretation, about which more later, offers the non-standard alternative explanation that it is a *field*, existing in addition to the electron and guiding the electron's motion, that goes through both slits). This standard conclusion is similar to what was inferred from violations of Leggett-Garg inequalities in our box scenario, namely non-localizability of the ball in general, despite the fact that position *measurements* always find the ball at definite positions.

The problems with classical objecthood go even further. In one-ball or one-electron scenario's, as discussed above, there seems no reason to doubt that at all points in time we are dealing with the same entity. So, there is no immediate conflict with the classical notion that objects possess synchronic and diachronic *identities*. Classical objects differ from each other at any given instant in at least one physical characteristic (they have synchronic identities), and they can be individually followed over time on the basis of their different trajectories (diachronic identities). But in quantum mechanics (again, in its standard form and interpretation) this is generally not the case. A collection of what we intuitively would like to call "n particles of the same kind" (for example, a collection of n electrons) is not represented quantum mechanically by a set of n individual one-particle wave functions. This is known as the "problem of identical quantum particles" (Dieks 2023b).

Suppose, to illustrate the point, that we have two electrons, described quantum mechanically. Suppose further that we perform initial position measurements, with results x_A and x_B, and that we repeat these experiments at a later moment, with results x_C and x_D. Now, in the general situation there is no answer to the question whether the electron initially found at x_A is the same as the electron found later at x_C, or whether it happens to be the electron found at x_D. The theory does not give us genidentity criteria for what happens between successive measurements.

Nevertheless, under certain circumstances patterns in measurement results may emerge that do suggest the presence of particles following definite trajectories and possessing individual identities. This may happen, for example, in the case of diluted gases (as argued by Schrödinger 1950) or in the presence of decoherence. In such cases a classical particle model may work well for certain practical purposes . However, precision measurements exploring fine-grained features of the situation will still be able to reveal that such a particle model cannot be taken literally. These models therefore function as pragmatic tools yielding useful results within a restricted context, but cannot be said to represent the physical world in a truthful fashion.

5 Emergence as a challenge for scientific realism

As emphasized in the preceding section, the applicability of the classical picture according to which the physical world is populated by objects with individual identities is something that *emerges* in circumstances not too far from those of our everyday experience. Here, emergence may be defined as the appearance of novel and unexpected patterns in the predictions of a theory as long as we stay within a restricted part of its domain of application. The classical domain, i.e., the set of conditions under which classical models can be used successfully, is determined by requirements like high temperatures, many degrees of freedom, and velocities low relative to the speed of light; it is a minute part of the total domain of quantum theory.

The principles of the underlying more fundamental theory remain valid within the domain where emergence occurs, and this is reflected by the fact that the emergent descriptions are only approximately valid. It always remains possible in principle to verify that emergent pictures are only adequate in a coarse-grained treatment; with the help of precision experiments the emergent "laws" may be falsified.

When in the history of physics new physical theories replace older ones, the phenomena predicted by the old theory typically resurface in a restricted part of the domain of application of the new theory. For example, thermodynamic regularities emerge from the theory of atoms and molecules for temperatures well above zero degrees Kelvin and in the presence of many degrees of freedom; Newtonian-like behavior emerges from special relativity when velocities are low relative to the speed of light; etc. In all such cases highly accurate experiments can expose the falsity of the principles of the emergent theories, and this is in fact usually (an important part of) the reason that the old theory was superseded at all.

The importance of emergence in the transition from one theory to the next suggests that the relationships between successive theories are usually not about incremental growth of our knowledge of objects we were already familiar with, but involve the discovery of completely novel entities and processes. Emergence thus poses a challenge to the brand of realism in which it is assumed that scientific progress consists in the addition of new details to our description of fundamental constituents of matter already figuring in older theories.

The problem is aggravated by the fact that the scope of newer theories is usually vastly greater than that of older and superseded theories. This entails that emergent patterns, although considered fundamental in older theories, occupy only a very tiny portion of the domain of applicability of successor theories. Thus, what were considered stable and fundamental building blocks of matter in previous theories later stop to be building blocks at all but rather become ephemeral patterns arising under special conditions.

In an earlier publication devoted to this topic (Dieks 2023a) we discussed how these considerations apply to the relation between Aristotelean and Newtonian mechanics. It is true that the Aristotelean laws of motion (using forces that impart velocities to objects) emerge from the very different Newtonian ones (with forces that cause accelerations) in circumstances where appreciable friction counteracts the accelerating forces. But despite this point of contact between the two theories, it appears inappropriate to maintain that the Newtonian world picture is a refinement of the Aristotelean one. Rather, the Newtonian framework completely replaced the Aristotelean doctrine, and the point of contact between the two is nothing but a logical consequence of the requirement that new theories should be able to reproduce the (limited) empirical success of their predecessors. Similarly, as argued in Section 4, the very concept of an object possessing an individual identity only becomes applicable in a coarse-grained description of a very small part of the quantum domain. Again, it is improper to comment that quantum theory merely adds details to our descriptions of submicroscopic particles (like electrons) that we already recognized as fundamental building blocks of matter in our pre-quantum theories. Rather, quantum theory introduces a completely new view on the nature of physical reality, according to which classical particles simply do not exist.

In the following section we will consider how realists might respond to this challenge.

6 Realist replies

The relation between the quantum realm in which there are no objects and the macroscopic world where objects abound, brings to mind Eddington's famous reflection about his two tables, the scientific and the ordinary one (Eddington 1948). The scientific table is mostly empty space, with here and there some protons and electrons, which themselves are "immaterial", Eddington says. By contrast, the ordinary table is solid and full of substance. As Eddington argues, from a modern scientific point of view, ordinary tables do not exist.

This paradoxical situation may be addressed by pointing out that there are stable object-like patterns in what can be observed on the macroscopic level, and that the object-language that we use is tailored to deal with such patterns. Within the context of that linguistic practice, we are entitled to say that the statement "tables exist" is *true*; indeed, the everyday term "table" in this case refers to phenomenal patterns whose existence can be verified. As Steven French (2014) argues, this is one of several available strategies for making true the statement "There are tables", without commitment to tables as parts of our physical ontology.

The question that should be answered in order to judge the viability of accumulative realism is whether strategies of this kind succeed in salvaging the intuition that science progresses by gradually adding details to our knowledge, thus refining our picture of the world. *Prima facie* this seems a tall order given our specific problem situation, namely that quantum mechanics questions the very notion of an object instead of discovering additional properties of objects. But let us take a closer look.

A standard realist move for reducing the conceptual distance between successive theories is the introduction of the notions of *approximate* and *partial* truth. The idea is that although descriptions of entities given by serious and mature but now superseded scientific theories did not get it completely right, they were not completely wrong either: they were close to the truth. The idea behind "partial truth" is that only some parts of old theories, namely the parts essential for the empirical success of those theories, can have this claim to approximate truth. With these conceptual refinements the central tenet of accumulative realism becomes that the evolution of science is a process in which parts of theories that were essential for their empirical success are preserved and updated, while inessential parts are discarded.

This strategy appears to be of little help if the discontinuity between classical theories, which are all object-based, and quantum mechanics is at stake. Indeed, the concept of an object is absolutely essential for classical physics. For example, Newton's laws of motion only make sense for material bodies following well-defined paths and undergoing accelerations. The empirical success of classical mechanics depends completely and essentially on these laws and the predictions made with them. So, it must be expected that objecthood will be retained in the transition from classical mechanics to quantum mechanics, if something like accumulative realism is to be right. However, we have already concluded that objects do not occur in the conceptual framework of standard quantum theory.

According to accumulative realism, this is an occasion where the notion of *approximate* truth should be invoked. The idea is that although objects as characterized within classical theory do not figure in quantum mechanics, they have quantum counterparts that are quite close to them. This might appear a plausible thought. Indeed, the jargon of quantum physics is full of terms like electron, proton, and so on, that evoke images of little balls—and in the physics literature pictorial representations of quantum experiments with such imagery (black dots indicating electrons, for instance) are often used.

However, equally often the picture of propagating waves is employed. In fact, as has been a subject of discussion since the early days of quantum mechanics, both particle and wave images are merely flawed pictorial tools born out of necessity, since there exist no satisfactory classical "anschaulich" representations of quantum "systems". As we have seen, such "systems" in standard quantum mechanics do not even possess individual identities, so that the very talk about "them", "entities", and similar, is already an abuse of language. The conceptual gap with the classical modes of description is deep. There is no way in which small refinements of the classical notion of a particle can bring us close to the concept of a "quantum particle" (a term used for lack of a better one).

This is not to say, of course, that there is no connection between classical particle theory and quantum mechanics. As discussed before, in certain limiting situations quantum predictions exhibit patterns that closely approximate patterns predicted by classical particle theory. This is a typical case of emergence. But what emerges are patterns in predictions; possibly also patterns in *events* that occur independently of measurements, although the latter is not part of standard quantum mechanics. This emergence in the classical limit does not change the quantum concepts in any way: quantum systems never turn into classical particles, even though in certain restricted limiting situation classical particle models start working well on the phenomenal level.

So, the appeal to approximate and partial truth seems ineffective if accumulative realism is to be saved. An alternative and possibly more promising strategy is that of giving a "functionalist" twist to the realist position (e.g., Cordero 2024). The core idea of functionalist realism is that objects should not be characterized via the basic ontology of theories, but rather by their observable (in the sense of measurable) manifestations. As Cordero (2024) puts it, we should think in terms of "functional" entities, individuated by their *causal effects*. In other words, functional entities are characterized by what they *do* rather than what they *are*. Following this idea, we can have functional classical particles within the classical regime of quantum theory, leaving it open what their "deep quantum ontology" is. Of course, quantum predictions never fully coincide with the predictions of classical theory, not even in the classical limit. Therefore, the emerging functional entities are only "effectively" classical: they closely approximate the behavior of the particles from classical mechanics.

So, in functionalist realism quantum particles are defined as the things responsible for quantum behavior, whereas classical particles are defined by patterns resembling trajectories and other familiar particle-like structures.

Since quantum mechanics makes predictions that in the classical limit are close to those of classical mechanics, the functionalist realist account allows us to argue that within the classical regime of quantum mechanics classical particles are actually present (even though this existence claim must be understood as relative to a coarse-grained, effective description). From the functionalist realist point of view it is not just patterns in predicted phenomena that emerge; the classical particles *themselves* emerge from the quantum realm, as functional and effective entities.

This way of speaking about entities at different levels of description and precision resembles the strategy for handling Eddington's tables mentioned at the beginning of this section. As such, it has the merit of being close to practice. Indeed, who would deny the existence of tables, even in the face of what fundamental physics tells us? But as already noted by Eddington, the relativization with respect to context and degree of precision make effective functional entities less attractive for realist purposes. Clearly, tables cannot figure in any fundamental ontology; even on the macroscopic level improving the precision of measurements makes it possible to put the substantiality of tables in doubt. "Tables", characterized by solidity and substantiality, thus becomes a "for all practical purposes" concept. Functionalist realism therefore runs the risk of boiling down to a pragmatist position, according to which we may call real scientific models that work to a certain degree of precision within a limited domain of application.

The latter position would lead to difficulties for standard scientific realism. Scientific practice abounds with models that work well in restricted contexts; sometimes there are even several different models that may be used in the same situation. If all such models are to have an equal claim to being representative of physical reality, a fragmented and even incoherent picture results. Such a patchwork of descriptions is not what standard realism is striving for. The basic motivation for standard realism is the desire to find the unique description actually fitting the physical world as it really is. This "multiplicity objection" against functionalist realism relates to the more general problem of theoretical underdetermination, about which more in the next section.

With regard to *accumulative* realism, the prospects offered by the functionalist turn seem bleak. If the picture of the world provided by a theory is nothing more than a model functioning well within certain limits, there is no clear reason why newer and better theories, with more extensive domains of application and more precise predictions, will only incrementally extend and refine earlier models. The only certainty is that successes of the old theory will be reproduced by the new theory, with improved precision. But for this to happen emergence is sufficient; there is no need for retention of descriptive elements of the old theory. Therefore, to give accumulative realism a chance, not every possible empirically successful model should *ipso facto* be accepted as descriptive; some selection criterion enabling a distinction between models with fundamental content and merely pragmatic models is needed. But the turn to effective functionalism, with its emphasis on "things that work", does nothing to solve this hard and general problem for scientific realism.

A specific problem arises for the case of quantum versus classical because functionalist realism defines entities "by what they *do*". Quantum particles are characterized by their causal effects, and the hope is that the thus defined entities are sufficiently close to their classical counterparts to make accumulative realism a viable option. But any characterization of quantum particles by their causal effects presupposes that there *are* causally effective individual entities in the quantum domain. As we have noted before, however, according to standard quantum mechanics this assumption is unjustified. The worry that functionalist constructions possess a pragmatic character with a limited scope rather than that they are able to reflect reality "as it is" is thus reinforced.

Summing up, "functionalist realism" is steeped in considerations about coarse graining and restricted domains that relate to human interests and limitations. This raises doubts about its value as a proper realist position. Rather than operating with a correspondence notion of truth, it seems bound up with a pragmatic truth concept. Moreover, even if this pragmatic aspect is recognized and accepted, it remains unclear whether and how functionalist realism could offer a better chance of representing scientific progress as a process of accumulation than standard selective realism paired with approximate truth (the first position discussed in this section).

A final strategy to be mentioned is that of "structural realism". According to structural realism scientific knowledge is knowledge of structures rather than of *things* characterized by monadic properties. From the structural perspective, particles (and objects in general) are nodes in the network of relations that constitutes the structure representing the scientific picture of the world. The idea of accumulative realism is now transformed into the view that the structures posited by old theories survive as parts of new structures.

For our theme the important question is whether structural realism proffers new resources that make it possible to avoid the problems for accumulative realism encountered in the preceding discussion. In particular, does the structural conception make the transition from classical particles to the non-particle-like quantum world more continuous than other forms of realism?

It is difficult to see how this could be the case. The mathematical structure of quantum mechanics is very different from that of classical mechanics. On the quantum side we have the mathematics of Hilbert vector spaces, in which the vectors (and density operators) represent states and linear operators stand for physical quantities. The standard way of representing subsystems of the universe is by reference to the factor spaces in tensor product Hilbert spaces representing composite systems; the states defined in these factor space are usually called one-particle states. It is not evident how this standard account should be reworked into a completely structural one. But anyway, what will result will have the character of relations between one-particle states, i.e., vectors (or density operators) in Hilbert space. In this way one may also obtain relations between physical quantities, via the standard rule that an eigenvector of an operator represents a well-defined value of the physical quantity associated with the operator. By contrast, on the classical side particles are represented by points in phase space, so that a structural account will refer to the relations between such points.

But the relations between quantum states in Hilbert space generally have a very different character from the relations between points in phase space. The best that can be achieved, it seems, are structural similarities that are valid in a restricted domain and in a coarse-grained description. But this brings us back to the problems faced by functionalist realism, discussed previously.

Of course, a certain amount of partial and approximate agreement between successor theories will certainly exist, since new theories have to reproduce (and improve!) the empirical success achieved by their predecessors. This will also be true for structuralist accounts. But such limited continuity has to be expected even within an empiricist analysis of science and does not need accumulative realism for its explanation (Dieks 2023a).

Finally, structural realism faces the problem that the structure of quantum mechanics (or any other physical theory) is not something that is unambiguously given. Not all interpretations of quantum mechanics use the same mathematical formalism. This implies that different interpretations will often propose different structures as descriptions of the physical world. So, structural realism, like other forms of realism, faces the problems posed by theoretical underdetermination.

7 Theoretical underdetermination

The underdetermination of physical theories by empirical evidence is sometimes portrayed as an artificial problem, conceived by philosophers but not present in a serious way in scientific practice. For example, Musgrave (1985) states that typical examples of underdetermination from the philosophy of science literature are contrived constructions while he is aware of only one real (though harmless) case, namely that Newtonian cosmological models only differing in their absolute velocities (i.e., velocities with respect to absolute space) are all in accordance with the same empirical data (because of the Galilean principle of relativity). This verdict of lack of real significance is incorrect: even in classical physics, several classical theories have more than one version, which is reflected in different mathematical formalisms. In quantum mechanics, however, different interpretations, associated with different portrayals of the fundamental physical world, play a particularly important role and have become the subject of debate in a dedicated "foundations of physics" literature. For our theme, namely the viability of accumulative realism, the contrast between interpretations that rely on the standard quantum formalism and the so-called Bohm interpretation is especially interesting.

What we have pointed out before about the difficulties in quantum mechanics with the notion of objecthood presupposed the standard Hilbert space formalism of quantum mechanics. In fact, there are two versions of this standard formalism, depending on whether a special evolution mechanism is assumed for what happens during measurements, namely a "collapse" of the quantum state, or whether ordinary Schrödinger evolution is assumed to be universally valid—in the latter case one speaks of unitary quantum mechanics. The diversity does not stop here. For one thing, there are several conflicting proposals for how to construe the descriptive content of unitary quantum mechanics (one notorious proposal being the many worlds interpretation). But this variety need not concern us here since all these variants adopt the Hilbert space formalism as basic and represent physical systems by Hilbert space vectors (or, equivalently, by wave functions). This representation is the essential reason why objects with individual identities and with definite properties are problematic in standard quantum mechanics.

But there exists an alternative version of quantum mechanics, in which the notion of an object is not problematic at all, but rather fundamental. This is the Bohm interpretation of quantum mechanics (Bohm 1952). According to Bohm, quantum mechanics is a theory about the behavior of *particles*, i.e., objects in the classical sense, possessing definite positions and velocities at all times. So, the world picture provided by quantum mechanics according to Bohm is radically different from the world picture(s) yielded by standard quantum mechanics.

In the Bohm interpretation, the wave function is not viewed as the complete characterization of a quantum system, but is interpreted as an additional player—either a physical field or a new term appearing in the laws of motion. In both cases, the wave function influences the motion of the particles. As it turns out, this influence is such that the wave function corresponds to the probability that a particle will find itself at position x, via the equation $P(x) = |\psi(x)|^2$. Note the difference with standard ideas: the usual view is that quantum systems do not possess definite positions independently of measurements, but that nevertheless a well-defined result x will be created in a position measurement. Quantum mechanics, in this standard view, is indeterministic in the sense that it is generally not determined, before a measurement, what the exact outcome x of a measurement will be. The theory only specifies the probabilities of all possible outcomes, via the formula $P(x) = |\psi(x)|^2$. By contrast, in the Bohm interpretation a position measurement simply reveals the preexisting position of a particle. However, because of a lack of control of the precise initial conditions, repetitions of the experiment will generally not give the same results. There will be a statistical distribution of particle positions, represented by the same formula $P(x) = |\psi(x)|^2$. The meaning of the symbol x occurring in this formula is therefore different in the two cases: according to standard ideas it is a value created in a measurement, but in the Bohm theory it represents a particle property that existed already before the measurement.

The above is only a brief summary of a central idea of the Bohm interpretation. A more extensive discussion should deal with the precise form of the laws governing the motion of the Bohmian particles and with the way the wave function figures in these laws. But the preceding paragraph already suffices to make it understandable that standard quantum mechanics and the Bohm view strongly diverge with respect to their portrayals of physical reality. Nevertheless, the two interpretations make exactly the same empirical predictions. That is, the possible values x of outcomes of experiments, plus the statistical distribution of these values in repeated experiments, are identical in the two cases. What is different is the *meaning* of these outcomes, their place in the two respective worldviews; whether the outcomes are created during measurements or reveal preexisting particle properties.

This metaphysical difference is parallelled by a difference in mathematical structure of the two theories. The collection of all physical states in standard quantum mechanics, as represented in the mathematical formalism, forms a vector (Hilbert) space, as was mentioned before. One of the consequences is that two states (vectors) can be added, which will form a new state. This is the so-called superposition principle. In contrast, the particle state space of the Bohm theory has the structure of classical state spaces: it is a manifold of points with coordinates x, v (position and velocity) in which it makes no sense to add states.

We have argued in Sections 4 and 5 that accumulative realism faces a problem when dealing with the transition from classical physics to quantum mechanics, because the notion of an object, which is central in the classical theory, disappears in quantum mechanics. We now see that this conclusion should be qualified: its validity depends on the version of quantum mechanics that we are contemplating. In the Bohm version of quantum mechanics objecthood remains a central notion, and accumulative realists could here argue that in the classical-to-quantum transition more is learned about the true nature and behavior of fundamental particles like electrons and protons. (This is certainly not uncontroversial, though, since the Bohmian quantum particles possess characteristics that deviate strongly from those of their classical counterparts, so that the accumulative realist idea of incremental refinement is questionable; but this is a subject outside the scope of the present paper).

If the transition from classical mechanics to Bohmian quantum mechanics is a case of continuous growth of our knowledge about particles, this may seem a vindication of accumulative realism. If accumulative realism is the natural, intuitive and close-to-common-sense philosophical position that it proclaims itself to be, one would accordingly expect that the Bohm interpretation is the preferred version of quantum mechanics in actual physical practice. This, however, is not the case. The Bohm theory is only accepted by a minority of physicists, and the standard formalism (including such at first sight outlandish interpretative ideas as the many-worlds interpretation) is much more popular. So, the idea of continuity that is behind accumulative realism does not appear to be a driving force behind actual physical research. Even in the presence of what arguably might be considered a version of quantum mechanics that is continuous with classical physics, the majority of physicists opts for radically different ideas.

Of course, the presence of different but empirically equivalent theoretical schemes in the actual practice of physics poses a challenge for scientific realism in general. If there are several mutually conflicting pictures of reality that can equally be associated with our best physical theories, then how can the thesis be supported that physics provides us with a representation of the physical world as it really is? The further specification of the realist position to the effect that scientific progress is accumulative, consisting in the addition to and refinement of earlier obtained descriptive truth, does not make the position more plausible. It denies the possibility of radical conceptual change concerning essential elements of earlier theories, and thus makes itself vulnerable to empirical disconfirmation.

8 A skeptical conclusion

Accumulative scientific realism is an epistemically optimistic position. While it admits that we are unable to directly perceive what is hidden behind the surface of observation, it argues that scientific theorizing can nevertheless uncover hidden truths at least approximately. Moreover, when new and better theories supplant previous ones, accumulative realism posits that this refines and expands the kernel of truth already present in the older theories. The so-called no-miracles argument is usually cited as justification for these beliefs: the empirical success of our scientific theories would be incomprehensible, and nothing short of a miracle, if our theories did not come close to the truth in essential respects. Since we do not want to be forced to believe in miracles, we apparently have no alternative but to believe that the scientific method is truth-conducive. Apparent counterexamples from scientific practice (the notorious "pessimistic meta-induction") must therefore be able to be refuted by showing that radical conceptual changes involve only non-essential parts of older theories.

However, the comparison of classical mechanics and quantum mechanics does not confirm the leitmotif of continuous growth of truth during scientific progress. As we have argued, the transition from classical physics to quantum theory has completely overturned previous conceptual frameworks, including their essential properties. It follows that preserving essential elements of laws and ontology cannot be necessary to understand the empirical success of earlier, now obsolete, theories. Indeed, a different explanation is available: from the standpoint of standard quantum theory the empirical success of classical mechanics is a consequence of the *emergence* of classical-like patterns, in certain limiting cases. Such emergence does not require the preservation of laws or ontology. More generally, our analysis appears to lend support to the skeptical conclusion that successful scientific theorizing leads to the detection of general patterns and successful descriptive possibilities, but need not postulate a unique truth in order to do so.

References

Agazzi, E., (ed.) (2017). Varieties of Scientific Realism. Objectivity and Truth in Science. New York: Springer.

Alai, M., (2017). The debates on scientific realism today: knowledge and objectivity in science. In Agazzi (2017), 19–47.

Bacciagaluppi, G. (2016). Einstein, Bohm and Leggett-Garg. Chapter 4 in E. Dzhafarov, S. Jordan, R. Zhang, and V. Cervantes (eds.), Contextuality from Quantum Physics to Psychology. Singapore: World Scientific.

Bohm, D. (1952). A suggested Interpretation of the quantum theory in terms of "hidden" variables, I and II. Physical Review 85, 166–179; 180–193.

Callender, C. (2020). Can we quarantine the quantum blight? In S. French and J. Saatsi (eds.), Scientific Realism and the Quantum. Oxford: Oxford University Press, 57–77.

Cordero, A. (2017). Retention, truth-content and selective realism. In Agazzi (2017), 245–256.

Cordero, A. (2024). On the structure and accumulation of realist content. Epistemology & Philosophy of Science 61, 134–150.

Dieks, D. (2017). Underdetermination, realism and objectivity in quantum mechanics. In Agazzi (2017), 295–314.

Dieks, D. (2023a). Emergence, continuity, and scientific realism. Global Philosophy 33:44. DOI: 10.1007/s10516-023-09696-w.

Dieks, D. (2023b). Emergence and identity of quantum particles. Philosophical Transactions of the Royal Society A 381: 2022.0107. DOI: 10.1098/rsta.2022.0107.

Eddington, A. S. (1948). The Nature of the Physical World. Cambridge: Cambridge University Press.

Egg, M., Saatsi, J. (2021). Scientific realism and underdetermination in quantum theory. Philosophy Compass 2021, e12773. DOI: 10.1111/phc3.12773.

French, S. (2014). The Structure of the World: Metaphysics and Representation. Oxford: Oxford University Press.

Leggett, A. J., Garg, A. (1985). Quantum mechanics versus macroscopic realism: Is the flux there when nobody looks?, Physical Review Letters 54, 857–860.

Musgrave, A. (1985). Realism versus Constructive Empiricism. In P. M. Churchland and C. A. Hooker (eds.), Images of Science. Chicago: Chicago University Press, 197–221.

Schrödinger, E. (1950). What is an elementary particle? Endeavour 9, 109–116.

Models or theories: what is the real representation in science?

Jan Faye

Institut for Kommunikation, Københavns Universitet, Karen Blixens Plads 8, København S, Denmark

Abstract. To answer the above question, two interrelated issues have to be untangled and addressed. The semantic view of scientific theories takes models to be interpretations of theories. If this is a correct view of scientific models, we cannot have physical theories without models. A realist understanding of theories takes one of its interpretations to be true or approximately true with respect to either the posited entities or the corresponding structures of some mathematical relations. In combination, we have a view of scientific theories that finds support among many philosophers of science and physicists who all believe that scientific theories should be understood as providing a literal representation of the world.

However, in this paper I shall argue that models should be separated from theories in the sense that models represent a section of the world, whereas theories do not. Scientific theories have no representational role to fulfill at all. Instead, they function just as natural languages do, as linguistic systems that do not represent anything. It is not until we use the vocabulary and the linguistic rules of a particular natural language to formulate statements about the world that these sentences supposedly represent something and therefore are true or false. Similarly, scientific theories establish a vocabulary and linguistic rules by which scientists can ascribe properties to those entities that science introduces in their models. No entity, for instance, appears in Newton's laws and in the quantum mechanical equations. So not until we use the rules and vocabulary of scientific theory to formulate sentences to describe the entities in a model do these sentences become true or false. Now, if a scientific theory is formulated in terms of mathematics, the mathematical relations establish the rules for using a vocabulary that concerns some specific numerical properties, while non-mathematical theories establish the rules for using the vocabulary of some qualitative properties. I conclude that this understanding of scientific theories and models fits both the history of science and the evolution of human beings.

Realism in science is an ontological interpretation of theories that considers the basic equations to characterize laws of nature. In contrast, instrumentalism is an epistemological interpretation of scientific theories according to which the equations provide scientists with descriptions and predictions. Over the last fifty-odd years, the common trend among philosophers and physicists about understanding scientific theories has been realism due to the conviction that our best physical theories represent the world as it really is. Among declared realists within the community of philosophers of science, many agree about a formulation of realism maintaining that realists believe that well-established scientific theories are true or approximately true and that the entities these theories posit exist. In this paper, I want to take issue with both claims. Not because I question the existence of many different invisible entities, but because I think that science often posits these entities independently of theories. Hence, I agree with Ian Hacking and Nancy Cartwright that many of those entities are regarded to exist because they have an independent operational and explanatory function. What I do question is that our scientific theories posit these entities.

Here I shall argue neither for the ontological nor for the epistemological interpretation of theories. Instead, I defend what I call the linguistic interpretation of theories that regards the basic equations as implicit definitions of selected predicates. This interpretation separates theories and models, claiming that theories and models have different functional roles in science. Contrary to realism, I therefore hold that scientific theories presuppose the existence of already identified entities, and that our best scientific theories are neither true nor approximately true. Elsewhere, I have presented the linguistic approach to scientific theories in contrast to the syntax and semantic view (Faye 2002, 2016, Ch. 4.7 and Faye 2023, Ch. 8). In this paper, I shall elaborate on my earlier approach. I think that scientific theories consisting of the basic equations of, say, Newton's mechanics, Maxwell's electrodynamics, Einstein's relativity theories, and quantum mechanics, are language rules that enable us to describe the entities scientists believe are relevant to be described in terms of the respective theories. Such a description takes place in a model in which the wanted entities are introduced with their various structures and properties. This implies that the mathematical symbols used to formulate these equations already were subject to a physical interpretation by the originators of these theories. Thus, a model is not—as considered by the semantic view concerning scientific theories—an interpretation of a formal theory, but a physical or mental representation of some real system such that the system is describable in terms of the theory. If a model system is described successfully by a theory, this puts scientists in a position to make correct predictions. Hence, I think that theories are non-representational and that models are intended to be structurally representative. Model and theory are conceptually distinct.

What is a language?

Let me begin with an observation that seems to have been overlooked by many philosophers of science. Natural languages and mathematics are both languages. A natural language is a structured tool of communication by which humans can meaningfully describe their beliefs about the world, observations, and feelings to others. Similarly, mathematics is a structured tool of communication, which especially scientists use to describe their beliefs about the world and their observations. The difference between these two languages is that natural language is a language in which we ascribe qualitative properties to various observable entities, whereas mathematics is a language by which we ascribe numerical values to entities having quantitative properties. As long as we are dealing with experientially accessible entities, they can be described in terms of both languages. A red ball can be described in terms of its function, motion, solidity, elasticity, shape and color, but also in terms of its mass, kinetic energy, and momentum. The purpose of communication determines which of these two descriptions one wants to use in a particular context.

Ordinary people use natural language to communicate as part of their practical knowledge without thinking much about how words and sentences relate to the world, and the same holds for scientists' use of mathematics and their absence of consideration of how mathematical formulas relate to the physical world. Linguists understand the function and structure of the natural language, mathematicians know about the function and structure of mathematics, but these two groups know qua their profession only little about the relationship between the use of natural language and the use of the language of mathematics within a particular area and reality.

The first question is in which sense the structure of natural language is capable of representing the real world. A natural language consists of a vocabulary and a grammar. The vocabulary contains a number of the different words that are at the users' disposal, and the grammar states the rules for combining the words into meaningful spoken or written expressions. Children do not learn a language through these rules of language, nor are these rules explicitly grasped by the child. One needs a certain understanding of how a language functions in practice before one can understand these rules. The child is nevertheless indirectly able to learn the rules, just as the rules may contain many exceptions that he or she also learns without much instruction. The rules and exceptions are grasped in virtue of an induced practice without the user ever explicitly needing to know the rules that he or she has to follow in order to speak or write correctly. This description agrees well with Ferdinand Saussure's distinction between the two parts of language called *langue* and *parole*. *Langue* is the language system, including its syntactical and semantic rules, while *parole* is the actual spoken language, the concrete utterances, determined by the pragmatic rules of communication. The langue is the vocabulary and abstract linguistic rules that exist before the individual user gets to learn a certain language. In contrast, the parole refers to the concrete instances of the use of a particular langue. Today this distinction is fundamental in linguistics. For instance, Noam Chomsky makes a parallel distinction between *competence* and *performance* respectively, although his distinction refers to the user of a language, and not directly to the language as a medium of communication.

One of the consequences of this distinction is that it does not make sense to assign truth to the language system as such. Instead, the language system must be (maximally) consistent and coherent. The grammar has to be consistent to avoid confusion and misunderstanding, and the semantics must be unambiguous. So in order to get a higher degree of consistency the rules may operate with teachable exceptions. The formal requirement to a vocabulary is that it is relatively semantically stable, although the meaning of the words may change depending on the context in which the words are used. Hence, the language system contains both syntactic and semantic rules that determine the standards for how to use the vocabulary correctly. But sometimes the language system is used intentionally or unintentionally in ways that make its use ambiguous or meaningless. Whether the rules are broken intentionally or unintentionally depends again on the context.

It makes sense to talk about truth only with respect to parole or performance. Whenever somebody utters a statement, whenever somebody makes a declarative assertion, we think that such a sentence expresses a content that is either true or not. In English grammar, a declarative sentence is a complete sentence containing a subject, an object and a verb. Such a sentence makes a statement, provides a fact, offers an explanation, or conveys information. Because of its function to say something about the world, a declarative sentence has a capacity of being true. And the intention behind asserting a declarative sentence is to make other people believe that such a statement is true.

So much for the natural language. However, mathematics is also a language, but in contrast to the natural language that mostly deals with sensorily accessible qualities, mathematics is constructed to describe quantities. Originally, humans realized that some qualitative experiences come in degrees such as one stone feeling heavier than another, some animals moving faster than others, somebody being taller than someone else, and some sets of object being multiples of others. Thus, humans came to name such quantitative differences with numbers, and determined the rules of numbering. Eventually, the language of quantities evolved into the language of mathematics just as the language of qualities evolved into the natural language.

If this claim is correct, it seems reasonable to propose an analogy between the natural language and mathematics. We have to maintain the distinction between *langue* and *parole* in the use of mathematics in physics. Mathematics is pure syntax; it only acquires a semantics once we are able to assign the mathematical signs with reference to some non-mathematical entities. Thus, for instance in physics, the use of mathematics becomes semantically meaningful once one has provided the signs with a physical reading. But, as we shall see, such a reading does change the language of mathematics from *langue* to *parole*.

The realistic turn to representation

Before physicists began their study of the atom and their development of quantum mechanics there was little reflection among them about whether scientific theories represented the world. After the logical positivists had looked at scientific theory from a more instrumentalist point of view, the philosophy of science community began to turn towards a realistic interpretation of scientific theories. This happened around 1960. Forerunners were philosophers like Karl Popper and Mario Bunge. However, I think that Feyerabend and Kuhn's ideas about incommensurability between succeeding theories, and the accusation against both that incommensurability caused irrationality in science, paved the way for scientific realism. Where scientists were realists with respect to theoretical entities because of their empirical discovery at the beginning of the century, a new generation of scientific realists began to think that scientific theories directly posit there entities. One of the first post-positivist realists was Grover Maxwell who argued that, "well-confirmed theories are conjunctions of well confirmed, genuine statements and ... the entities to which they refer in all probability exist" (Maxwell 1962, 18). Since then, every decade has seen well-known philosophers of science expressing a similar point of view.

For instance, Richard Boyd said in 1980, "By 'scientific realism' philosophers ordinarily mean the doctrine that non-observational terms in scientific theories should typically be interpreted as putative referring expressions" (p. 613). In 1984 Jarrett Leplin announced that (1) our best scientific theories are true or approximately true, and (2) the central terms of our best theories genuinely refer to some objective entities, properties, or states of affairs (p. 1). Stathis Psillos said in 1996 "insofar as scientific theories are well confirmed, it is rational to believe in the existence of the entities they posit" (p. 70). And in 2020 Carl Hoefer characterized scientific realism as "the family of philosophical views that assert that we have strong reasons to believe in the truth or approximate truth of much of the content of our current scientific theories" (p. 19).

The realist's attitude towards scientific theories found strong support in the semantic account that Patrick Suppes proposed in 1960. As a logician, he proposed that scientific theories should be treated in accord with formal semantics where a theory consists of a set of axioms and theorems, which becomes true through a series of interpretations. Stated more systematically we have

1. The theory T must be formulated in a first- or second-order language L.

2. The language L can be given an interpretation I by postulating that the individual variables run over a domain of objects and that predicate variables run over a series of values and properties that satisfy the

predicates. An interpretation is the assignment of a class of objects and properties that will satisfy the axioms and theorems in L.

3. Every sound interpretation I that makes L's sentences true with respect to the postulated entities is a model of L.

4. A theory is identical with an entire class of models where each model is a consistent interpretation of L.

5. The set of models, a family of models, constitutes the truth conditions for the theory, i.e., all the possible interpretations that invest the theory with truth and falsity.

6. If one of these models represents the real world, the theory is true with respect to the actual facts.

An example of a scientific theory that meets such a model theoretical approach would be the formal expression of Newton's laws that supposedly get meaning from their assignment to any material objects and quantitative properties like position, mass, velocity and force. But the problem with such a solution as suggested by the semantic theory is that we must already know what we mean by saying that material objects have positions, mass, velocity and force before we can use the laws to describe a system.

The mathematical terms get their meaning from being associated with entities and quantitative properties whose meaning one already knows independently of the theory. If some unobservable properties, described by a theory, shall satisfy some predicates to have linguistic meaning there must be other observable properties that determine the meaning of the predicates. The predicates we use to designate observable properties must already have a meaning in virtue in virtue of their relation to our natural language. What the theory does is that it establishes a language in which the various unobservable properties are defined in terms of certain observable ones. As an empirical theory, Newton's theory has to connect to observations, and the basic quantitative properties of Newton's theory are therefore position and motion, which are directly observable by human sensations.

Newton himself was very much aware of the problem of introducing unobservable properties into a theory concerning observables. Before formulating the laws of motion, he therefore established a set of explicit definitions of some unobservable properties, which did not have a well-understood meaning in the natural language. He then began his Scholium by commenting on these definitions:

> Hitherto I have laid down the definitions of such words as are less known, and explained the sense in which I would have them to be understood in the following discourse. I do not define time, space,

place and motion, as being well known to all. Only I must observe, that the vulgar conceive those quantities under no other notions but from the relations they bear to sensible objects. (Newton 1687/1960, 77)

In other words, Newton used his definitions to specify a number of unobservable predicates in terms of some well-known observable predicates whose meaning is carried over from the natural language.

The empirical observations that brought Newton to his definitions and laws of motion were a set of experiments on the collision of bodies that John Wallis, Christopher Wren, and Christian Huygens carried out in the middle of the seventeenth century. They observed that the change of motion of two bodies before and after the elastic collision happened according to a constant. Thus, measuring motion in terms of velocity, we have:

$$\frac{\Delta v_1}{\Delta v_2} = \text{constant}. \tag{1}$$

Thus, motion and the change of motion are the basic observable properties of any material body. Moreover, if one body gains velocity after the collision the other will correspondingly lose velocity, and the gain and the loss is proportional to a coefficient associated to each of the two bodies:

$$k_1 \Delta v_1 = -k_2 \Delta v_2. \tag{2}$$

Newton then introduced his first unobservable properties by seeing the coefficients as expressions of an internal quantity of matter, which he denotes the mass of the body:

$$m_1 \Delta v_1 = -m_2 \Delta v_2. \tag{3}$$

The change of velocity is then referred to as acceleration:

$$m_1(a_1) = -m_2(a_2). \tag{4}$$

Newton could now introduce a further unobservable property in terms of an explicit definition of force, which we usually call Newton's second law:

$$f = ma. \tag{N2}$$

And by using this definition of force on (4) Newton reached his third law:

$$f = -f. \tag{N3}$$

Hence, Newton's first law follows directly from his definition of a force. If a body does not change its velocity, it is because the body either is at rest or moves uniformly in a straight line.

Nothing in Newton's own layout of his theory corresponds to the rational reconstruction given by the semantic theory. What is interesting about Newton's own description is, however, that he showed how his laws of motion offer a linguistic explication of how to describe motion and the change of motion in terms of the unobservable. First we define some unobservables in terms of observables, and them we refer to these unobservables to explain the change of motion. Later generations of physicists recognized this circularity. Here is Ernst Mach's remarks about Newton's laws of motion:

> We readily perceive that Laws I and II are contained in the definitions that precede. According to the latter, without force there is no acceleration, consequently, only rest and uniform motion in a straight line. Furthermore, it is a wholly unnecessary tautology, after having established acceleration as the measure of force, to say again that change of motion is proportional to the force. (Mach 1960, 242)

Mach refers among other definitions to Newton's definition IV:

> An impressed force is an action exerted upon a body, in order to change its state, either of rest, or of moving uniformly forward in a right line. (Newton (1687/1960)

This definition seems rather to be an afterthought. The second law tells us only that there is a relation between a force and the change of motion. However, Newton's definition states that a force *is* the unobservable cause of the change of motion.

Similarly, Henri Poincaré acknowledged that the force law is empirically derived from experimental observation:

> The principles of dynamics appeared to us first as experimental truths, but we have been compelled to use them as definitions. It is *by definition* that force is equal to the product of mass and the acceleration; this is a principle, which is henceforth beyond the reach of any future experiment. Thus it is by definition that action and reaction are equally and opposite. (Poincaré 1905, 104)

Since Ernst Mach and Henri Poincare first argued that Newton's laws were definitions, several philosophers and scientists have suggested that we understand such expressions as implicit definitions. As Brian Ellis writes,

> In the tradition that succeeded Mach, Newton's second law of motion has been widely regarded as a definition of force. (Ellis 1965, 52)

For instance, Stephen Toulmin thinks of the laws of nature as definition, holding that they

> resemble other kinds of laws, rules and regulations. These are not themselves true or false, thought statements about their range of application can be. (Toulmin 1953, 89)

This view is quite understandable, although we often talk, as Newton wanted us to do, as if a force is the cause of acceleration. But if we take into consideration that for a force to be regarded as a causal entity, we need to be able to specify its identity conditions independent of its effect. As Quine claimed: No entity without an identity. However, forces lack such identity conditions. From a different perspective, Norwood Russel Hanson regarded Newton's laws of motion as umbrella titles because they function in many different ways depending on the context in which they are used (Hansson 1958, 112). Similarly, Thomas Kuhn called such expressions symbolic generalizations about which he said,

> they function in part as laws but also in part as definitions of some of the symbols they deploy. Furthermore, the balance between their inseparable legislative and definitional force shifts over time. (Kuhn 1962, 183)

Of course, one may argue that it depends on the context whether an expression like $f = ma$ is considered as a law or a definition. As a law, the expression is assumed to represent some state of affairs, but as a definition the expression determines the rules for using a specific term of an unobservable with respect to some sensible properties. However, it is important to separate these two functions. My suggestion is therefore that when such an expression is part of a theory, it is part of a linguistic system, and thus function as an explicit definition. However, whenever the theory as a linguistic system is used to describe a particular physical system, scientists construct a model assuming that the description represents certain regular aspects of the system. We then think of them as laws.

This brings me to the second reason why I think realism with respect to theories fails. A theory, like Newton's mechanics, introduces a set of physically interpreted mathematical symbols as numerical predicates standing for various quantitative properties. It does not mention which entities satisfy these predicates. The equal sign connects predicates, it does not state which objects are describable in virtue of these predicates. The pragmatic solution suggested by Russell Hanson and Kuhn according to which the so-called laws of nature sometimes function as definitions and sometimes as empirical generalizations depending on the context can be traced back to this fact. Even if we think of the so-called laws as implicit definitions, they are not arbitrary. They depart from something we can experience but something we want to understand further. However, such definitions are not factually true, but useful. They may be helpful and adequate in describing some intended entity or model system.

The third reason why I deny theories to be realistic representations is that I do not think they are either true or false. Definitions of unobservable predicates in terms of observable predicates are not declarative sentences. No theory in and of itself contains declarative sentences. A declarative sentence consists of a subject-verb-object structure, but no expression in any physical theory acts as a subject for the ascription of an object predicate because no theory refers to entities that have independent identity conditions.

It seems to me that one can only be a realist about scientific theories if one ignores a number of facts pointing to a separation of theories and models. In perspective, such a separation may seem understandable if we take into consideration that science is a social activity by which we acquire advance knowledge. Considering such an activity there might be many sensible ways to conceptualize such a social practice. Both realists and I accept that within this activity, it makes sense to talk about theories, models, predictions, explanations, and entities. What is open for discussion is how we are to understand these concepts, how they should be interconnected, and what can be said in favor of one position rather than the other. It is in this light that I say that the realist ignores some, in my view, important facts.

Take the theory of quantum mechanics. When Heisenberg and Schrödinger gave it its final formulation physicists only knew two subatomic entities, namely the electron and the proton, which at that time they believed made up the atom. Later many more elementary particles have been discovered by advanced experiments just as physicists discovered the electron and the proton years before the formulation of quantum mechanics. So it seems preposterous to suggest that quantum mechanics posits all these subatomic entities if their discovery happened uninfluenced by the theory. Moreover, it is often said that quantum mechanics is a universal theory in the sense that it applies to all objects regardless of whether these are subatomic entities, atoms, molecules, or macroscopic objects. No one will argue that quantum mechanics posits all these things. Instead, human beings constructed quantum mechanics because they already knew that entities such as atoms existed, but classical physics was unable to explain their behavior.

The central element in a physical theory is a set of mathematical equations which scientific realists regard as expressions of some natural laws. Indeed, realists of different sorts considered these expressions to have a structure or a content that allows them to be true. However, one should not be fooled by the fact that Newton's so-called 'laws' are historically referred to as laws of nature. In contrast, let me give three reasons why I believe that the realist view is wrong and why these so-called laws are definitions or language rules.

Do mathematical theories represent real structures?

Realists concerning scientific theories might have a trump card up their sleeve. Today's realists are often structuralists and may therefore agree that scientific theories do not posit entities. Instead, theories are true or approximately true because the laws of the theories reveal certain real structures of the world. The mathematical structure of these laws shows what these real structures are. The argument is that when a new theory succeeds an older one, we will often see that there exists a correspondence between the structure of the old theory and the structure of the new one, although some of the important predicates may change meaning. For instance, Ladyman and Ross (2007) argue that a theory is true if its mathematical structure maps the relevant part of reality because structures are everything there is. These authors insist that we have structures without physical objects being their relata. The relata are themselves structures. They believe that the mathematical structures of our best theories represent the physical structures of the world.

I am sceptical. A representation is not identical to what it represents. It therefore seems reasonable to claim that if we characterize an item as a representation that we then have independent identity criteria of both the object that represents and the one being represented. To say a photo is a representation of me, we must be able to identify both the photo and me independently of each other. Likewise, we must be able to specify the identity criteria for the physical structures independently of the mathematical structures said to represent these physical structures in order for them to exist. Until somebody presents us with such conditions, structural realism is in its ontological version pure speculations.

Two languages

English and mathematics are both languages. English is a natural language. Such a language is a structured system for communication by which, among other things, humans can meaningfully describe the world in terms of qualitative predicates. Similarly, mathematics is a structured system for communication, which especially scientists use to describe the world in terms of numerical predicates. Linguists normally distinguish between the system of language and the use of language for communication. Saussure saw this distinction as one between *Langue* and *Parole*.

Langue is the language system consisting of a vocabulary as well as a syntactic structure and semantic categories that determine how to apply the vocabulary. As an abstract system, *Langue* does not represent anything factual since it can be specified in isolation from the user's concrete intentions of using the language system. In contrast, *Parole* is the performative use of the language system for communication in which meaning partly depends on the context in which we use the various words. Sometimes the context is such that the utterances are intended by the speaker/writer to describe something about the world. In such situations, the intention behind a particular utterance is that it represents some facts of the matter. Much communication consists in situations in which we utter sentences that are neither factually true nor factually false. Only when we describe something in terms of *declarative sentences* does it make sense to say that sentences are intended to represent and therefore to ascribe a truth value to what we say.

Analogically, we may distinguish between theory and model where the function of a particular theory corresponds to *Langue* and the function of a model to *Parole*. The theory gives us a vocabulary of predicates and specifies the syntactical and semantic rules we may use to talk about entities introduced by model. First, when we have presented such entities into a model is it possible to form well-formed declarative sentences and therefore to describe the behaviour of these entities to make proper predictions.

Models and scientific entities

The consequences of considering so-called laws as implicit definitions may not be as devastating as they might seem. Science is much more than its formal theories. Physics makes many declarative statements that are true or approximately true by stating facts, providing explanations, and conveying information. All this happens in connection with physicists' construction of models. Either a physicist introduces into his or her model entities by hand or by classificatory prediction, since the identity conditions of these entities are independent of the theory that may be used to describe them.

A mathematical model is an idealized representation of actual entities that scientists regard as the constituents of a physical system. The structure of the model is intentionally designed to correspond to the empirically discovered structure of the target system. Thus, a model functions as a representation because it contains proper elements that refer to some real entities placed in an intended structure, and the elements have been constructed such that the predicates of a particular theory are applicable to these elements. Usually, a model in physics represents some entities by attributing properties to them that satisfy the numerical predicates of a theory, and then though observation provides these predicates with initial values. Whenever the model has been constructed, scientists may use it to make predictions and explanations concerning a target system. Hence, if the predictions fail to accord with observations, it may either be due to the use of an inadequate theory in the description of the assumed entities or to the existence of yet undiscovered entities.

Let me illustrate these claims with a number of examples. Newton was already familiar with the existence of five planets we can see with the naked eye. The heliocentric model and Kepler's Laws assumed that the planets move around a central object in elliptic orbits. So Newton had a model of the solar system. However, Newton's merit was to provide us with the mathematical theory that could be used to describe and predict the behavior of the planets. He told us the numerical predicates to be used in describing the motion of planets such that physicists could predict their positions and explain their movements in relation to each another around the sun. This planetary model later allowed Urbain Le Verrier to predict the existence of a new planet, Neptune, based on mathematical calculations of its predicted positions due to observed perturbations in the orbit of the planet Uranus. It is by using the same model that some physicists today believe that there is a ninth planet, planet X, in the solar system. But it is not always the case that wrong predictions indicate an undiscovered entity. The postulation of Vulcan based on a Newtonian description of the heliocentric model in order to explain Mercury's observed perihelion movement failed. Although a Newtonian description of the heliocentric system might be useful to predict the existence of a new planet, this description must be replaced by an Einsteinian description if and when physicists want to make an accurate prediction of Mercury's perihelion. In other words, the heliocentric model is one thing and the language of the mathematical theory that enables us to describe the orbits of the plants is quite another.

The second example is the discovery of the neutron in 1932 by James Chadwick. When Bohr set up his semi-classical model of the hydrogen atom, he did it by rethinking the structure of Rutherford's planetary model of the atom with the intention of explaining the hydrogen's radiation patterns. Rutherford's model was a result of Rutherford's interpretation of Hans Geiger and Ernest Marsden's experiments with the bombardment of a gold foil with alpha particles. The planetary model places most of the mass of the atom in a very small nucleus. The nucleus was positively charged and identified as consisting of protons around 1920 by Rutherford. The nucleus was surrounded by elections whose number corresponded to the number of positively charged particles in the nucleus. Moreover, around 1920 isotopes of the same chemical elements had been discovered, and the mass of the other elements had been found to be integer multiples of the mass of the hydrogen atom.

During the 1920s there were speculations that the nucleus of the various elements other than hydrogen might contain electrons that outbalanced the extra protons in the nucleus, but none of the speculations added up to the experimental observations. So the physicists had to look for yet an unknown particle, and the hunt for such a particle in the atom bore fruit with Chadwick's discovery. This discovery was not made possible by the quantum mechanics, and the corrections this theory had on Bohr's model. Quantum mechanics does not enable the physicists to predict the existence of the neutron. The theory puts only some limits on the possibility of using classical predicates, like position and momentum, simultaneously to predict their trajectories of elementary particles.

The third, and last, example is the discovery of quarks, which are some of the constituents of the so-called standard model. Before Murray Gell-Mann and George Zweig independently of each other suggested the existence of quarks, particle physicists had discovered hundreds of strongly interacting particle named hadrons due to the rapid development of detector technology. All hadrons were considered elementary because they could be assigned different intrinsic properties. Therefore, physicists began to contemplate a possible classification of these particles by using abstract mathematics in the form of what is called the representation theory. This theory studies abstract algebraic structures by representing their elements as linear transformations of vector spaces. These elements may form different groups based on various reflections and symmetries. A couple of years after Gell-Mann and Zweig came forward with their proposal, physicists began to find evidence for the existence of quarks of which the standard model operates with kinds of six. But let us not forget that no free quark has ever been detected.

The three examples of models presented here are mathematical models but they also play different roles in the physical science. But before we consider these functions, we should say a bit more about the construction of mathematical models. At the center of a mathematical model is the representation of some entities such that their description satisfies the vocabulary of a certain theory. The construction of a model is carried out such that all entities represented by this model may have many properties not represented, but those represented should be the ones that can be described by the intended theory. In a Newtonian model of the solar system, for instance, the structure of the model is based on the heliocentric system and Kepler's first law according to which each planet moves in an ellipse around a central body located in one of the focal points of the ellipse. Hence, apart from this structure the Sun and the planets are constructed as idealized objects such that they are assigned properties, which satisfies the predication of Newton's theory. In other words, if we regard this as a paradigmatic example of how scientists construct models, the structure of a scientific model stems from, or is suggested by, experimental observations and not from the theories scientists use to describe what happens with entities fulfilling such a structure.

Thus, models are intentional constructions that introduce target objects to have certain properties corresponding the predicates specified by a particular theory, and which scientists believe must have a certain structure obtained by observation of the target system and empirical generalizations. The appropriate model allows scientists to construct the reference to the target system as the subject in the mathematical statements, a system assumed to satisfy numerical predicates of a theory. It allows the scientists to use the predicates of a specific theory to describe the objects in terms of declarative sentences. A scientific model enables a scientist to use such sentences to make predictions about the target system just as a model enables a scientist to use the model to make explanations. Although predictions and explanations are declarative statements that are either true or false, it seems reasonable to say that the model itself, which aids us in formulating predictions and explanations, is an idealized representation of a given physical system that may be more or less correct and therefore more or less useful. Indeed, as several philosophers have pointed out, a model does not represent just because of an isomorphism between itself and reality, but because somebody has the intention that the elements and the structures of the model have a representational function. This observation alone implies that the semantic notion of theories cannot be correct.

Summary and conclusion

I have argued that a scientific theory consists of a set of interpreted mathematical formulas that we consider to be laws of nature. To connect any formal theory to physical reality we need to interpret the mathematical formulas into terms of an observable language with its indexical terms and with the help of pointing. The mathematical formulas explicitly define a set of unobservable predicates in terms of a set of observable predicates. I also maintained that as a system of interpreted formulas a physical theory does not posit which entities it can be used to describe. Neither Newton's laws nor the laws of quantum mechanics contain reference to which kind of objects it may be successfully applied. Hence, none of these theories represents the world, as scientific realist would have us to believe.

Considering mathematics as the language of quantities, I hold that physical theories do not represent the world just as the natural language as the language of qualities does not represent the world. With respect to the natural language, linguists separate the language system, which is an abstract entity, and the performative use of this system in communicative situations. Similarly, a physical theory is to be considered as "langue", the abstract system of defined predicates that may be used to describe physical entities whenever they are introduced in a model. Thus, a scientific model plays an intermediary role between "langue" and "parole" by enabling us to construct model objects in such a way that the predicates of a particular theory can be used for communicative purposes. The structure of the model is taken over from observations and experiments (sometimes thought experiments), and together with the language borrowed from the theory, scientists hope to say something correct about a particular area of the world. The concrete predictions and explanations provided by the model belong to "parole". Indeed, these concrete quantitative statements are either true or false just as qualitative statements are.

In contrast to concrete statements expressed based on a model, scientific theories are neither true nor false as they merely consist of a set of implicit definitions of unobservable predicates in terms of observable predicates. A realist may argue that these predicates refer to universals, whereas the nominalist would say that predicates do not refer but only have extension. But as long as we only regard the so-called laws of motion as a codification of how some predicates should be used to describe some model objects, the metaphysical disagreement is irrelevant because it touches only on concrete statements and not on abstract relations between predicates. Not until some specific model is constructed to represent some entities can we form declarative sentences by using the "laws" of the theory. Before that no predicate can have a referential status. Scientists and scientific philosophers' understanding of theories may benefit from linguists' distinction between the language system and concrete statements using the system. Linguists have, in contrast to scientists and philosophers of science, not only used language, but studied the use of language. If we follow their insight, it makes sense to argue that the relationship between a scientific theory and scientific model is similar to the one that exists between *Langue* and *Parole* in the natural language. Only statements based on a model are true or false.

References

Boyd, Richard (1980). "Scientific Realism and Naturalistic Epistemology." *PSA: Proceedings of the Biennial Meeting of the Philosophy of Science Association 1980*, Vol. 2: 613–662.

Ellis, Brian, "The Origin and Nature of Newton's Laws of Motion" In R. G. Colodny (Ed.), *Beyond the Edge of Certainty*. Englewood Cliff. Prentice-Hall.

Faye, Jan (2002). *Rethinking Science*. London: Ashgate/Routledge.

Faye, Jan (2016). *Experience and Beyond*. London: Palgrave-Macmillan.

Faye, Jan (2023). *The Biological and Social Dimensions of Human Knowledge*. London: Palgrave-Macmillan.

Hanson, Norwood Russell (1958). *The Pattern of Discovery*. Cambridge: Cambridge University Press.

Hoefer, Carl, 2020. "Scientific Realism without the Quantum." In S. French and J. Saatsi (Eds.) *Scientific Realism and the Quantum*, 19–34. Oxford: Oxford University Press.

Kuhn, Thomas S. (1962). *The Structure of Scientific Revolutions*. Chicago: Chicago University Press.

Mach, Ernst (1883/1960). *The Science of Mechanics: A Critical and Historical Account of its* Development (6th ed.) LaSalle: Open Court.

Ladyman, James & Ross, Don (2007). *Every Thing Must Go. Metaphysics Naturalized.* Oxford: Oxford University Press.

Leplin, Jarrett (1984). *Scientific Realism.* Berkeley: University of California Press.

Maxwell, Grover. 1962. "The Ontological Status of Theoretical Entities." In H. Feigl and G. Maxwell (eds.) *Minnesota Studies in the Philosophy of Science Vol. III*, 3–27. Minneapolis: University of Minnesota Press.

Newton, Isaac (1687/1960). *The Principia: Mathematical Principles of Natural Philosophy.* Edited by I. B. Cohen and A. M. Whitman. Berkeley: University of California Press.

Poincaré, Henri (1905). *Science and Hypothesis.* New York: Dover Publication.

Psillos, Stathis (1999). *Scientific Realism: How Science Tracks Truth.* London: Routledge.

Suppes, Patrick (1960). "A comparison of the meaning and uses of models in mathematics and the empirical sciences." *Synthese* 12: 207–301.

Toulmin, Stephen (1953). *The Philosophy of Science.* London: Hutchinson.

The structural view of representation: a defence

Michel Ghins

Institut Supérieur de Philosophie, Université Catholique de Louvain, Place Cardinal Mercier 14, 1348 Louvain-la-Neuve, Belgium
E-mail: michel.ghins@uclouvain.be

Abstract. After having presented the objectifying attitude typical of science, this paper discusses various—scientific and non-scientific—examples of representation and shows that representation is an action that involves a user, a context, a target and a transfer of structure from the target to the representing artefact. It is argued that a transfer of structure from the target to the representing artefact by means of a representational isomorphism or homomorphism is a necessary (*albeit* not sufficient) condition for the success, and *a fortiori* the correctness, of a representation.

1 The objectifying attitude

To construct theories which predict and explain observations and measurements, scientists must adopt a particular attitude or stance towards the world. When looking at concrete entities given in perception, i.e., phenomena[1], they must see them as *systems*. A system is a set of parts or elements organised by means of relations. When I look at the *Madeleine à la veilleuse* by Georges de la Tour in the Louvre, I am immediately overwhelmed by its beauty. Yet I am also able to detach myself from this state of wonder to direct my attention to specific components of the painting such as the flame of the candle, the table, the left arm of Madeleine as well as the spatial relations between them. In doing so, I look at the painting as a system, namely an ensemble of selected parts or elements that stand in spatial relations.

To perceive phenomena as systems, I have to distance myself from immediate perception and to refrain from any feeling or emotion, whether aesthetic or otherwise, that I might experience. This distancing permits to select some properties of interest while disregarding many others. An astronomer interested in celestial phenomena might focus on the planetary orbital revolutions rather than their brightness or colour. In the same way, a chemist studying a gas could select its properties of pressure, volume and temperature, instead of its colour or smell.

In doing so, scientists adopt a selective *démarche*. First, they separate a concrete thing, such as a gas, within the thickness of phenomena. As a

---

[1] The term "phenomenon" can mean either something purely subjective such as a sensation or a perceived external thing. When I use the word "phenomenon", I mean something perceived or observed, which is external to us. Phenomena are not *sense data*.

second step, they will pick out particular characteristics or properties, such as pressure, volume and temperature, and organize them into a structure by means of specific relations. As a consequence, a perceived entity, such as a gas, is reduced to a system the elements of which are the properties of pressure, volume and temperature, organised into a structure. Within such approach, scientists identify properties in the phenomena which they consider to be cognitively interesting, and structure them with relations.

By proceeding in this way, scientists construct a scientific *object*, which is nothing else than a system of properties structured by relationships between them. A system is a structure of properties.[2] For instance, in the case of a gas at constant temperature, the domain of values of pressure, volume, temperature, can be organized using an equality relation, such as "the product of the values of pressure and volume divided by the temperature is equal to a constant".[3]

Thus, within the objectifying attitude, an entity is reduced to a system or object that is constructed by taking into account a limited number of properties and relations between them and neglecting many others. For science, an empirical object is nothing else than a system of properties chosen among the properties instantiated in the observed entity.[4]

In his book *The Empirical Stance*, Bas van Fraassen (2002) portrays the scientific attitude as "objective distancing". To construct a scientific object, scientists must in the first place adopt a distancing attitude regarding to the entities chosen as targets of investigation. Such attitude is very different from spatial distancing. To see phenomena as systems, scientists are compelled to establish a separation between themselves as human subjects on the one hand, and the entity from which they construct an object-system on the other. In most cases, a scientific object has the same status it had in seventeenth and eighteenth centuries experimental sciences, that is to say, "an object that is collected, labelled, put in a museum, that is sliced, dissected, solidified, dyed, and put under a microscope." (Wilson 1997, p. 37)[5] When looked at in this way, a thing or entity[6] is reduced to a scientific object that is completely deprived of intrinsic value. As reduced to an object, an entity

---

[2]The notions of system and structure are closely related. Systems are mostly taken to be real worldly objects which exemplify a structure. In this case, "structure" refers primarily to the organisation of elements. But in mathematics sets of related elements are regularly referred to as "structures". I will often use the words "structure" and "system" interchangeably since there is no structure without elements—whether elements are mathematical or not—in relation. For a general definition of system, based on Da Costa's notion of partial structure, see Bresciani Filho & D'Ottaviano (2018).

[3]Pressure × volume / temperature = constant. This is the Boyle-Charles formula.

[4]Of course, scientists do not always start from experience but also devise theoretical hypotheses and construct possible objects, as it will be seen later.

[5]Quoted by van Fraassen (2002, p. 157).

[6]By "thing" or "entity" I mean any kind of existent, be it a substance, a process etc. I favour an ontology of instantiated properties. An entity is a set of spatiotemporally

becomes available for cognitive purposes without any constraints or limits. Being devoid of any intrinsic value, a scientific object can be manipulated, altered and even destroyed to serve merely scientific purposes.

The objectifying approach is a defining feature of scientific practice. But it can be adopted in other fields as well. I can decide to see the *Madeleine à la veilleuse* as composed of parts, study the relations between them, and attempt to understand the arrangement between shapes, colours, proportions ... Embracing an objectifying attitude requires a reversal of our spontaneous attitude towards the world. When we look at entities around us, whether human or not, we immediately grasp them not as systems but as *singular totalities*. If we pause to reflect on this, we realise that the entities we immediately see are undivided totalities implicitly endowed with intrinsic value, whether positive or negative. A child spontaneously attributes some value to the entities he perceives, typically in terms of their intrinsic powers to cause pleasure or pain. The same is true for the people—undeservedly called "primitive"—who envision the world as populated by things inhabited by ancestors or spirits. Some entities, like some trees in New Caledonia, are directly grasped as undivided units with which it is possible to enter into a personal relationship. Such singular and unique entities have an intrinsic value which commands respect. Far from assigning negative connotations to such an attitude, we must see it as fundamentally positive, capable of revealing important aspects of the entities which make the natural world.

As we saw, the objectifying attitude typical of science consists in seeing phenomena as systems. It requires a detachment, a bracketing, a suspension of our personal, immediate and spontaneous grasp of the entities given in perception.[7] I call such a suspension of our natural relationship to things the *primary, primordial* or *original abstraction*. Primordial abstraction consists in seeing any entity as an object, that is, as a system of *properties*. I call it "abstraction" because it requires *neglecting* or *omitting* most of the properties of a concrete thing given in perception. Even though an object is constructed by abstraction, it is real if its properties and relations are. In science, the elements in relation are often (but not always[8]) quantifiable properties, such as the pressure and volume of a gas. These elements are not things in the usual sense of the term, but properties. It is these properties and the relations among them that are studied within the objectifying approach. The choice

---

instantiated properties or relations. Thus, an entity is not quite a "bundle" of properties since these properties generally stand in some relations.

[7]It seems to me that we are unable to simultaneously take both an objectifying attitude and what I call below a holistic (emotional, aesthetic, religious etc.) attitude. We certainly can move very quickly from one kind of attitude to the other. The scientist, *qua* scientist, must strive to avoid holistic influences.

[8]There are scientific domains, typically in social sciences, in which the properties put in relation are not quantifiable.

of the properties of interest is constrained by the requirement for scientists to introduce a distance, to control their emotions and to refrain from attributing intrinsic values to objects. In adopting some form of asceticism, scientists must strive to curb any personal—subjective or emotional—involvement with the object of study. Although this ideal is only partially attainable in practice, it is consciously and deliberately pursued by scientists. This is one of the most important aspects of the search for the highest possible degree of objectivity, which would be achieved by the complete elimination of any influence linked to a particular scientist, whether experimenter or theorist.[9] In fact, the scientific object-system cannot be a singular and unique thing but must be indefinitely reproducible and repeatable. Such a system could in principle be constructed or reconstructed by any scientist, regardless of personality and context of research.

The second step typical of the scientific *démarche*—although most often simultaneous with original abstraction—consists in *selecting* in a given phenomenal entity (or set of phenomenal entities) some properties, quantities or magnitudes taken to be relevant from the perspective of a given discipline: chemistry, sociology, psychology etc. In such a way, the field of research is circumscribed in a precise and restrictive way. Such process of selecting specific properties or quantities is what I call *secondary abstraction*. Within this second step, scientists take a particular point of view or *perspective* with respect to the targeted phenomena. This leads them to neglect or make abstraction of a vast quantity of objective properties.

Although many properties and structures can be selected in the same phenomenon depending on one's interest or point of view, this does not in any way prevents possible justified belief in their reality. The term "abstraction" can be misleading since in some contexts abstract objects are deemed to be in principle inaccessible to perception, such as in mathematics. Here, the term "abstraction" means that some properties, including relational properties, of the phenomenon are disregarded or omitted. Admittedly, the selection of certain properties and relations implies neglecting other ones, but sometimes the properties called "abstract" are the properties on which scientists focus their attention within their modelling process, especially when these properties are mathematical properties. According to the terminology used here, these abstract properties are *extracted*[10] *f*rom the phenomenal thing. From now on, I will understand by secondary abstraction (or simply abstraction when there is no risk of confusion with the primary abstraction) the operation that consists in selecting or extracting from a phenomenal entity some properties and relations while disregarding many others. By

---

[9]For an in-depth discussion of objectivity, see Agazzi (2014).
[10]See Portides (2018).

this process we construct an object of enquiry, which is real provided its properties and relations are instantiated.[11]

Idiosyncratic preferences, personal feelings, circumstances etc., play a decisive role in motivating scientists to engage in scientific disciplines rather than others. Some prefer physics to chemistry, others psychology to demography or economics. Nevertheless, the extracted *properties* themselves can belong to the entities that are the targets of investigation. They can exist independently of individual scientists and the way they are selected or observed. Therein lies the most common meaning of "objectivity". It is imperative in science that the relevant properties be observed or measured by any observer or experimenter, that is to say, by anyone who uses the appropriate observational or measuring instruments.

For example, a planet is a concrete thing which has an indefinite number of properties, objective or not. Yet in celestial mechanics a planet is reduced to a very restricted set of properties such as position, velocity, orbital period ... These properties are in principle observable, directly or indirectly, by anyone, anywhere and at any time. The scientific object is not a unique, singular entity, but a system that can be multiplied and replicated indefinitely. An electron is just a system of instantiated properties: charge, mass etc. with a precise value and always present simultaneously. These properties form a system: their organisation consists at least in their simultaneous presence or instantiation. Nothing resembles an electron more than another electron: they all share identical properties. As John Earman once said, there is nothing more boring than an electron: once you have seen one, you have seen them all ... This holds true for any scientific system-object. Yet this does not prevent scientific activity from being exciting. Every day new properties are discovered, new objects constructed, and novel theories developed.

Far away from the city lights, looking at the sky on a cloudless night, some verses of the *Chanson du mal-aimé* may come to your mind:

> *Voie lactée ô sœur lumineuse*
> *Des blancs ruisseaux de Chanaan*
> *Et des corps blancs des amoureuses*
> *Nageurs morts suivrons-nous d'ahan*
> *Ton cours vers d'autres nébuleuses*[12]

Poets and scientists adopt strikingly different attitudes towards the sky. Instead of dissecting the Milky Way into a system, the poet sees it as a totality in which we immerse without making any distinction between us as

---

[11] On this, see Agazzi (2014, p. 104).
[12] *Milky Way, O bright sister / Of the white streams of Canaan / And white bodies of lovers / Shall we, dead swimmers, follow with ahan / Your course towards other nebulae* (My literal translation).

subjects and the sky as an object. More generally, in the aesthetic attitude, natural entities as well as works of art such as paintings, sculptures etc. are perceived as unique, singular totalities with which, instead of maintaining a distance, we try to achieve closeness, even fusion, by entering into the work of art itself to the point of forgetting that we are looking at it. This is the right way of seeing when we look at the *Madeleine à la veilleuse*. Otherwise, we would fail to sense its beauty. I call this attitude *holistic, sapiential* or *contemplative*. We spontaneously adopt such attitude in our friendly and loving relationships with persons. Such contemplative attitude should be embraced in relation to natural entities in order to be able to value and respect it.

Do not be mistaken however in believing that I value the objectifying attitude more than the sapiential attitude, or the other way around. Both play important roles in human life and knowledge. Yet we must carefully distinguish them. We surely want to avoid falling into a pervasive materialism that would make the scientific approach exclusively and universally cognitively valid, or into a romantic holism that would unduly value the sapiential attitude to the point of despising the scientific attitude.

2 Modelling and representing

How do scientists proceed to construct models that could represent something?[13] Representing is an action that can succeed or fail. According to the *structural view* of representation which I favour, a representation is successful *only if* it involves a transfer of structure from its target (the represented entity) to the representing artefact.[14] This requirement of *structural similarity*—distinct from resemblance—is a *necessary* condition of success. However, as we shall see, it is far from being sufficient.

2.1 What models are

Take a very simple and familiar empirical example drawn from astronomy.[15] In order to construct a model, the initial step consists in isolating and identifying from the bulk of celestial phenomena concrete entities such as immobile bright spots called "stars" and moving ones baptised "planets". Individual planets can be identified by means of their colour and brightness. They receive names such as "Mercury", "Venus" or "Mars". Like all concrete things, they have many objective as well as holistic properties. Within the

---

[13] Here I propose a philosophical approach to modelling and theory building. I do not claim that scientists actually work in the way I describe.

[14] A structural conception of representation is defended, with variations, by Suppes (1967, 2002), Da Costa and French (2003), Bartels (2005, 2006) and Chakravartty (2010), among others. It is criticized by Suárez (2003), Contessa (2007), Frigg (2010), Pero & Suárez (2016), and others.

[15] Old fashioned examples have the advantage of being well-known and understood by all ...

primary abstractive *démarche*, scientists first view the ensemble of planets as an object-system. Then, by secondary abstraction, they select some monadic and relational properties in order to construct specific object-systems, i.e., sets of specific properties. For example, an astronomer can decide to focus on the observed orbital periods, namely the times planets take to return to the same position with respect to the stars. (Positions are attested by observing properties of brightness and distances to the stars). In proceeding thus, the astronomer omits mentioning most of the other properties of planets. Model construction is always *incomplete*.

When observed from the earth the planetary return periods are not constant. This is due to the motion of the earth around the sun. But these return periods are *on average* equal to what we mean today by orbital period, which is the return period of the planet to the same position with respect to the stars, *as seen from the sun*. The duration of a complete revolution of the planet earth around the sun is approximately 365.25 days.

The next step is to construct a scientific object-system. In the present example, the object is a *perceptual* or *phenomenal system* or *structure*, whose elements are some selected observed properties of the various planets, namely the *average* orbital periods observed directly with the naked eye from the earth. Orbital periods are evaluated by observing the positions of the planets relative to the stars over long periods of time. The values of the planetary orbital periods are then structured by a "smaller than" relation, which is an order relation.

Notice, and this is an important point, that the elements of the perceptual structure are not concrete things but properties. Periods of revolution are properties instantiated in concrete things, namely planets. A specific planet, say Mars, is a concrete thing with respect to which we can adopt a holistic attitude (for example aesthetic or religious) or a scientific attitude. The planets themselves are not components of the constructed perceptual system. Only some of their properties are. A perceptual system is a system of perceived properties and relations selected among those instantiated in the concrete things which have been selected for research.

By constructing an object—which in this case is a specific perceptual system—a scientist performs the first step of the *modelling process*. *A model can be first characterised as a system of properties, that satisfies, that is, makes true, some propositions*. In the empirical example discussed above, the perceptual system makes true the propositions that describe the relations between orbital periods. For example, the perceptual system satisfies the following proposition: ⟨the orbital period of Venus is smaller than that of Mars⟩. The constructed scientific object is thus a model in the sense just defined, which may be called the "veridical sense" or "alethic sense".[16] Obviously, models in this sense are not propositions.

Of course, scientists are not satisfied with the construction of perceptual systems. By direct observation we often get rough values that must be made precise by using instruments or measuring devices. In our planetary example, the measurement results are also structured by the relation "smaller than". In this manner, we obtain what is usually called a *data model*. Such data models satisfy the propositions that describe relations between the data, namely measurement results. Like the perceptual structure, the data model makes true propositions such as ⟨the orbital period of Venus, equal to 224.7 days, is smaller than that of Mars, equal to 686.98 days⟩.

In addition to making some propositions true, models can play another important role. Models are used by scientists to *represent*. In the above example, the data model represents part of the sky (the set of planets) *as* a system of orbital properties. The dual role of models is reminiscent of the Roman double-faced god Janus, with one face looking to the past and the other looking to the future.[17] Similarly, models in science have a dual function: they make propositions true and can represent at the same time. But, how and what can models represent?

2.2 Photos and maps

When we talk of representation, mundane examples such as photos or maps that may represent a person or a landscape immediately come to mind. In the context of our present culture (but not in the context of other cultures, such as precontact tribes in Amazonia), things like photos or figurative paintings are immediately seen as artefacts that represent. When I look at someone's photo, I implicitly establish a correspondence between properties I select in the photographed person and some parts of the photo. A given coloured area on the photo corresponds to the face, while another area corresponds to the hair of the person who is represented. This kind of correspondence is called a "function" in mathematics. When I look at a coloured piece of paper which I recognise as a photo of someone, I associate properties of the person who is represented with elements of the picture, mostly unconsciously. But I can also consciously construct a function that *codifies* a correspondence between what the photo represents and the photo itself. If each selected property of the person who is represented corresponds to one and only one element of the photo, and vice versa, I have constructed what is called a "bijective function" or "bijection". In this case, the properties selected in the photographed target and in the photo are equal in number.

---

[16]This sense corresponds to what Alfred Tarski and Patrick Suppes understood by model in mathematical logic, namely a set-theoretical structure satisfying or making true the sentences of a theory (see Suppes 2002, p. 21).

[17]Da Costa and French insist on the dual role played by models (2003, p. 67).

Moreover, I choose a function that preserves specific relations of a certain kind, such as spatial relationships. What in the photo corresponds to the mouth is located below what corresponds to the nose etc. A bijective function that preserves relations is called an "isomorphism". The relations organise the elements into a structure, a form, as hinted by the Greek etymology of the word "isomorphism":[18] the person who is represented and her photo share the same structure or form, but only with respect to the construction of a specific correspondence, which is always based on selected elements and relations. Such construction—implicitly taken for granted in some cultural context—disregards some aspects of the photographed person, like three-dimensionality. The photo is a partial and thus incomplete representation of its target.

A function that maps some properties of a person into properties of her photo while preserving selected relations is called a *representative* or *representational function*. The representational function performs a *transfer of structure* and thus establishes a *structural similarity* between the person and the photograph. According to the structural view, some structural similarity between the representing artefact and what is represented is a necessary—but quite insufficient—condition for a representation to be successful.

Let us now look at an unfamiliar quite exotic example shown in the figure below.

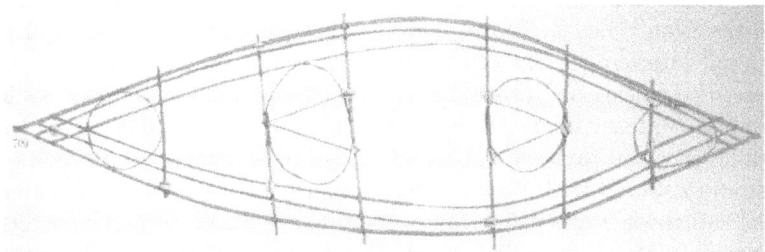

The above artefact is easily recognised as representing a specific target in some cultural contexts only. Most people are unaware that it was used as a sea chart by Micronesians living in the Marshall Islands.[19] In constructing this artefact, the cartographer intended to convey useful information to a navigator. How did the Marshall Islands navigators manage to extract

---

[18]"Μορφή" in Greek translates as "form" and "ἴσος" as "same". Homomorphisms (many-to-one functions) are more general than isomorphisms. For the sake of simplicity, I will limit the discussion to isomorphisms. Homomorphisms, just as isomorphisms do, can ground structural similarity.

[19]This sea chart is in the Linden Museum in Stuttgart. I am grateful to Anthony Meyer (1995, p. 616, figure 709) and Ulrich Menter, curator of the Oceanic art collection of the Linden Museum, for permission to publish this reproduction.

interesting information from this map? In order to obtain correct, and therefore useful, information, I need to know the code. This code is not included in the map: it is *external* to it. Taken by itself, this artefact does not represent anything at all. Yet it is obviously true that it has internal properties. It is made of wooden sticks tied by knots, contains shells placed at some intersections and exhibits other features. When told that it is a maritime chart, I realize that the Micronesians mapped some elements and relations relevant to steering a canoe into elements and relations of the artefact, but I do not know which ones. In order to be able to see and use this artefact as a map, and not look at it as a work of art, I must know the code, that is, the function—more precisely the isomorphism—that connects selected relevant properties and relations of the maritime environment— which is the intended target—to selected properties of the map and selected relations among them.

In order to be able to use this artefact as a helpful instrument for navigation, I must know that the maker of the map intended to establish a correspondence between islands and shells. In addition, to detect the presence of a distant island, the Micronesians relied (besides the bearings of stars and other clues) on observing interference patterns of swells. Swells are quasi-permanent waves produced by persistent and strong winds, especially the trade-winds near the equator which blow from the east, called "easterlies". When an island is present, it reflects and refracts parts of those swells (refraction here means the bending of the inshore ends of swells by friction with the island coast). To put it briefly, the presence of an island distorts the swell interference pattern of the open ocean. Such distortion can be observed (by seeing but mostly by the body feeling the waves under the boat) by experimented navigators up to about a 100 km distance to an island. Swell interference patterns were rarely taken to be relevant to navigation by Western explorers ... However, what is represented by the arrangement of sticks and shells is the distortion of the ocean swell interference pattern by the presence of one or more islands. The map is used to partially represent the maritime environment—the concrete target—*as* a system of swells.

Yet such a map was not used during navigation. In fact, it is a pedagogical and mnemonic tool.[20] Only oral tradition in a specific context could initially reveal what and how it represents. What is more, the information encoded in this map is quite insufficient to serve as a guide for navigators in Micronesia. Such sea charts are far from being complete since no information from the bearings (azimuths) of stars, among other relevant guiding information, could be acquired from them.

---

[20] For a detailed explanation of how these maps were used, see David H. Lewis (1994, pp. 224–252) and Ascher (1995).

Suppose now that I am on a beach on the Ailinglaplap Atoll (where the above stick chart comes from) in the Marshall Islands. To be able to use such a map, I must first locate myself on it, *i.e.* I must know which shell the Ailinglaplap Atoll corresponds to, according to the intention of the maker of the map. I also need to correctly orient the map in relation to my surroundings. This information is not contained in the map! The map is "impersonal" in the sense that it can be used by different people at different locations. Location involves both position and orientation. If I locate myself at the wrong place on the map, I will be unable to make correct statements such as: if I sail in this direction, I will reach that particular island. Thus, proper use of the map presupposes the truth of the statement: I am here on the map. Such statement contains indexical terms. "I" and "here" have different denotations depending on who is making the assertion and where the map user is located. Again, just as the code was, the referents or denotations of these indexical terms are determined by information *external* to the representing artefact.

The examples of the photo and the Micronesian sea chart teach us valuable lessons. Firstly, something never functions by itself as an artefact representing something else. As van Fraassen insists *"There is no representation except in the sense that some things are used, made, or taken, to represent some things as thus or so."* (2008, p. 23) From the outset, a photo or a map must be *appropriated* by a user for some practical purpose or aim with reference to a particular target. My grandmother's photo is not in itself the photo of my grandmother. It only becomes the photo of my grandmother because I *decide* to take such piece of coloured paper as a photo of someone and also specifically the photo of my grandmother. The decision to take the piece of paper as a photo is of course strongly suggested by familiar implicit conventions that permeate our cultural context and our knowledge of the production of photos by cameras, but it is not compulsory.

The example of the Micronesian artefact makes it clear that something does not immediately and obviously present itself as having a particular representing role, except for users in a specific cultural context. In order to represent, something must in the first place be appropriated by a user who determines its target. In themselves, a photograph or an arrangement of sticks, knots and shells do not provide any identification of a possible target. Such identification is achieved by a user who takes some artefact as a picture of a person or as a map that represents a swell pattern. The *intention* of the user is paramount: the decision to employ something to represent a chosen target belongs to the user. Different users could use the same artefact to represent different targets. The identification of the target is the result of the intentional act of the user which may or may not correspond to the intention of the maker of the artefact. Of course, this intentional act is also external to the target and the representing artefact. As van Fraassen says:

> Given this intentionality, it is perhaps not surprising that, in the case of a representation, the relations can change with context of use. The very same object (...) can be used to represent different things in different contexts, and in other contexts do not represent at all. (van Fraassen 2008, p. 27)

The direction or asymmetry of the representation also depends on the intention of the user: a photo or a map represents its target and not the other way around. Since the user's intention and the context play a crucial role in the success of a representation, the relation between a representing artefact R and its target T cannot be reduced to a two-place relation. The representational relationship is a four-place relation: a user U represents T as such and such by means of R in some context C. Given that the intention of the user and the context are external to the representing artefact and what is represented, the established structural similarity between R and T is far from being sufficient, although according to the structural view of representation it is necessary.

2.3 Truth and correctness

To identify a target, we could simply point to something which is immediately perceptually present. In other situations, we must formulate a description that mentions some properties actually possessed by the target. Identifying the target of a representation is similar to identifying the referent of a word. Referential success can be achieved either in accordance with Kripke's causal theory of reference or (at least partially) true descriptions. In the latter case, the (partial) truth of some propositions is necessary for the identification of the target.

The main point is that identifying the target of a representing artefact is arbitrary, just as a given word can be made to denote anything. Of course, conventions in place in some context determine in practice the denotations of linguistic signs, as a given context does for the targets of some representing artefacts. But such external facts do not eliminate the fundamental arbitrariness in attributing a target to a representing artefact. As a consequence, mistargeting understood by Suárez (2003) as applying a representing artefact or a model to "an object that it is not intended for" or to the "wrong target" (Pero & Suárez 2016, p. 74) cannot occur. Indeed, mistargeting is meaningless in the same way as misreferring for a word is, except in the external sense that a word may sometimes be used without complying with the conventions in place in some cultural linguistic context. For example, it could happen that someone who is not proficient in English uses the word "rat" to denote a mouse. Similarly, nothing intrinsic to a

Micronesian stick chart prevents it from being appropriated by a user as a map of Brussels. Then, its intended target would be Brussels. (I am insisting on this, because it helps to understand why a successful scientific model can be applied to a target which is very different from its initial target, when for example the liquid drop model is used to represent the atomic nucleus)[21]. Obviously, it could be the case that no intended target has been attributed to an entity or an object, as is the case for most entities in the world. Then, such entity does not qualify as a representing artefact in the first place and *a fortiori* cannot misrepresent.

Once a target has been identified, some selected properties, which are intrinsic to the target, are made to correspond to selected properties of the representing artefact, the photo or the map, in order to construct a representational function which preserves some selected relations. Such an operation, which is tantamount to specifying a code, is most often implicit in a given context. When performing a representation, the user always relies (often unconsciously) on a function which performs, as we have seen, a transfer of structure from the target *to* the representing artefact, be it a photo or a map.

It is crucial to realise that the construction of this function is based on the *assumed truth of some propositions* that attribute properties and relations to both the representing artefact (the photo, the sea chart) and its target (a person, a maritime environment) such as ⟨the stick chart contains shells⟩ and ⟨the maritime environment comprises islands⟩. This is the case even if the representation is incorrect, that is to say, misrepresents its target. However, such construction does not commit us to a constructivist antirealist position according to which our representations never provide cognitive access to external real things. It is certainly true that in this construction process a thing acquires the status of a representing artefact, but it is also true that it has intrinsic properties. If a photo is used to represent a person it is because people have properties which are put in correlation with properties actually possessed by the photo. This representational action is *successful* only if the target has been identified *and* a transfer of structure from the person to the photo has been carried out by the user, namely someone looking at the photo.

Suppose now that I decide to use the photo of a particular person as a representation of my grandmother. I might do that because at some place on the photo there is a black area above a light area, and my grandmother had black hair. Yet I could have used other identifying clues and other conventions. On the other hand, a photo of my grandmother is considered *correct* or "good" if propositions (which do not have to be uttered or written)

---

[21]The liquid drop model of the nucleus is carefully discussed by Da Costa & French (2003, pp. 50–51).

about relevant aspects of her physical appearance as well as propositions about some characteristics of the photo are true. The correctness of the photo decisively depends on the isomorphism, which has been established and which conveys to the user some information about my grandmother. If the photo is accurate (in some respects), it is because, among other things, the area and the photo corresponding to the nose is comparatively small and because my grandmother had a small nose, a fact that makes true the proposition ⟨my grandmother had a small nose⟩.

The very same photo may be intentionally appropriated by someone else to represent my great-aunt. In this case, the photo will *not* represent my great-aunt correctly, i.e., it will *misrepresent* her in some respects because, for example, my great-aunt's nose was larger than my grandmother's. However, it will be a photo of my great-aunt, a successful representation of her based on the truth of propositions (descriptions) identifying her as the intended target.

A representing artefact such as a photograph is neither true nor false. Only statements or propositions can be true or false, such as the proposition ⟨my grandmother's nose was small⟩. Artefacts and propositions belong to different categories that should not be mixed up.[22] If one speaks of the truth of a representation, it only can be in an indirect or derivative sense. The correctness of an artefact endowed with a representational use rests on facts on which we rely to construct representational functions. Those facts make some propositions true, but an artefact is neither an assertion nor a proposition. For this reason, I will not speak of true or false representations but of correct or incorrect representations.

In what sense can a representing artefact be incorrect or misrepresent? Since the choice of an artefact to represent a particular target is always intentional, the visual resemblance between an artefact and some entity does not determine that the artefact represents something specific, nor *a fortiori* that it represents it correctly in some respects. What is more, it is not true that an artefact must visually resemble its target to be a representation of it. This point is made clear by the example of the Micronesian sea chart. Is it plausible to claim that this chart resembles a maritime environment? If it did, it would immediately be recognised as a sea chart in most contexts. Does a sheet of paper with straight parallel lines and small elliptical patches immediately appear to anyone, in any cultural context, as a music score? Does the score look like the music it represents? Obviously not.

---

[22] According to my regimented construal of representation, true propositions do *not* represent their truthmakers. No representational function can be constructed from the truthmaker to the proposition it makes true. The failure of Wittgenstein's "picture theory of meaning" in the *Tractatus* is a case in point. (Wittgenstein 1971) Although I advocate a correspondence view of truth, the relation between a true proposition and its truthmaker is not representational in kind but rather referential. (Ghins 2024, pp. 51–52).

This is why Nelson Goodman could write:

> The most naive view of representation might perhaps be put something like this: "A represents B if and only if A appreciably resembles B". Vestiges of this view, with assorted refinements, persist in most writing on representation. Yet more error could hardly be compressed into so short a formula. (Goodman 1976, pp. 3–4; quoted by van Fraassen 2008, p. 11)

Visual resemblance can certainly play a representational role provided it is encoded in a (usually tacit) representational function that connects identical or nearly identical properties and relations. Obviously, this is implicit in the case of a photograph, which always resembles something or someone by virtue of the very process of its production by means of a particular technical device, such as a camera. Despite of this, a photo can misrepresent. It all depends on the target intentionally chosen by the user. As in the example discussed above, if I decide that the picture of my grandmother is the picture of her sister (who looks very much like her), then I certainly represent her sister. It is the intentional act that decides the target or referent of the representation, and thus its *asymmetry* (the photo represents my great-aunt and not the other way around).[23] However, I could claim that the photo *mis*represents my great-aunt by pointing out that, unlike my grandmother, her nose was large, as we saw. Again, the incorrectness of the photo depends on an actual physical property of my great-aunt.

2.4 Some objections

Let us now have a look at two standard objections to the structural view of representation I proposed. According to the first objection, the structural view fails to account for cases of *non*-representation, i.e., when no target has been identified and also when the intended target does not exist. According to the second objection, structural similarity is not a *necessary* condition for representational success in examples such as Stolz's caricature that represents the chancellor Bismarck as vainglorious, which is a case of what I will call "symbolic or metaphorical representations".

Firstly, if no target has been identified, there is no representation. As seen above, target identification is akin to denotation, since it is arbitrary (anything can represent anything ...) just as any entity can be made the referent of a given sign or word. Without target identification, it is obvious that no transfer of structure from a target to a representing artefact can be established by a user. Thus, objecting at this stage that isomorphisms (or, more generally, homomorphisms) have not been instituted or that they are unable to account for the identification of targets is irrelevant.

---

[23] On the asymmetry issue see also Bueno (2010).

Granted, in everyday language some objects are often called to represent other things even when no transfer of structure has been established. For example, in board games such as the Game of the goose, it is often said that coloured pieces *represent* the players. But in such instances, no representation takes place. Actually, it would be more appropriate to say that coloured pieces *stand for* or *denote* the various players.

It must also be emphasised that when an intended target has been properly identified, it need not to be real. Imaginary or ideal targets can be described and theoretically constructed, especially in scientific contexts. Mathematical models are routinely constructed, that may or may not match— approximately—selected properties of real targets. Such activity of model construction plays an important heuristic role in science. Mathematical models or ideal structures such as perfect gases or ideal pendulums are *necessarily* correct (or very nearly so) by construction, in the sense that they exactly (or very nearly so) satisfy the laws[24] of perfect gases and ideal pendulums.[25] Indeed, ideal structures are constructed in such a way that they satisfy some propositions. They are models in the alethic sense. Representation happens only when such models are claimed to partially represent real systems previously identified—independently of theoretical construction—as targets. If an ideal model does not correctly represent its target in some relevant respects, it can be called a misrepresentation of its target, as explained before.

A successful and partially correct model for specific targets, can be tentatively applied to very different targets in accordance with the claim that anything can represent anything. In science, such attempts are heuristically guided by analogies supposed to be present between the target (seen as a system) of the previous model and the intended target (seen as system) of the tentatively constructed model, as Mary Hesse (1970) famously contended.[26] In this paper I am more interested in the relation between scientific models and reality. Thus, I will not further delve into the (admittedly very important) heuristic role of models.

---

[24]More precisely, ideal structures satisfy nomological formulas such as $PV = kT$; more details on this in Ghins (2024, p. 27).

[25]It has often been pointed out that mathematical structures such as the ideal pendulum are contradictory. To get the law of isochronism of small oscillations ($T = 2\pi(\ell/g)^{\frac{1}{2}}$), where T is the period of oscillation, ℓ the length of the pendulum and g the gravitational acceleration), one supposes that the angle of oscillation is equal to 0 and thus that the pendulums does not move! Nevertheless, the ideal pendulum with small angles of oscillation nearly satisfies the law of isochronism. And observations of real pendulums approximately agree with the law when oscillations are small ...

[26]As Da Costa and French (2003) nicely showed, Hesse's notions of positive, negative, and neutral analogies can be precisely captured by the notions of partial structures and partial isomorphisms.

The issue of misrepresentation brings us to the second objection, namely when distortion is used to represent the target *as* having properties (or relations)—which I call "symbolic" or "metaphorical"—that are not mapped into properties (or relations) of the representing artefact by some isomorphism (or homomorphism).

Let us look more closely at this through one of van Fraassen's examples, namely Stolz's caricature of Bismarck (who was chancellor of Germany at the end of 19th century) as vainglorious.[27]

First, for the caricature to function as a representing artefact *of* Bismarck its target must be identified. In the present case, the referential intention is determined by propositions, which are implicitly supposed to be true by the user. These propositions attribute to Bismarck's visage specific properties that resemble some features of the face pictured in the caricature. Thus, the identification of the target relies on facts: Bismarck was bald, wore a moustache etc. These facts make the relevant propositions true. Moreover, a significant part of the structure of Bismarck's visage is mapped (by a user in some context) into the structure of part of the caricature. Thus, the target of Stolz's caricature is Bismarck.

Yet in the drawing Bismarck's head, chest and feet substitute the head, neck and legs of a peacock which displays his tail feathers. Evidently, the drawing was not intended by Stolz to be taken to be a resembling portrait of Bismarck but as a caricature that represents him *as* vainglorious. How is

---

[27]This caricature is in the public domain (Wikimedia Commons). It is discussed by van Fraassen (2008, p. 14).

Stolz's aim achieved? As van Fraassen stresses, success in achieving such aim relies on some *distortion* of Bismarck's physical features. Bismarck's arms are replaced by wings, his chest looks like a long neck etc. If implausibly believed to be a resembling portrait of Bismarck, such representation is obviously incorrect and is thus a misrepresentation of him in some respects. However, the drawing contains properties and relations—notably the displayed tail feathers—which are typical of peacocks. In our cultural context, peacocks are metaphorically or symbolically associated with vanity. Hence, appropriated by a user in a Western culture, Stolz's drawing successfully represents Bismarck as vainglorious, whether he was actually vainglorious or not.[28] Here again, representational success is grounded on an isomorphism between parts of Bismarck's body as well as properties of peacocks on the one hand and properties of the drawing on the other hand.

Although metaphorical or symbolic representations are not usually used in scientific contexts, distortions are. The representation of a planet-star system as a structure of two mass points is a clear and frequently cited example of distortion. Clearly, planets and stars are voluminous entities ...

2.5 Scientific modelling

Today, many philosophers of science rightly emphasise the prominent role of models within scientific practice. For the proponents of the "semantic view of theories",[29] theories are primarily sets or classes of models. Such a conception, defended by Patrick Suppes (1967, 2002), Bas van Fraassen (1980, 2008) and Ronald Giere (1988), among others, gradually became prevalent in reaction to the "syntactic conception" according to which theories are just sets of statements or propositions. This syntactic view was embraced by the logical positivists of the Vienna Circle in the early 20th century, such as Rudolf Carnap, Moritz Schlick and Otto Neurath, to mention only a few. The syntactic conception dominated philosophy of science until the late 1960s.[30]

In the *Scientific Image*, Bas van Fraassen endorses the semantic view and claims that "models take centre stage" (1980, p. 44). He of course acknowledges that theories also contain propositions. Nevertheless, a theory is primarily a set of models that fulfil the dual role of representing phenomena as well as making propositions true. Yet theories are not maps or photographs. Models in science can be systems of real properties (like the DNA double

---

[28]The caricature could have been appropriated to represent a peacock as Bismarckian. Given the context, this would have been somewhat far-fetched ...

[29]The name "semantic" is justified because the semantic conception of theories is primarily interested in models and these, as we saw, can make true some statements and propositions.

[30]Look at Frederick Suppe's (1974) classic work for a presentation of the reasons that led to the abandonment of the syntactic conception in favour of the semantic conception of theories.

helix modelled as a system of spheres and rods), but also mathematical structures whose mode of reality is controversial and which I qualify as *ideal*.

In the example of the orbital periods of the planets presented above, the aim of representing a perceptual structure by a data model is reached by establishing a correspondence between two distinct sets of properties, one which contains directly observed quantities while the other contains measurement results. If the domains of the perceptual structure and the data model contain the same number of elements, a one-to-one correspondence between them can be constructed by means of a bijective function F. Such function maps an element of the domain of the perceptual structure to an element of the domain of the data model, in such a way that there are no unpaired elements. In the example above, the orbital period of planets observed by the naked eye are mapped to their measured orbital periods.

In addition, we can arrange things in such a way that the correspondence preserves selected relations between the elements of the domains. Two elements a and b connected by a relation R in the perceptual domain are mapped by F to data that stand in a relation R^*. In the example we are discussing, R and R^* are the same relation "smaller than". Let us call two observed orbital periods "a" and "b". $F(a)$ and $F(b)$ are the corresponding elements (images) in the data model of a and b. If a is smaller than b, then $F(a)$ is smaller than $F(b)$: if aRb, then $F(a)R^*F(b)$. The representative function F is an isomorphism. Thus, this set of data can be appropriated by scientists as a model to represent the perceptual or phenomenal structure of orbital periods.

For a data model to represent a perceptual structure, a representational function operating a transfer of structure must have been constructed beforehand by a user. This is the central point of the *structural* conception of representation in science which I favour. Granted, a mathematical model, such as a data model, does not appear to have the material solidity of a photograph or a map. Although models are not propositions, they can be conveyed by means of symbols like written signs on a piece of paper, just as propositions also can. It seems to me that the relation between a mathematical model and those signs is analogous to the relation between a proposition and a corresponding sentence or propositional sign. In the same way as a proposition can be expressed by various sentences in different languages according to distinct conventions, a model can be conveyed by various material symbols.[31]

We saw above that the *context* can play a crucial role in indicating some representational function when some artefact is seen as a photograph or a map. A given cultural milieu includes a wealth of conventions which deter-

---

[31] Let me recall that the relation between sentences and propositions is not representational.

mine, most often implicitly, the code assumed by a user in appropriating an artefact as a map, a photo ... I also emphasized that the representational relation is complex since it involves four ingredients: the representing artefact, the represented target, the user and the context. However, once the representative function between two structures has been explicitly and clearly specified, as is often the case in science, one can limit the representational relationship to a two-place relation between two structures, while remaining silent about the other ingredients, which are taken for granted. I also insisted that I use the word "representation" in a precise, regimented, technical sense, which does not correspond to its usual meaning in some contexts, such as when we say that some piece on a board game represents a player. Besides, in attributing a property P to an entity S, we commonly say that we *represent* S as instantiating property P. However, in this case we are not establishing a representational relationship (in the structural sense) between a property P on the one hand and an entity S on the other, let alone a relationship between an "image", an "idea" or a "representation" in our mind and an external entity.

A successful action of representation—in the technical structural sense—requires constructing an isomorphism (or homomorphism) between two structures. A scientist can succeed in representing a targeted phenomenon only by selectively extracting a perceptual structure from it. Then, a data structure and an isomorphism between them is constructed in order to finally get a representing data model. Proceeding in this fashion within the objectifying approach seems to lead to the following counter-intuitive consequence: the data model does *not* represent the targeted phenomenon, but only the system of perceived properties which is extracted from it, that is, a scientific object. At first sight, the representing process seems to imply the unwelcome consequence that scientists loose contact with concrete real things. This is not so! Success and correctness of a representation are grounded on instantiated properties, that is, on facts, described by true propositions as we saw earlier.

For sure, the elaboration of a scientific theory cannot remain limited to the construction of a data model, if only because a data model has no explanatory power. The data model only represents the perceptual structure and does not explain *why* the durations of orbital periods increase with the distance to the sun. In order to explain the measurement results, scientists immerge or "embed" the data models into larger, more encompassing structures, called "theoretical structures". What does such *embedding* consist in?

Embedding a data model in a theoretical structure amounts to constructing an isomorphism between a substructure of the theoretical structure and the data model. By extension, we can speak of the embedding of perceptual structures (and even of phenomena themselves according to van

Fraassen, 1980) in theoretical structures, which make true (or nearly so) the laws of the theory. In this broad sense, phenomena are embedded in theoretical structures although phenomena are not systems. Theoretical structures are mathematical structures. They often are set-theoretical structures capable of representing structures of properties instantiated in an intended target. Furthermore, theories contain structures that cannot be instantiated in reality. The world does not contain completely isolated systems of two massive bodies which exactly match the mathematical models of Newtonian mechanics. Real systems are represented by mathematical models only in an approximately correct way.

In celestial mechanics, the structure of orbital periods can be embedded in the set of models of Newtonian mechanics that deal with two masses in gravitational interaction. As a first approximation, when looking at the orbital motion of a planet such as Mars we focus on Mars and the sun only and disregard the gravitational influence of other planets. Since the mass of the sun represents more than 99% of the total mass of the solar system, such omission is justified when a high degree of precision is not required. Moreover, we take planets and the sun to be point masses. When simplifying assumptions disregard properties which are known to be relevant (such as the presence of more than two gravitationally interacting bodies), this is a well-known feature of the abstracting process. However, the simplifying assumptions may not conform to some relevant properties of the target. In such cases, some relevant properties are modified or distorted. In situations like these, we should speak of *idealisation* as Portides recommends. (Portides 2018) As a consequence of omissions and idealisations, a proposed model can be incorrect in several relevant respects. Scientists are aware of this. This is why they strive to construct less incomplete and more accurate models by taking into account relevant factors that have first been omitted by abstraction and also by modifying or cancelling idealisations. In practice, simpler or more sophisticated models are used in different contexts in function of the demanded degree of precision.

Newtonian theory contains a theoretical substructure isomorphic to the data model of orbital periods. But the availability of an isomorphism does not imply that the theoretically calculated values of orbital periods conform the data. In addition, we want the theoretical values to be sufficiently close or *adequate* to the measured values. Otherwise, the two-mass-point model would be useless for delivering correct predictions. A theoretical substructure susceptible to be isomorphic and also adequate to the data model is called an *empirical substructure* (van Fraassen 1980, p. 64). It is empirical because the properties of its domain, such as the orbital period values, are measurable. Yet an empirical substructure is also theoretical since it is obtained by calculation within the framework of a theory. Given that its adequacy can be tested empirically, there is no contradiction for an empirical substructure to be both empirical and theoretical. When for any data model belonging to the domain of investigation of a theory, the theory always contains an empirical substructure that adequately, i.e., correctly (at least approximately), represents the data model, the theory is said to be "empirically adequate".

Obviously, an empirically adequate theory must also permit calculating and predicting *novel* measurement results. This is a challenging requirement. Empirical adequacy is not limited to available data but must encompass *all* possible future measurements. A theory is empirically adequate if and only if it contains empirical substructures that are isomorphic (or homomorphic) to the set of data models that can be constructed for the set of perceptual structures that fall within its domain of investigation. It may happen that new data do not conform to the predictions of the theory. A scientific theory always runs the risk of being falsified: there is no guarantee that future data will always match the predictions of the theory. This typically occurs when more accurate measuring instruments are developed. If the predictions of the theory deviate too much from new measurement results, then it can no longer be taken to be empirically adequate.

The process described above can be summarised in the scheme given in Figure 1.

It should be clear that this scheme is not supposed to reflect the actual manner in which scientists proceed, let alone the way classical mechanics has been elaborated. Rather, it is meant to be a conceptual epistemological analysis of the connection between theoretical models and observed things. Once the laws of classical mechanics are known, structures that make true those laws—or rather solutions of them in disciplines like physics—can be constructed and studied independently of experience. Such purely theoretical models could then be applied to some real systems, including systems that do not pertain to the domain for which a theory was originally designed. In other words, a theoretical model can play a heuristic role as mentioned earlier.

I acknowledge that the presentation above offers a very simplified view of the complex process of model construction in science, as the abundant current literature on models testifies. However, the value of simplification lies in its ability to facilitate generalisation. I submit that the proposed framework generally applies to successful modelling in science.

3 Conclusion

To conclude let me first recall that representing is an activity or an action, as van Fraassen stresses. It involves a user appropriating an artefact to represent an intended target as such and such by stipulating a code and

Phenomenon (sky)

@

Perceptual structure (perceived orbital periods)

isomorphism
↓

Data model (measured orbital periods)

isomorphism
↓

Empirical (*and* theoretical) substructure (calculated orbital periods)

∩

Set of theoretical models (two-mass models)

∩

Class of models (theory) of classical point mechanics

FIGURE 1. The symbol @ stands for abstraction, i.e., selection and omission of properties and relations, and ∩ stands above for strict set-theoretic inclusion.

adopting conventions in a certain context. An action is neither true nor false; it can succeed or fail, insofar as the user succeeds or fails to achieve some intended aim. To successfully represent a target, two conditions must be met. First, the user must identify the target. This identification is achieved by an intentional action in the first person: I decide to represent a particular thing (or class of things), recognisable by some of its specific properties, whether it exists or not. This is the reason that mistargeting cannot occur, but non-representation only, in the same way that a word sign can lack denotation. As a next step, the user must establish, consciously or unconsciously, a transfer of structure from the target to the artefact used to represent it. This requires extracting from the target some properties and relations that are mapped, by an isomorphism (or homomorphism), to selected properties and relations of the artefact. For example, if I decide to use the liquid drop model to represent an atomic nucleus, I must establish a mapping between some properties of the nucleus into some properties of the liquid drop model as seen earlier. The success of these two actions (target identification and transfer of structure) presupposes the truth of some propositions about the properties of the target and the representing artefact. I can also successfully represent a person, *albeit* incorrectly in some respects, when using my grandmother's photograph to represent my great-aunt. Since a representing artefact is never true or false, its correctness or incorrectness depends on the code determined by the representative function and—crucially—on some facts which make certain propositions true or false. The code as well as the facts are external to the representing artefact.

When I represent a given target using some artefact, I always adopt a particular perspective with respect to certain properties and relations. By appropriating a piece of coloured paper as a photograph, I represent the chosen target according to some of its visible aspects; in other words, I represent its target *as* a visual system. By appropriating a Micronesian artefact *as* a sea chart, I represent an environment as a system of properties relevant to navigation. In other words, I adopt a particular point of view on a target by representing it as such and such, that is, according to some highlighted respects. Of course, many other respects are disregarded: my representation is never complete. It is even hugely incomplete because my representation disregards the vast majority of the properties and relations instantiated by the target.

Discussing some mundane examples of representation helped us to better understand how model construction works in science. Starting from some phenomena, the first step is to extract from them a perceptual structure, that is, a set of perceived properties organised by specific relations. The next step is to construct a data model to which the perceptual structure is connected by a representative (isomorphic or homomorphic) function. The data are measurement results often smoothed out to produce a continuous structure. Then, an empirical structure is constructed to represent the data model. Such empirical structure is then embedded in a theoretical structure, such as a two point masses model as illustrated above. Obviously, scientists do not usually proceed in the way just described in their actual practice. More often than not, phenomena are not directly observable, and no perceptual structure can be constructed by extracting properties from them. Scientists often work within the theory to produce empirical substructures susceptible to guide them towards collecting new measurements and data. Be it as it may, I submit that the relationships between data models, empirical substructures and theoretical models generally obtain as presented above.

References

Agazzi, E. (2014), *Scientific Objectivity and its Contexts*. Berlin: Springer.

Ascher, M. (1995), "Models and Maps from the Marshall Islands: A Case in Ethnomathematics", *Historia Mathematica* 22, 347–370.

Bartels, A. (2005), *Strukturale Repräsentation*. Paderborn: Mentis.

Bartels, A. (2006), "Defending the Structural Concept of Representation", *Theoria* 55, 7–19.

Bresciani Filho, E. & D'Ottaviano, I.M.L. (2018), "Basic Concepts of Systemics" in Pereira Jr, A., Pickering, W. A., Gudwin, R. (eds.), *Systems, Self-organization, and Information: an Interdisciplinary, Perspective*, 47–63. New York: Routledge.

Bueno, O. (2010), "Models and Scientific Representations" in Magnus, P. & Busch, J. (eds.) (2010), *New Waves in Philosophy of Science*, 94–111. Basingstoke: Palgrave Macmillan.

Chakravartty, A. (2010), "Informational versus functional theories of representation", *Synthese* 172, 197–213.

Contessa, G. (2007), "Scientific Representation, Interpretation, and Surrogative Reasoning", *Philosophy of Science* 74, 48–68.

Da Costa, N. & French, S. (2003), *Science and Partial Truth. A Unitary Approach to Models and Scientific Reasoning*. Oxford: Oxford University Press.

Frigg, R. (2010), "Models and Fiction", *Synthese* 172, 251–68.

Giere, R. (1988), *Explaining Science: A Cognitive Approach*. Chicago: University of Chicago Press.

Ghins, M. (2024), *Scientific Realism and Laws of Nature. A Metaphysics of Causal Powers*. Synthese library 483. Cham: Springer.

Goodman, N. (1976), *Languages of Art: An Approach to a Theory of Symbols*. Indianapolis: Hackett Publishing Company.

Hesse, M. (1970), *Models and Analogies in Science*. Oxford: Oxford University Press.

Lewis, D. H. (1994), *We, the Navigators. The Ancient Art of Landfinding in the Pacific*. Edited by Sir Derek Oulton. Honolulu: University of Hawaii Press.

Pero, F. & Suárez, M. (2016), "Varieties of Misrepresentation and Homomorphism". *European Journal for Philosophy of Science* 6, 71–90.

Portides, D. (2018), "Idealization and Abstraction in Scientific Modelling", *Synthese* 198, 5873–5895.

Suárez, M. (2003), "Scientific Representation: Against Similarity and Isomorphism", *International Studies in the Philosophy of Science* 17, 226–244.

Suppe, F. (1974), *The Structure of Scientific Theories*. Chicago: University of Illinois.

Suppes, P. (1967), "What is a Scientific Theory?" in Morgenbesser, S. (ed.) *Philosophy of Science Today*, 55–67. New York: Basic books.

Suppes, P. (2002), *Representation and Invariance of Scientific Structures*. Stanford: CLSI.

van Fraassen, B. (1980), *The Scientific Image*. Oxford: Oxford University Press.

van Fraassen, B. (2002), *The Empirical Stance*. New Haven: Yale University Press.

van Fraassen, B. (2008), *Scientific Representation. Paradoxes of Perspective*. Oxford: Oxford University Press.

Wilson, C. (1997), *The Invisible World. Early Modern Philosophy and the Invention of the Microscope*. Princeton: Princeton University Press.

Wittgenstein, L. (1971), *Tractatus Logico-Philosophicus*. Transl. by Pears, D. F. & McGuinness, B. F. London: Routledge & Kegan.

Model and normativity
On the relation of nature—technology—ethics

Elisabeth Gräb-Schmidt

Lehrstuhl für Systematische Theologie II, Evangelisch-Theologische Fakultät, Eberhard-Karls-Universität Tübingen, Liebermeisterstr. 12, 72076 Tübingen, Germany

1 Introduction: The significance of models and problems of normativity in the transitional situation of modernity

Models are created and varied in situations of transition and crisis. When traditional assumptions of truth become fragile or questionable, the challenge arises to develop new models. In the natural sciences, this is obvious when we think of atomic models, or the discovery of the benzole ring by Kekulé, to whom this model appeared in dreams. Or let us think of the conceptual change in physics by Galileo and Newton, in terms of looking at the function of objects rather than their cosmological order as a law of nature, that is, studying what objects do rather than what they are. Models are created and varied in the search for suitable meaningful explanations for certain factual observations. Less noticed is this method of understanding and self-understanding through models of explanation and making reality tangible through models in the humanities or even in theology. And it is precisely in theology that models are present from the very beginning. Such models can be seen in all mythological narratives, which can be understood as origin stories. Especially in the development from tribal religions, in archaic societies, to high religions, models of reference to God and transcendence emerge, as Jan Assmann has shown, for example, for the development of monotheism in ancient Egypt[1].

My thesis is that theology, as a meta-level of understanding the Christian faith, always represents a model—or is represented by a model. Theology virtually stands for modelling, insofar as its object—God—is the permanently withdrawn, an unobjectifiable entity, which is why theology cannot go beyond being a model. To be a model corresponds—at least in modern perception—to the character of theology. It is part of this character to represent a model in order to approach the object and to test and plausibilise its truthfulness by discussing different models. The question of theology as a model thus directly concerns theology as a science, i.e., Christian theology as a meta-level of understanding the Christian faith.

---

[1]Cf. Jan Assmann, Moses der Ägypter, Entzifferung einer Gedächtnisspur, Berlin 2000.

From the very beginning, however, we find such a meta-level of attempts at understanding, which resemble models, in the formations of myths already mentioned. Therefore, they too can be regarded as models in a certain sense, even if only on a pre-reflective level, and they already point to the scope of models in theology, namely to the fact that with religion or the object of theology we are dealing with something that cannot go beyond models at all. The fact that it is precisely the non-rational or supra-rational aspect of faith that plays a role here does not detract from the rationality of models. So it can apply to models in general: They can be based on and stimulated by experiences of evidence. However, these are subsequently consolidated by arguments ex post and, above all, made communicable, but always within the limits of the model.

With the model character of theology we therefore enter the meta-level of rational understanding of religious worldviews, their values and norms. These worldviews themselves meet as certainty of experience in contrast to certainty of knowledge, which would have as its flip side scepticism or the denial of truth knowledge. However, it is precisely this level of certainty of knowledge that must account for the accuracy of models.

Therefore, when we speak of models in theology, we must distinguish between the level of faith and the level of reflection of faith. It is this meta-level of reflection on faith that characterises theology as a science, which leads to the concept of theology as a model. The value of self-reflexive theology is to be aware of this model character. For it is precisely for theology that there is a danger of overlooking or ignoring the model character of its doctrinal statements, since theology is concerned with understanding reality. Therefore, there is always the possibility of confusing models with reality. But the insight into the reality of faith is based precisely on the fact that such models cannot represent reality as such, that is, reality in the form of the wholeness of a world view, but that models want to refer to this wholeness, namely in and through the reality of experience and the experience of reality of individuals. This experience of reality manifests itself in evidence that cannot be generalised. This generalising approach has been the endeavour of metaphysics. But we have to face the critique of metaphysics, according to which a general reference to truth, to reality, as represented by metaphysics, is regarded as speculation—at the latest since Kant's destruction of the proofs for the existence of God. The modern turn of philosophy to the subject—for example with Descartes—exposes and therefore demands the model as model instead of a direct reference to any truth, if one holds on to a concept of reality and normativity at all.

This way of making models/concepts explicit confirms the modern insight that knowledge of reality cannot be generalised and therefore cannot be rationally grasped. Nevertheless, the search for reality and normativity can claim its own place as experience through the figure of the individual. Now we have to consider that it is this experience of the individual that makes it possible to establish a reference to reality at all. There, in the individual, the grasp of reality goes hand in hand with the claim to appreciate something universal in the individual. And this is possible with regard to a certainty that is legitimised by an experience that is somehow evidential.

The general is therefore to be distinguished from the universal when it comes to the question of an epistemological access to reality. This distinction between the general and the universal is possible because the universal can be seen as transcending the general—and thus human reason—while at the same time offering a unique evidence and certainty about reality that can be glimpsed, so to speak, at certain moments. It is therefore obvious that the focus on the individual, the individual as the guarantor of access to reality, represents a spiritual and intellectual-historical transition within modernity. The individual represents an entity that provides a contingent insight into reality. This leads to a shift in the broader cultural context, expressed through the development of new models that, among other things, validate the concept of the model itself.

This validation occurs through a particular emphasis on the individual and the particular, in contrast to the modern concept of the subject. Unlike the modern subject, which sought to grasp the whole or the general, the individual now represents experiences of certainty about reality within specific areas and times, giving it only a model-like character. This perspective is consistent with a radical critique of metaphysics. The question of my paper is now concerned with the effort to maintain interest in the possibility of normative orientation, that is, the possibility of grasping reality, so to speak, in a post-metaphysical world or in a world of cognition in which models as models are the only honest way to stay within the reality of the scientific approach.

Ratiocentrism, for example, can be understood as a model of human emancipation and maturity that took place during the Enlightenment. It is characterised precisely by the fact that reason becomes in a prominent way the standard for dealing with the world, and thus the problematic relationship between reason and religion becomes an issue. This new modelling of man's relationship to the world included the fact that religion is no longer, as it used to be, the realm of man in his self-understanding of his being in the world, as was the case in antiquity and the Middle Ages, which included metaphysics and ontology as ontotheology, including ideas of nature, of the cosmological order and of natural law.

This view of unity, or of the possibility of unity through the integration of reason into a whole, superordinate cosmological order or conception of natural law, broke down in modernity and modernity and in the name of modern rationality. The so-called ratiocentrism that grew out of it designated the new intellectual-historical model of the explanation of the world and of the self, which created a new model of the possibilities of cognition, by which theology, in the course of the critique of religion, now saw itself challenged to develop new models of the relationship between transcendence, rationality and reality.

However, with this post-metaphysical turn towards understanding reality only through models, the pressing question arises: to what extent did philosophy, in its turn away from ontology and metaphysics during the Enlightenment, not only abandon its normative foundations, but also fail to compensate for this loss? In other words, the urgent question is: how can this loss of orientation through the loss of metaphysics be countered with models alone? To answer this question, we must consider the two levels of reference to reality.

I would like to illustrate this problem with an example of a changed understanding of normativity, as it is challenged by the new technologies in their new determination of the relationship between nature and technology. This problem becomes evident in the modern hybridisation of technology and nature. The traditional distinction between technology and nature, which has been maintained since antiquity, no longer seems appropriate. Historically, the concept of nature symbolised normativity, acting as a guiding horizon and an ethical boundary for the limits of technological research and development. This model—in which nature was unquestionably seen as the boundary and standard for ethical guidelines—has already been abandoned in modern times. Today, with the rapid pace of technological progress, the notion of nature, or even 'natural law', as a boundary is increasingly disregarded. The exemplary nature of ethical guidelines or normativity can be illustrated by the concept of human nature itself, understood as humanity's unique cultural capacity expressed through specific forms of technology.

A brief look at the understanding of technology can illustrate this. When we think of technology, we usually think first of artefacts, of tools, or of specific technologies in our actions. We often overlook the dimension of technology that accompanies this—the aspect of securing our place in the world, which affects the conditions of both the world and the self for humanity as a whole. Yet it is precisely this dimension of technology that is directly linked to humanity's normative self-understanding, helping us to cope with the contingency of our existence. It seems to me crucial that we keep in mind this aspect of technology, as it relates to self-understanding and coping with contingency, if we are to determine its ethical-normative significance for human beings. Although technology has an instrumental character as a compensation for the lack of instinct of the "deficient being" (Mängelwesen[2]), it also fulfils a normative function by securing humanity's position in the world. Both aspects reflect human freedom. However, with regard to this second dimension—which shapes humanity's self-understanding—technology risks undermining freedom itself, since the ambivalence inherent in freedom can threaten freedom itself.

This is illustrated by newer technologies, which place us at the centre of questions about the possibility and validity of norms in modernity. It's important to consider how both dimensions of technology—the instrumental, artefact-based aspect and its role in mastering the self and the world—are intertwined. When this interweaving blurs the distinction between these two dimensions, it has significant implications for our understanding of nature in its traditional, normative sense. This development of technology can thus illustrate the change in the concept of nature in relation to technology—and, what is important for us, it can also somehow illustrate the model character of nature in relation to human freedom.

2 The transformation of the concept of nature in its normative dimension and its relation to technology

Since Greek antiquity, "nature" has functioned as a decisive normative concept of orientation in ethical and legal debates.[3] In antiquity and the Middle Ages, for example, this normative function also found expression in the concept of natural law. For our Western thinking, this orienting dimension of the concept of nature as a normative boundary and background dimension has become indispensable for the orientation of our self-understanding and our understanding of the world. The concept of nature has traditionally served to set limits—both for the orientation of culture and in relation to the scope of technology. In this respect, nature had a cultural, legal and ethical normative function. We recognise this in the expressions as "against nature" or "unnatural".

The German philosopher Gernot Böhme also has this dimension of the concept of nature in mind in a monograph: "The Other of Reason"[4]. This "other" is not only the "objective" or the "excluded", but at the same time an entity that accompanies us as the inaccessible, as the background dimension of all our thinking and perceiving. And it is precisely this background

---

[2]Cf. Arnold Gehlen, Der Mensch. Seine Natur und Stellung in der Welt (1940), Frankfurt 2016.

[3]See also the remarks on the relationship between nature and technology in: Elisabeth Gräb-Schmidt, Art. Umweltethik, in: Handbuch der Evangelischen Ethik (HEE), ed. by Wolfgang Huber, Torsten Meireis and Hans-Richard Reuter, Munich 2015.

[4]Böhme, Gernot/Böhme, Hartmut: Das Andere der Vernunft. Zur Entwicklung von Rationalitätsstrukturen am Beispiel Kant, Frankfurt/Main (^{2}1992) 1983.

dimension that is important for defining the character or even the existence of human freedom.

However, this normative boundary and background function of nature is threatened by those newer technologies which imply a hybrid form of nature and technology. Such hybridisation, for example in biofacts, is then referred to as "enabling technologies" or "converging technologies"[5]. At this point, the question arises as to whether the claim of nature as the other to be the background and boundary dimension of our actions and conceptions is attacked or even dissolved by such a mixture. Does nature lose its previous normative power with such a hybridisation of nature and technology?

In any case, if biofacts lead to a hybridisation of technical and biological components in humans, it is already apparent that the traditionally taken for granted Aristotelian distinction between nature as that which has become natural and technology as that which has been artificially made is beginning to waver, and with it the distinction between two aspects of nature: (a) as material for technical shaping, (b) as a background dimension for ethical norms.

This also has consequences for the understanding of the possibility of normativity, because freedom is affected. It becomes a mixture of its instrumental function, as it is given within technology, and the ethical dimension of freedom, as it is given within the function of self-determination and world domination of human beings, which is granted by the fact that the possibility is embedded in a background dimension. Both aspects of freedom, that of the technical shaping of nature and that of the ethical responsibility for the shaping of the word, including through technology, must be considered. But since both dimensions are related to nature in different ways, the normative status of nature becomes problematic. It disappears in the hybridisation of nature and technology. Nature is now objectified as a whole, i.e., nature as such is subordinated to the feasibility of technology and loses its unavailable background dimension.

With the blurring of the two dimensions of nature, the object and the background dimension, the different functions of freedom are leveled out: freedom as creativity in craft and art, i.e., in technology, on the one hand, and freedom as self-management of human openness to the world ("Weltoffenheit"[6] , i.e., as the given in nature, on the other. It is this de-differentiation of freedom, however, that endangers the possibility of a normative dimension at all. For this mixture draws ethical freedom into technical freedom, so to speak, in that nature as such in its givenness, i.e., in its unavailability, is "made", technically "made", and is thus subordinated to human controllabil-

---

[5] Mihail C. Roco, William Sims Bainbridge (eds.), Converging Technologies for Improving Human Performance. Nanotechnology, Biotechnology, Information Technology and Cognitive Science, Dordrecht/Boston/London, 2003.

[6] Cf. Arnold Gehlen, op.cit., footnote 2.

ity. This means that the previous conception of nature as not made, but as that which has become and as such determines the background of our creative actions, now itself becomes an object and thus something that is "made". Precisely the former, fundamentally uncontrollable, because unavailable, which is conventionally symbolised in "nature" as a background dimension, now, in the newer technologies, seems to be subjected to technology itself.

In this way, however, all that is left is technology. Technical freedom is then identified with freedom as such. This can be illustrated in its radical consequences in the new technologies of artificial intelligence. These radical consequences are that fantasies of dominating and optimising nature through technical processes can also be directed at human nature as feasible, as is promised, for example, in transhumanism, where the limits of life itself are to be pushed out or even abolished. In the immortality visions of Google engineer Ray Kurzweil[7], human nature itself appears as technically feasible and extendable. But as a threatening scenario, as Peter Sloterdijk has already shown in his "Rules for the Human Park"[8].

These scenarios of modern technologies in the field of artificial intelligence have drastic consequences for the relationship between technology and nature or for the understanding of human freedom. One could even speak of a paradigm shift. For the cultural distinctions between nature and technology that have so far determined the normative model can no longer be clearly defined when what is technically made and what is natural become intertwined, when the boundaries between nature and technology become blurred, for example, as already mentioned, in the biologisation of technology, in biofact.[9]

Up to now, nature has been an object of technology, but at the same time a boundary concept of technology. The new technologies now threaten not only to determine the extent to which nature is penetrated by technology, but also threaten the creative space of human freedom itself. For the space of freedom has always been linked to nature as the ground and counterpart of freedom. By symbolising the given and thus, in a certain sense, the unavailable, nature has always represented the enabling space of freedom. But freedom atrophies when it is no longer understood in relation to nature or to a horizon that provides criteria for definition, but rather as a mania for feasibility that believes it can exploit or usurp this relation itself.

Thus, although at first sight technology seems to increase freedom as an extension of man's technical possibilities, in the end, in its mania for feasibility, it turns out to be its abolition. It erases the background dimension

---

[7] Cf. Ray Kurzweil, The Singularity is Near, When Humans Transcends Biology. 2005.

[8] Cf. Peter Sloterdijk, Regeln für den Menschenpark. Ein Antwortschreiben zu Heideggers Brief über den Humanismus, Frankfurt a. M., 1999.

[9] Cf. Nicole Karafyllis (ed.), Biofakte. Versuch über den Menschen zwischen Artefakt und Lebewesen, Paderborn 2003.

of nature, which could be seen—symbolically—as a condition of freedom and normativity. If this background function of nature is dissolved by technology, then in a sense freedom also disappears, although technology itself is an aspect of freedom.

Together with the change in the concept of nature, technology or technical intentionality usurps the traditional place of freedom. However, if this de-differentiation is to be stopped, a new model of nature is needed that can preserve and value human freedom in its two dimensions, the technical and the normative. However, a return to traditional models of nature is impossible if we do not want to fall back into pre-modern metaphysical and ontological patterns.

If we look at what characterises freedom, human freedom not only in its technical quality of creative power, but also in its ethical capacity of responsibility, it is clear that freedom is not exhausted in technical operations, in technical progress. Freedom is then also seen in its power of judgement— also as a counterpoint to a merely reduced, technical ability. And this power is the decisive factor in preserving freedom in its ethical character of responsibility.[10]

The precondition for such a capacity to judge is that freedom remains related to its enabling condition, which in the philosophical tradition was symbolised by nature and which also held the potential for normative orientation. In this respect, Jürgen Habermas rightly points out that we must hold on to a natural basis, to a "naturalness" of our humanity, if we want to preserve our autonomy, namely our capacity to judge.

But it is precisely here that we come to the problem of understanding nature in the light of modern technologies and the change in the model of the concept of nature. The concept of "naturalness", as Habermas uses it[11], can lead to misunderstandings here, because it is now inaccurate. For we have seen: With the biologisation of technology and the objectification of nature, the boundaries between technology and nature become blurred. The problem then lies in the concept of the natural. The natural is no longer given as "natural", as in the ancient and medieval understanding of nature. Rather, as we have seen, the further technology develops and the more nature becomes the object of technology, up to and including human nature as such, the less technology can be defined simply as the opposite of the natural, since it is human nature that expresses itself in this technical way. Insofar as technical feasibility no longer recognises biological nature as a boundary, nature as a biological or cosmological basis has (rightly) lost the function of determining boundaries and backgrounds.

---

[10]Cf. Philip Clayton, In Quest of Freedom, The emergence of Spirit in the Natural World, Göttingen 2006.

[11]Cf. J. Habermas, The Future of Human Nature. On the Way to a Liberal Eugenics? Frankfurt a.M. 2005.

In order to escape this misconception or misunderstanding, nature must be perceived not as biological or cosmological, but in its symbolic dimension as background determination. Even if nature as a biological basis has lost its normative function, this does not apply to the "unavailable" that nature symbolises, the unavoidable of its boundary determination. But this is misleadingly called "natural growth" in the Habermasian sense. Indeed, the understanding of naturalness runs the risk of a biologistic narrowing of the understanding of nature or of nature as a normative criterion. If nature now becomes the designation of a symbolic place of the unavailable, of a space of human freedom, then nature can continue to symbolise the unavailable and thus preserve a space of primordial freedom. This given freedom as a space of possibility now corresponds to nature as a given background dimension that can form the normative criteriology of ethical action.

The criterion itself is and must be an orientation towards the preservation of freedom. In a sense, then, it's a formal criterion that is open to various material contents. But this also makes it clear that our task of preserving freedom is now made more difficult: for we now have to decide for ourselves what we must or want to preserve as "nature" or as unavailable in relation to technology. This is a question that cannot be answered once and for all, but it is the task of ethics, which must be oriented towards the preservation of human freedom as the ability to judge and to choose a goal. To do this, it needs a symbolic model of nature, which is not available. Then we see: Not only the ancient model of nature, but also such a model of a symbolic space of the (possible) conditions of freedom offers a limit for technical action. But this limit is not naturally given, it is not without a criterion. The criterion is thus given where the space of freedom, in its unavailability, does not dare to be attacked, i.e., when the root of freedom, which is expressed in the reflection and judgement of the self-experience of the individual, is itself technically appropriated, then we have to stop, at least to observe our technical goals.

The orienting criterion of such a symbol or model of nature is therefore whether ethical freedom—and this is the power of judgement of the individual—is preserved, expanded, strengthened, or whether it is diminished, surrendered and lost in a technological imperative, i.e., where the original space of freedom is usurped by technology and freedom is in danger of being destroyed.

3 Model and reality: normativity as a heuristic variable

We can say: The philosophical change in the understanding of nature and technology is to be met by specifying the considerations of freedom, which remain dependent on nature as a symbol, as a given background dimension that entails freedom as an ethical power.

It is true that already in modern times freedom and thus ethics were understood as the other of nature, but in a dichotomous sense. In Kant's case, this sharp separation was enforced to the extent that he kept the natural, such as human inclinations, out of ethics. But this was a problematic path to take. For in this way only a reduced understanding of nature—in the sense of the other of reason—became dominant. The dimension of nature as a normative background was abandoned in favour of its objectification and at the expense of its technical instrumentalisation.

As a result, nature came to be seen simply as raw material for technical manipulation, and freedom lost its dual role as both technical creativity and ethical reflection. This second dimension of freedom would correspond to nature as the normative background to the criterion of freedom—a dimension that cannot be technically dominated, but rather cultivates the capacity for judgement. Both dimensions can only be sustained by a symbolic understanding of nature that allows for normativity and thus an ethical framework. In this model, nature retains a normative function as a symbol of such normativity. What cannot be transcended here is not nature in a strictly biological or cosmic-ontological sense, but rather nature as an unavailable space that shapes our reflective, self-aware experience of freedom.[12] In this light, nature is neither opposed to reason nor, as in the modern tradition, to freedom or technology. For both reason and technology, nature remains the "other" that serves as the essential point of reference in humanity's creative endeavour. The boundaries of such a symbolic conception of nature may shift, but they can never be completely dissolved if human freedom and self-determination are to endure.

By treating nature as the "other"—not as an object, but as an elusive background—the normative dimension of a symbolic understanding of nature for freedom emerges. However, nature should not be reduced to a biological or metaphysical entity. Such a reduction would contradict its symbolic role, which allows for cultural shifts in the relationship between nature, technology

---

[12]Precisely here, in this unavailability, the inwardness dimension of self-experience comes into play, which stands for a qualified concept of freedom, which symbolizes the unavailability dimension and ties it back to self-experience. We are thus led to the unavailable dimension of existence, when it comes to this freedom. But the place of unavailability is now no longer simply nature in a cosmic or biological sense as natural, but at the place of inner self-experience. Nature in this sense can therefore now be determined as the space of origin of freedom. This constellation of the relation of cognition to inner experience points us to precisely that epistemologically unusual category of trust as the category that can make plausible the unavailable. This is also the quintessence of Protagoras' Homo Mensura theorem, which by no means denotes human hybris, but on the contrary—quite modernly—anticipated the limitedness and perspectivity of human cognitive capacity.

and freedom, affirming humanity as a being capable of judgement and action, grounded in a space of freedom symbolized by nature, or by a nature made symbolic. In this model, nature serves as a realm of possibilities for the realisation of freedom. This perspective brings us back to the role of the individual. The relationship to reality is forged through the fluidity of the given and the adaptability of our individual self-understanding, which must ultimately be communicated within a pluralistic context.

Thus, the concept of nature as a model—a space for freedom—does not imply a diminished view of reality after the end of metaphysics. It does not represent less reality, but rather illustrates how we can engage meaningfully with reality. This model of nature offers a deeper and more appropriate understanding of the cognitive conditions of subjectivity under finite and embodied cognitive conditions. Here, cognition does not simply assert the existence of being, as in Kant's approach, but aims at genuine access to and recognition of being. In this sense, the importance of the individual and the particular is emphasised. All claims to truth and reality in modernity depend on the validation of individual access to reality, represented by models. These models do not aim to transcend themselves, but in their flexibility and adaptability allow us to continually test, verify or challenge our understanding, thus enhancing humanity's capacity for judgement.

What do models represent in theology?

Hans-Peter Grosshans

Seminar für systematische Theologie, Evangelisch-Theologische Fakultät, Westfälische
Wilhelms-Universität Münster, Universitätsstraße 13–17, 48143 Münster, Germany

Modelling is popular in many areas of our contemporary life, be it in the geosciences for climate change or in medicine for epidemiology, as we have seen in recent years. In theology, it is a very old scientific intellectual practice. If we distinguish between theology and religion—a distinction relevant in theology in the 18th century at the latest and has since remained relevant—then the term "religion" refers to the more material aspects of religion (including its practice), such as praying, praising God, singing religious songs, performing rituals, doing acts of kindness such as helping one's neighbour, feeding the hungry, giving to the poor, sheltering the homeless, visiting the sick, and so on. Theology, then, as opposed to religion, is any kind of reflection—academic or non-academic—on religion and faith.[1]

As in other sciences, the plausibility of theological models depends on the symbiosis of material and theoretical aspects, i.e., religious life or practice and theological reflection—a symbiosis similar, for example, to that in other experimental sciences and mathematics (as we find it in the natural sciences, as well as in economics). Science in general is "a means of increasing our knowledge of empirical phenomena by explaining them in terms of theoretical entities". The specificity of theology here is to be "a means of increasing our knowledge of the phenomena of the human condition by explaining these phenomena in terms of the relationship between man and God"[2] or, to put it more generally, in the horizon of transcendence.

Theology, as a reflection on the practice of the Christian faith, developed very early in the history of Christianity. As I have shown elsewhere, theology can be understood as a uniquely European way of dealing with religion.[3] In Christian theology, the models were constructed early in its history. Since then, models have played an important role in theology.

In fact, models were built within religious practice itself. One example, which has received recent attention, is the understanding of the temple in Jerusalem as a model of the cosmos. Such a concept was worked out in the priestly writings—an important tradition of the Pentateuch in the

---
[1] Cf. Pieter J. Huiser, Models, Theories and Narratives. Conditions for the Justification of a Religious Realism, Amsterdam 1997, 62.
[2] Ibid., 63.
[3] Cf. Hans-Peter Grosshans, Europa und die Theologie – der besondere europäische Umgang mit Religion, in: Europa? Zur Kulturgeschichte einer Idee, ed. by Tomislav Zelić, Zaneta Sambunjak and Anita Pavić Pintarić, Würzburg (Königshausen & Neumann) 2015, 121–136.

Hebrew Bible—in which the Temple in Jerusalem is understood as a model of the cosmos (a concept that was then realised in the new Temple after the return from the Babylonian exile). In visiting the Temple of Jerusalem, human beings experience a specific understanding of the cosmos and their own place in it: a cosmos where heaven and earth are transcended by the divine Creator, who relates in a specific way to his creatures and who, in his transcendent invisibility, is concretely present in the Temple of Jerusalem, as he is present in all his creation. We find a similar modelling of the cosmos and the relationship between the divine and human in Christian conceptions of church buildings and the liturgies that take place within them.[4]

Similar modelling can be found in many areas of religious practice. However, in this article, I want to concentrate on models in theology. The examples of the use of models in religious practice only show that models in theology are also relevant to religious practice. They also show that there is a close connection between religious practice and theological models—at least in Christian theology.

To address the question asked in the title of this article, what models in theology represent, I would like to reflect on what is the most well-known model in Christian theology: the Trinitarian model of God.

The Trinitarian model of God, in the form in which it has become the standard model for Christian talking about God and faith, was developed in the 4th century. The most important contribution came from three theologians in Cappadocia, present day Turkey: Basil of Caesarea, Gregory of Nyssa and Gregory of Nazianzus. Their Trinitarian model of God more or less concluded a long discourse on the Christian understanding of God.

The main challenge for the new religion of Christianity at this time was how to understand the relationship of Jesus Christ to the divine. Was he himself divine? Was he a human being inspired by the divine spirit? Questions like these also necessitated a model of the witness of Jesus Christ in the biblical texts, which led to different Christological models. All these questions became urgent when a discourse ensued surrounding a claim made by Arius that there was a time when Jesus Christ did not exist. According to Arius, even if Jesus Christ, the Son of God, had come into being long before the beginning of the universe, he would still have to be regarded as a creature of God who was not characterised by an originless and causeless eternity, as was the case with God by definition. Understood within the conceptualities of the 4th century, Jesus Christ was finally conceived in Greek

---

[4]Originally, the specific Christian church building was a model of the relationship between transcendence and immanence, between the transcendent divine and the human. This becomes interesting when we come to more Platonic understandings in religious practice. In Orthodox Christianity, the liturgy of worship is understood as corresponding to the heavenly worship in the direct presence of God. In fact, the model here is the heavenly worship, which is copied in all worship on earth with the divine liturgy.

as *homoousios*—of the same essence—of the Father (ὁμοούσιος τῷ πατρί), while at the same time holding firmly to monotheism, to the singular unity of God.

Actually, the criticism that we are faced with a contradiction or at least a paradox was already part of the discourse given the differences in Greek and Latin terminology. In this distinction, one can see a semantic irrationality between different languages. The Latin equivalent of the Greek *homoousios* was *consubstantialis*. In Latin, the Greek *ousia* became *substantia*. There is a similar asymmetrical equivalence in the terms used for the three realisations of the one God. In Greek, the formula was: μία οὐσία—τρεις ὑποστάσεις: the one divine essence has three hypostases (realisations resp. actualisations). In Latin, the basic Trinitarian formula was: *Tres personae—una substantia divina*: three persons—one divine substance.

The interpretive problem was that the Latin *substantia* was actually a translation of the Greek *hypostasis*. The Romans therefore considered the Greek understanding to be polytheistic: a belief in three gods. On the other hand, the Latin *persona* was πρόσωπον in Greek, meaning a mask of a face used in the theatre to play a particular role. The Greek-speaking theologians therefore regarded the Roman understanding of God as a simple monotheism that ignored the complexity of the divine reality.

The challenge was then to develop a model of God that did justice to God's unity and complexity. Simply put, the challenge was to develop a model that coherently combines oneness *and* plurality, or diversity.

The need for such a model came, on the one hand, from biblical texts in which the relationship of Jesus to God, as well as the relationship of the Spirit to Jesus and to God, is described as one of intimate closeness and even identity. In the New Testament, for example, there are statements about God sending the Son and the Spirit, but also about the Son sending the Spirit: "When the time was fulfilled, God sent his Son" (Gal 4:4); "God did not send his Son into the world to condemn the world, but to save the world through him" (John 3:17). The Son says that God "will give you another Comforter, who will be with you forever, even the Spirit of truth" (John 14:16f.). Then the Son says that he himself sends the Spirit: "But when the Comforter comes, whom I will send to you from the Father, the Spirit of truth" (John 15:26). Then there are statements in the New Testament that reverse the direction of activity and speak of an event between the Spirit and the Son, in that the Spirit testifies to the Son (cf. John 15:26; 1 Jn 5:6–12), or of an event between the Son and the Father, in that the Son glorifies the Father (cf. John 17:1ff.) and in the end will give dominion to God the Father (cf. 1 Cor 15:24). Ancient Christianity was therefore confronted with the task of "thinking about Jesus Christ as about God: οὕτως δεῖ ἡμᾶς φρονεῖν περὶ Ἰησοῦ Χριστροῦ ὡς περὶ θεοῦ". The reason for this is soteriological: "For if we think less of him, we expect less from him" (2Clem 1:1).

The main challenge for building models on these relationships was certainly the brutal execution of Jesus, the divine Son. The divine was by definition eternal and infinite. Death was the opposite, a sign of finitude and temporality. Jesus Christ could not be of the same essence as God and thus be considered divine. Arius' conclusion was then:: the Son could not be *homoousios* (of the same essence) with God the Father. The Son is dissimilar to the nature and character of God the Father, being by nature "mutable" and endowed with "freedom of will" like all other human beings. The Son's moral self-determination thus makes him actually (but not necessarily) "unchangeable".

The initial trinitarian models of God concentrated strictly on monotheistic oneness, the singular unity of the divine. Various modalist models were often used: in the appearance and activity of the one divine essence there is a succession of Father, Son and Spirit—similar to the three states of water: solid, liquid, and gas. In all these attempts to construct a Trinitarian model of God, the various activities and effects of the Divine as experienced and conceived by human beings were combined with a specific concept of singular unity.

These early Christian models followed the conviction, generally accepted in the first centuries, that there is only "one God". This philosophical monotheism represents the idea of the one world monarchy of the one God. The unity of the world corresponded to the strictly singular unity of God.

The Cappadocian Fathers were thus innovative in the 4th century in that they used basic monotheism while trinitarianly overcoming the monotheistic monarchism. When a concept of singular unity is used, the One cannot be shared or communicated.

Such a concept of singular unity was also popular in political theory and in politics in general. According to Aristotle, only one can and should rule, having multiple rulers is evil. In ancient Greece, of course, one thought of the gods on Mount Olympus, who fought each other as rivals to the detriment of the common good—which had already been effectively criticised by the ancient philosophical critique of religion. In Rome, the Pax Romana ensured the subjugation of other Mediterranean countries since all power emanated from the one (singular) Roman emperor.

An idea of unity that included plurality and diversity did not seem reasonable at the time, neither in terms of political rule nor divine rule. Therefore, some theologians used the modalist model: the one, indivisible God appears in the world in different forms; first as Creator and Lawgiver, then in the form of a human being, who is considered the Son of God and Redeemer of the world, then in the form of the Spirit as the inspiration of life and the completion of what God began in creation. Father, Son and Spirit were seen as three manifestations of the one unique God. However, the singular One—apart from the three manifestations—remains unrecognisable and inexpressible. Metaphorically speaking, one might say the One God is the eternal and simple light whose rays are refracted in different ways in the world of human beings according to their receptivity.

Another popular model tried to preserve the strict singularity of God by subordinating Jesus Christ to God in such a way that he could not be considered equal to God in any way. The idea here was: Since the one God is incommunicable (because He is indivisible), he needs the mediation of mediary beings. The mediary being between the one God and the diverse world is then called "Son" or "Logos", which is a creature of the one God, through whom God communicates himself through a medium. The basic form of this model is: one God—one Logos (as mediator)—one world—one world monarchy.

To these models—the modalist and the subordinate models—the Cappadocian Fathers constructed their alternative model, which then became the standard model. This model of the Trinitarian God was expressed in the formula: one substance and three persons, respectively, one essence (μία οὐσία) and three realisations (τρεῖς ὑποστάσεις).

This formula was supplemented by descriptions of the relationships between the three persons. The various works or activities of God in relation to the world and human beings were also attributed to one of the persons or hypostases. In the internal relationships, God the Father begets (not creates) the Son and breathes the Spirit. The Son is begotten (passively) by the Father. There was a later addition to the Cappadocian formula, which claimed that the Spirit proceeds not only from the Father, but also from the Son. In a sense, the Spirit was breathed by both the Father *and* the Son.

In terms of the acts and activities of the Divine, the creation of heaven and earth was attributed to the Father. Salvation, final judgement, perpetual government and co-creation were attributed to the Son. The renewal of life, the formation of a new form of human sociality, the forgiveness of sins, the resurrection of the dead and eternal life—in short, sanctification—were attributed to the Spirit.

The concept of *perichoresis* was then introduced to avoid the idea that the three persons of the divine being were acting alone. The *perichoresis* of the three persons (*hypostases*) indicates a mutual permeation, a reciprocal and mutual participation of all three persons in divine activity.

The family categories used (Father, Son) are in a sense metaphorical, following biblical terminology, but adapted to the need of the complex Trinitarian model of God to express the simultaneity of activity (such as creation) and receptivity (sonship) or passivity (such as suffering) in the Divine.

Throughout the reception history, this standard model has been debated and newly developed in theology and philosophy. In particular, at the beginning of the 19th century, the standard model was adapted to the new philosophy of German Idealism—which then became the main understanding of the Trinitarian model of God in Christian theology. One reason for this development was that, in modern Europe, the concept of God as the highest substance was replaced with the idea of God as an absolute subject. Since German Idealism, the divine unity has been interpreted as that of an absolute, self-identical subject. Accordingly, one speaks of God's "self-revelation" and "self-communication". This conception of God has parallels in the modern conception of human subjectivity: the absolute subject in heaven corresponds to human subjectivity in relation to nature and history, and the personal God corresponds to the bourgeois culture of personality.

But with the conceptual shift from substance to subjectivity, new problems arose for the Trinitarian model of God. The modern concept of subject seems to make the traditional talk of the three persons of the Trinity impossible. Instead of the old formula *una substantia—tres personae*, it became popular again to speak of the one divine subject in three different modes of being. If the one God is the subject (that acts, etc.), then the three persons must be downgraded to modes of being of the one self-identical subject. The three persons, which in the modern sense would be understood as subjects, are dissolved in favour of the one God—and consequently God as a Trinity of persons becomes less important.

The Trinitarian model of God, in this understanding, was developed from the logic of God's self-revelation. But this divine self that reveals itself and its reign cannot be conceived otherwise than as an absolute subject. We find such a reductive model, for example, in the theology of the Protestant theologian Karl Barth in the first half of the 20th century. In the course of the second half of the 20th century, this reductive model of God's subjectivity was vehemently criticised, insofar as it was a recourse to the concept of a singular unity that did not do justice to the true Trinitarian understanding of God. The inspiration for such a critique came from the ancient Greek tradition, which was still alive in Orthodox Christian theology. The starting point for a stricter trinitarian model of God was therefore not the unity, but the three persons of the divine. These three persons were not understood as different modal manifestations of the same absolute subject. Rather, the starting point of a Trinitarian model of God was the three persons, followed by the question of their unity. According to the Protestant theologian Jürgen Moltmann, this unity cannot be assumed, but is an "eschatological question about the completion of God's Trinitarian history". Consequently, the "unity of the three persons of this history ... must be understood as a communicable unity and as an open, inviting, integrating unity".[5] The correct term for this kind of unity is unanimity or concord. And so, according to Moltmann, it is a matter of the "unity of the three persons among themselves, or: the unity of the three-in-one God".[6] Then the Trinitarian model of God is about personal, not modal, self-differentiation. Only persons can be united in unanimity or agreement, not modes of being. The unity of the Trinity is then communicative and consists in the communion of the divine Father, Son and Holy Spirit. The unity of the three divine persons must then be perceived in the mutual relationships between them. As mentioned earlier, the theological term for this mutuality of relations is the *perichoresis* of the divine persons (mutual permeation).

Another Protestant theologian, Eberhard Jüngel, summarized this concept in the following way: the triune God is the "community of mutual otherness".[7] In this Trinitarian model of God, instead of sameness, otherness forms a unity—a unity of otherness in itself and in its activity. Regarding the latter, a classical element of the Trinitarian model is that the works of the Trinity are indivisible (*opera trinitatis ad extra sunt indivisa*), but nevertheless the various activities of the divine are attributed to the respective divine persons (although all three persons are always involved in each divine activity)—also taking up an idea of early Christian theology.

An important feature of the Trinitarian model of God, emphasised in its modern version, is the involvement of the observers, i.e., the believers, who see and believe themselves to be involved in the divine activities—in the divine creativity, redemption and reconciliation, in the consummation and perfection of human beings to become truly human.

On the one hand, the Trinitarian model of God is intended to make the relational community—and history—between God and God conceivable and accountable, but also the community and history between God and human beings. Therefore, the Trinitarian model also implies that God's activity in relation to human beings—God's history with human beings—is salvific

---

[5]Cf. Jürgen Moltmann, Trinität und Reich Gottes. Zur Gotteslehre, Werke, Vol. 4, Gütersloh 2016, 167: „Die Einheit des Vaters, des Sohnes und des Geistes ist dann die eschatologische Frage nach der Vollendung der trinitarischen Geschichte Gottes. Die Einheit der drei Personen dieser Geschichte muß folglich als eine *mitteilbare Einheit* und als eine *offene, einladende, integrationsfähige Einheit* verstanden werden."

[6]Cf. ibid.: „die Einigkeit der drei Personen untereinander, oder: die Einigkeit des drei-einigen Gottes".

[7]Cf. Eberhard Jüngel, Die Wahrnehmung des Anderen in der Perspektive des christlichen Glaubens, in: ibid, Indikative der Gnade – Imperative der Freiheit. Theologische Erörterungen IV, Tübingen 2000, 205–230, 214; cf. Hans-Peter Grosshans, The Concrete Uniqueness of God. The Contribution of Trinitarian Thought, in: The Unique, the Singular, and the Individual, ed. by Ingolf U. Dalferth and Raymond E. Perrier, Tübingen 2022, 131–146.

and participatory. It implies that God, who communicatively relates to himself in mutual otherness, also relates to human beings in a similar way as others. The inclusion of the observer in the Trinitarian model of God thus expresses that God in his eternity is determined by his temporal history with humanity. Through the incarnate Son, man is present in eternity in the divine as revealed to humanity in Jesus Christ—that is, God does and gives everything for the salvation and perfection of man.

The Trinitarian model of God therefore also has a hermeneutical function in relation to the life situation of human beings, and especially of believers, who think about the Divine in the Trinitarian model, but also about themselves in the horizon of the transcendent Divine. The Trinitarian model of God makes the human situation understandable in such a way that "we find ourselves as human beings created by God and fallen with him, that we are found as such by God through Jesus Christ, and that we are guided by the Holy Spirit to find the right way to the goal and the end of life",[8] as Gerhard Ebeling formulated.

On the one hand, the Trinitarian model helps in understanding God as a relational being in concrete vitality. On the other hand, the model illuminates the life of faith in its richness of relationships and in its concrete vitality.

After this reflection on the Trinitarian model of God, an answer to the question of this essay can be provided: What do models represent in theology?

In Christian theology, models—here exemplified by the Trinitarian model of God—represent, first of all, the texts of Holy Scripture. They are a consequence of the diversity and complexity of these texts on various topics, which require models for their interpretation, providing them a certain consistency and coherence. Modelling a diversity of statements on a given topic in a set of texts is the alternative to ignoring those that seem to be incongruous or disturbing. The modelling of diverse statements in Scripture avoids a reductionist and selective kind of interpretation.

Models in Christian theology also represent the purpose of theology. The aim of theology goes beyond certain texts, although the biblical texts also address the aims of theology using a variety of means, such as narratives, metaphors, myths, confessions, moral advice, and spiritual instruction. In theology, models are constructed through rational reflection. They must be grounded not only in the thoughts and ideas expressed in the biblical texts, but also in rational standards, including the adequacy of the model to the "thing" it is meant to represent. In this paper, I have focused on the example of the Trinitarian model of God in Christian theology. Here we can see that

---

[8]Gerhard Ebeling, Dogmatik des christlichen Glaubens, Vol. III, Tübingen 1979, 545.

the terms used in the model must be clearly defined in order to construct a model adequate to a rational understanding of divine transcendence.

Moreover, models in theology also represent human religious experience and practice. In general, then, models are more oriented to the data given by human religious experience and practice. Models represent the mental awareness of religious individuals and the mindset of believers. The construction of such models can be done in a more empirical way or in a more idealistic way. In empirical theology, for example, believers are interviewed about their religious beliefs and practices using social science or psychological methods. The data collected can then be interpreted and generalised in statements and models. Idealistically, the beliefs and practices are doctrinally reconstructed in order to show what believers should believe and what their practices should be if they were ideally realised.

In the first way, empirically, it is shown how the beliefs and practices of a religion are actually believed and practised. At the beginning of the 19th century, the German theologian Friedrich Schleiermacher proposed statistics as a new subject in theology for this very purpose.[9]

In the second way, the idealising, knowledge is gained about the potential of beliefs and practices for the lives of believers and religious communities. This knowledge then has mainly a heuristic value and is useful for the orientation of the religious life of believers and religious communities—in fact, for the whole of their individual and community life. This second approach was also taken by Schleiermacher in his work entitled "Der christliche Glaube nach den Prinzipien der evangelischen Kirche" (The Christian Faith according to the Principles of the Protestant Church).[10] His approach begins with human consciousness and shows how it is determined by Christian faith when faith is inscribed in its idealising form.

Models in these latter theological approaches represent human consciousness and practice: the religiously determined mental states and religious practices of individuals and communities.

These models must also depict the essence of faith—understood as religious human consciousness—and religious practice. Since in Christianity faith and religious practice are about a human life in relation to the divine and in the horizon of the divine, these models must also concenr the divine. However, in such a subjective and cultural approach, the model of God is not—one might say—direct, but about God as reflected in human consciousness and as related to human practice. Therefore, in

---

[9] Cf. Friedrich Daniel Ernst Schleiermacher, Vorlesungen über die kirchliche Geographie und Statistik, ed. by Simon Gerber, Kritische Gesamtausgabe II/16, Berlin/New York 2005.

[10] Cf. Friedrich Schleiermacher, Der christliche Glaube nach den Grundsätzen der evangelischen Kirche im Zusammenhange dargestellt. Zweite Auflage (1830/31), ed. by Rolf Schäfer, Berlin/New York 2008.

such an approach, in which models in theology represent religious human consciousness (i.e., faith) and practice, the Trinitarian model of God is rather a second-order model. It is a modelling of what appears in the models at the level of faith, religious experience and religious practice, which is multifaceted, diverse and complex. The Trinitarian model of God then relates this complexity to the activity of the triune God and constructs a second order unity of diverse, inconsistent, conflicting, contradictory and incomprehensible life in the horizon of the transcendent triune God. We can say, then, that the theological model of the Triune God represents the horizon that gives orientation to human beings in the twilight of their contingent lives and in all that is generally indeterminable.

What do models represent in theology? There is more than one possible answer, because at least some of them—like the model of God—represent plural realities. The Trinitarian model of God represents the complex God-talk in the texts of the Christian Bible; it represents the reality of God; it can also represent the religious consciousness of believers and their practices in their relations with the divine; it can also represent the complex interpretation of human life in the horizon of the divine or in the horizon of transcendence. It is the challenge of theology to bring these different dimensions together consistently in the complex Trinitarian model of God.

Scientific cognition based on models as epistemic warfare
Do scientific models serve as epistemic weapons or fictions?

Lorenzo Magnani

Department of Humanities and Computational Philosophy Laboratory, University of Pavia, Piazza Botta 6, 27100 Pavia, Italy

E-mail: lorenzo.magnani@unipv.it

Abstract. Using the idea of "epistemic warfare", which views scientific exploration as a complex battle for rational knowledge in which it is critical to distinguish between epistemic (such as scientific models) and non-epistemic (such as fictions, falsities, and propaganda) weapons, I will demonstrate in this article how scientific modeling activity can be better described. I will go into more detail about a dynamic perspective on models as well. It is incorrect to evaluate models in research by confusingly combining dynamic and static elements of the scientific research processes. To an epistemologist, scientific models presented from a static perspective (as in a textbook, for example) undoubtedly seem fictitious, but when a dynamic perspective is used, this fictitious quality vanishes.

1 Do scientific models serve as epistemic weapons or fictions?

As a result of current cognitive research, we are aware of the following implicit assumptions that Charles Sanders Peirce made: The way in which nature nourishes the mind is by means of the mind's disembodiment and expansion in nature—a process that might be described as "artificialization"—which in turn influences the mind. In more contemporary terms, models are constructed, for instance, by the scientist's mind, which first assigns "meanings" to external objects of various kinds. In this way, "internal" representations are "extended" in the environment, and subsequently, processes that take place outside will reshape them while also taking into consideration the constraints found in the external representation (a *model*, for example). Following the external model's alteration, the ensuing aspects of those modifications/movements are "picked up" and in turn re-represented in the human brain of the scientist.

This viewpoint allows us to enjoy the speculative Aristotelian prediction that *"nihil est in intellectu quod prius non fuerit in sensu"*, now inside a naturalistic context. These modifications can readily coincide with (or lead to) new guesses—either instinctive or reasoned, depending on the brain areas involved—that is, plausible abductive hypotheses about the external extra-somatic world. In the case of science, this is because the information flowing from the model allows the scientists' internal models to be rebuilt and further refined. The process may be viewed from the standpoint of the notion of cognitive niches:[1] when the mind constructs the so-called cognitive niches over the history of culture, it grows up with its representational delegates to the outside world. The complex cognitive niche of a scientific laboratory at the same time is an "epistemic" niche, specifically designed to advance knowledge through cognitive processes, in which "people, systems, and environmental affordances" (Chandrasekharan 2009, p. 1076) interact harmoniously. Nersessian and Chandrasekharan's (2009) research on various cognitive processes that characterize a scientific lab focuses on models that heavily refer to movement and ignores models that are not essentially based on it, it still offers a helpful example that highlights the distributed nature of scientific models and the true kind of abstraction and ideality they possess, reinvigorating ideas from the history of philosophy of science.

Recasting Contessa (2010)'s definition of a model as "an actual abstract object that stands for one of the many possible concrete objects that fit the generative description of the model" (p. 228) in the context of the current naturalistic perspective, this perspective would benefit of the analysis of models as material, mathematical, fictional, and "abstract objects." "Yet, it is important to notice that the model- system is not the same as its [verbal] description; in fact, we can re-describe the same system in many different ways, possibly using different languages. I refer to descriptions of this kind as model-descriptions and the relation they bear to the model-system as *p*-representation", states Frigg (2010), introducing a fictionalist viewpoint. Indeed, Contessa's reference to models as "actual abstract objects" and Frigg's reference to models as abstract "model-systems" would take advantage of the cognitive perspective I am presenting here, which can easily answer the question "where are models located, from a naturalistic point of view?"

From this angle, scientific models cannot easily be considered fictions because, at least when it comes to the cognitive processes involved in scientific discovery, scientists do not intend to put forth fictions; rather, they provide models as instruments that help reshape a general cognitive niche as an epistemic niche in order to carry out a sincere effort to represent the outside

---

[1]The cognitive human acts that convert the natural world into a cognitive one are known as representational delegations to the external environment that are configured as elements of *cognitive niches* (some of which may be seen as pregnances; see Magnani, 2022, Lexicon of Discoverability). According to research conducted in the field of biosciences of evolution by Odling-Smee, Laland, and Feldman (Odling-Smee et al., 2003; Laland & Sterelny, 2006; Laland & Brown, 2006), humans have created enormous cognitive niches that are characterized by informational, cognitive, and ultimately computational processes.

world. Models, the war machines employed in this conflict, which I refer to as "epistemic warfare", are only concrete, clear-cut, and well-designed tactical intermediate weapons capable of strategically "attacking" nature (the target systems to be studied) in order to further reveal its structure. They emphasize the determined—strictly epistemic—dynamism of the adopted tools that are at stake. On the other hand, fictions in fiction works aim, for instance, to expose human life and characters from fresh artistic angles and/or to critique them via a moral lesson, whereas fictions and military tactics aim to deceive the adversary and potentially destroy the eco-human targets (the target systems) in order to expose the structure of those targets even more.

I argue that even while the "military" character of various cognitive processes is not immediately apparent in different features and applications of syntactilized human natural language and in abstract knowledge, epistemologists do not need to ignore it. It is challenging to identify this "military intelligence"[2] in the various *epistemic* roles that natural language serves. For instance, it is difficult to observe this "military intelligence" at work when language is merely used to transmit scientific results in a classroom setting or when we obtain weather information from the Internet that is expressed in linguistic terms and numbers. However, we must not lose sight of the fact that information packages entrenched in certain language use—and in hybrid languages, such as mathematics, which includes a substantial amount of symbolic language—even with their more abstract nature, still have a tremendous impact in modifying the moral behavior of human collectives. In human social groupings, for instance, the creation and dissemination of new scientific knowledge involves not only the operation of information but also the implementation and distribution of roles, talents, limitations, and action options. This process has intrinsic moral value because it produces precise distinctions, powers, duties, and opportunities that may either modify pre-existing conflicts or lead to the emergence of new, violent, intragroup conflicts.

Allow me to give an example. Two opposing moral/social effects are typically associated with new theoretical biomedical knowledge about pregnancy and fetuses: (1) improved social and medical management of childbirth and related diseases; and (2) possible escalation or modification of conflicts regarding the legitimacy of in-vitro fertilization, abortion, and other related practices. All things considered, even the most abstract bodies of knowledge and seemingly harmless bits of information are subject to the semio/social

---

[2] I am borrowing this expression from René Thom (1988), who links "military intelligence" to language and cognition's role in "coalition enforcement," or the level of their complementary effects in confirming morals and associated behaviors and, ultimately, carrying out potential violent penalties. It is clear that the term "military" has in this case a metaphorical meaning.

processes that determine the identities of groups and their capacity for aggression when forming coalitions. Argumentative, deontological, rhetorical, and dialectic elements are all too often present in declarative knowledge and deductive reasoning. It is difficult, for instance, to distinguish between the argumentative or deontological function of language and a type of "pure" (such as deductive) inferential one in an eco-cognitive context. It is clear that the deductive function of language, for instance, may simultaneously play an associated argumentative role. But the arguments that are conventionally acknowledged as "fallacious" are the ones that help us better understand the military character of human language and, in particular, and especially of some hypotheses reached through fallacies.

Therefore, we must recognize that while science positions itself as a paradigm for generating knowledge in a particular "decent" way, it also inadvertently participates in the cross-disciplinary conflict that is the hallmark of modernity. Science engages in conflict with other non-scientific fields, as well as with literature, magic, religion, and other non-scientific fields. It also subtly orders and norms societies through the use of technological products that enforce morality and behavior. Of course, propaganda plays a role in scientific cognitive processes—sensu strictu, inside scientific groups as coalitions—as Feyerabend notes (Feyerabend 1975). For example, propaganda may be used to persuade colleagues about a hypothesis or a method. However, propaganda also plays an external role, reaching out to other private and public coalitions as well as the general public in order to obtain funding—a crucial issue that is frequently ignored in modern science is the cost of producing new models—or to persuade about the value of scientific knowledge. However, when the creation of its own regimen of truth is at risk, its core cognitive processes are based on avoiding fictional and rhetorical devices. Ultimately, science is precisely that endeavor that generates the types of realities that articulate the paradigms for distinguishing fictions and, hence, "irrational" or "arational" modes of knowing.

I am aware that epistemological fictionalism views fictions as something "we cherish" (Frigg 2010, p. 249) and something "far from being execrable"; however, to say that literary and scientific fictions are equally "good" fictions would be oversimplifying the problem a little bit, as science is the one that created new types of models that go beyond poetry and literature and are dedicated to a particular production of a rational truth, *constitutively* aiming at *not being fictional*. Admittedly, I fail to understand how the perfect pendulum could be discussed in the same vein as Anna Karenina: it seems to me that we are running the risk of inadvertently opening the gates of epistemology to a kind of relativistic post-modernism à la mode, even if fictionalists seem to avoid this possible confusion by producing—often useful—taxonomies about the slight differences between fictions in science and in other cognitive practices.

Frigg and Nguyen (2017) wrote a lengthy piece discussing models and representations, just released in the *Handbook of Model-Based Science* (Magnani and Bertolotti 2017): the many ideas of scientific models (structuralist, inferential, fictionalist, representational, in terms of stipulative fiat or of similarity) are shown in great detail by the writers. When discussing fictionalism, they cite my article (Magnani 2012) and note that I reject the fictionalist view because it misinterprets the role that models play in the process of scientific discovery. I contend that these models cannot be indicated at all as fictional because they are the foundation of new empirical domains and scientific frameworks. They claim that because falsities are unable to contribute to the formation of new empirical domains, my criticism appears to be predicated on the idea that fiction is false. Finally, they respond that the fiction perspective is not subject to my issue since it is not devoted to the "fiction as falsity" account.

I can agree that fictions do not always contain falsity and that within literary frameworks, fictions can be understood as imaginations rather than as falsities—presumably carrying some sort of truth or at least potential truth—but that is precisely the problem. I continue to believe that there is a distinct difference between what are referred to as works of fiction (literature, for example) and non-fiction (science, for example), and that even if we choose to attribute to both types of knowledge some positive cognitive functions, we are dealing with very different kinds of cognitive processes that cannot be completely confused.

Furthermore, I read the article "Models and explanation" by Bokulich (2017) that was also included in the quoted *Handbook of Model-Based Science*. It illustrates numerous instances of the constructive and unavoidable roles that idealizations—as well as those that are considered "fictions"—play in science, not only in cognitive creative processes. She contends that certain so-called fictions are actually informative and produce true scientific cognition because they are able to authentically depict real patterns of structural interdependence in the real world in their fictional representations. However, as I said I came to the conclusion that it is strange to adopt the term "fiction" in epistemology. The reader should consult this text in order to receive a concise and well-written response to the remaining queries: do some highly abstract and mathematical models exhibit a non-causal form of scientific explanation? How can a "how-actually" model explanation be distinguished from an exploratory "how-possibly" model explanation? Do modelers have to make trade-offs such that, for example, a model that is best at producing explanatory outcomes may not be the most accurate predictor, and vice versa?

The in-vitro model and Anna Karenina are quite unlike. In true scientific practice, a model only qualifies as fictitious when it is acknowledged as such by the research community due to its *inability* to fruitfully describe the target systems. In these situations, a model is just abandoned within the changing context of scientific research.

Instead, Tolstoy would have replaced Anna Karenina with another, equally fictional character who would have remained unreal forever. Tolstoy might have rejected Anna Karenina as an inappropriate fiction for some modern aesthetic—not scientific—purpose, for example, had she failed, in her author's opinion, to authentically represent a female member of Russia's high society at the end of the 19th century. Giere helpfully points out that, conversely, "Tolstoy did not intend to represent actual people except in general terms" and that, on the contrary, a "primary function [of models in science], of course, is to represent physical processes in the real world" (Giere 2007, p. 279).

2 A dynamic perspective on scientific models as fictions

A scientific model can be abandoned, as I mentioned a few lines above if it is unable to effectively reflect the target systems and contribute to scientific cognitive processes. It is simpler to recognize that a scientific model can be more accurately classified as "fictional" in a cognitive (sometimes creative) process when it is determined to be ineffective by applying the *negation as failure* (Clark 1978; Magnani 2001). This is because a scientific model becomes fictional in the sense that it is falsified (even if "weakly" falsified by failure), and as a result, it ceases to be relevant in the "rational" life of scientific cognition. Regarding the compelling and cohesive examination of relationships between theories, which encompasses the issue of inaccurate model representation—as well as the replacement or modification of models—and the incompleteness of scientific representation, concerning partial structural similarity, see (Bueno and French 2011) and the seminal work (da Costa and French 2003).

The process of eliminating something through negation is methodologically similar to what Freud describes when constructions (the stories the analyst creates about the patient's past psychic life) are dropped because they do not advance the therapeutic psychoanalytic process: if the patient does not offer new "material" that expands the suggested construction, "if," as Freud states, "[...] nothing further develops we may conclude that we have made a mistake and we shall admit as much to the patient at some suitable opportunity without sacrificing any of our authority". The "opportunity" of rejecting the proposed construction "will arise" just "[...] when some new material has come to light which allows us to make a better construction and so to correct our error. In this way the false construction drops out as if it has never been made; and indeed, we often get an impression as though, to borrow the words of Polonius, our bait of falsehood had taken a carp of truth" (Freud 1974, vol, 23, 1937, p. 262).

Similar to this, in the process of scientific discovery, for instance, the old model is buried in the necropolis of the no longer useful—dead—models and is simply eliminated and labeled as "false" because "new material has come to light" to provide a better model that in turn will lead to new knowledge that supersedes or refines the previous one. However, in the entire scientific endeavor, a successful scientific model (like the ether model) may also be arbitrarily eliminated along with the theory that supported it. As a result, the outdated model is buried in yet another necropolis—that of the abandoned "historical" models—and in this instance, it is indeed plausible to reclassify it as a fiction.[3]

Woods and Rosales (2010) provide a thorough and convincing logico-philosophical investigation of the issue at hand, leading them to a conclusion that is in line with my suspicions regarding the fictional nature of scientific models. They argue that applying the notion of literary and creative fictions to science and other branches of cognition is incredibly perplexing. There is "nothing true of them in virtue of which they are literary fictions", regardless of what we say about the fictions of science and mathematics (p. 375). "Saying that scientific stipulation is subject to normative constraints is already saying something quite different from what should be said about literary stipulation" as they properly point out.

In my previous research, I always emphasized what I called "mimetic" external scientific models: in the case of semiotic cognitive processes occurring in science, the external scientific models are *mimetic*, to emphasize the fact that the mind disembodies itself, performing a cognitive interplay between internal and external representations, and possibly, *creative* (in this last case, they are not necessarily mimetic). This distinction reflects the one Morrison made between idealized (mirroring the target systems) and abstract models (more creative and finished to generate new scientific intelligibility), as we will see in Section 4 below.

I find this interplay crucial for analyzing the relationship between meaningful semiotic internal resources and devices and their dynamic interactions

---

[3]The importance of "understanding" in science is also connected to this issue in contemporary literature: de Regt (2015, p. 3782) addresses the perplexing relationship between scientific understanding, false models, and realism. The author claims that understanding can be—and frequently is—achieved through models that are unrealistic, highly idealized representations of the target system, or on the basis of theories that are, in and of themselves, false, or through models and theories that, despite being disproven now, did not stop them from adding to our understanding of phenomena. These insights are supported by the practice and history of science.

with the externalized semiotic materiality already stored in the environment (scientific artifactual models, in this case), as I am attempting to demonstrate in this article through the description of an intellectual framework that considers models material and distributed. Because this outward materiality shows (and functions within) its own cognitive limits, it plays a particular role in the interaction. Therefore, minds are artificial and "extended" in nature. It is in this perspective that I also have to emphasize the significance of what I dubbed manipulative abduction at the level of that ongoing interplay between online and offline intelligence.

As I have explained (Magnani, 2001), manipulative abduction is a process that is commonly used in scientific reasoning to form and evaluate hypotheses. It primarily involves extra-theoretical and extra-sentential behavior that aims to create communicable accounts of new experiences in order to integrate them into systems of experimental and linguistic (theoretical) practices that have already been established. As I have stated, manipulative abduction is a sort of redistribution of the cognitive and epistemic effort to handle things and data that are not readily represented or located internally. The building of external models by humans with the intention of performing observations and "experiments" that might change one's cognitive state in order to reveal new characteristics of the target systems is precisely an example of manipulative abduction. The more impromptu and unconscious action-based cognitive processes that I have described as types of "thinking through doing" are also included in the definition of manipulative abduction.

3 We do not need to mix up static and dynamic aspects of the scientific enterprise

At this point, I may also argue that, in the case of creative processes, the produced external scientific model is precisely the opposite of a fiction as well as a general process of make-believe (neither is a barely credible world (Sugden 2000, 2009) nor a mere surrogate, as (Contessa 2007) puts it). Instead, it is a *regulatory* tool *stabilized* in "some exterior form", a sort of reliable anchorage, and it is not purposefully constructed as fiction, unlike a romance author who may purposefully create the character of Harry Potter. The usage of the term "fiction" in epistemological fictionalism about models is typically justified by the absence of empirical systems that match, for instance, the ideal pendulum (and its equation).

The label creates a paradox that is easy to comprehend by using the example of scientific models that are seen as "missing systems," which is a fresh metaphor that resembles the fictional one. In fact, the description of a missing system might be a fiction. According to Thomson-Jones (2010), science is rife with "descriptions of missing systems," which are ultimately regarded as abstract models. Furthermore, Mäki (2009) expands on the missing systems framework by providing an additional metaphoric conceptual apparatus: missing systems are also "surrogate" systems expressed as credible worlds, as models. Mäki (2009) acknowledges that scientific models are "pragmatically and ontologically constrained representations." Godfrey-Smith (2009, p. 114) makes similar arguments: "To claim that talking about model systems is a psychologically unusual way of looking into conditionals (and the like) is not enough to overcome the problem by itself. It is normal to assume that the useful output that comes from modeling is often a conditional, i.e., a statement that would be true if a specific configuration existed. The challenge of elucidating the empirical use of this type of information resurfaces, nevertheless, as the configurations in issue are often known not to exist".

Similar arguments are advanced by Godfrey-Smith (2009, pp. 114): "To say that talk of model systems is a psychologically exotic way of investigating conditionals (and the like) is not itself to solve the problem. It is natural to think that the useable output we get from modeling is generally a conditional—a claim that if such and such a configuration existed, it would behave in a certain way. The configurations in question, however, are usually known not to exist, so the problem of explaining the empirical usefulness of this kind of knowledge reappears".

In my view, the missing system (Thomson-Jones)—at least in the creative scientific cognitive processes—is not the one represented by the "model," but rather the target system itself, which is still essentially unidentified and un-schematized. This system will only appear to be "known" in a novel way upon acceptance of the research process results, which are then admitted into the theory T and considered worth *staying* in T thereafter. The same is true of models, which Godfrey-Smith refers to as configurations. While they are undoubtedly conditional, models do not necessarily need to be regarded as "known *not* to exist" in Godfrey-Smith's sense because at the very moment a scientific model is introduced during a discovery process, it is the only thing we can reasonably know to exist (for example, a diagram on a blackboard, an in-vitro artifact, or a mental imagery).

Once a final scientific result has been achieved, together with the description of the related experimental side, everything that does not fit that final structure is a fiction, and so models that helped reach that result itself. This is an exaggeration which Morrison corrects when she is pretty clear about the excessive habit of labeling fictional scientific models simply because they are superficially seen as "unrealistic": "Although there is a temptation to categorize any type of unrealistic representation as a 'fiction', I have argued that this would be a mistake, primarily because this way of categorizing the use of unrealistic representations tells us very little about the role those representations play in producing knowledge" (Morrison 2009, p. 133).

In the framework of an account of scientific representation in terms of partial structures and partial morphisms Bueno and French (2011, p. 27) admit that they agree in the fact that an important role for models in science is to allow scientists to perform the so-called "surrogative" reasoning, but they add the following constraint: "Indeed, we would claim that representing the 'surrogative' nature of this reasoning effectively rides on the back of the relevant partial isomorphisms, since it is through these that we can straightforwardly capture the kinds of idealizations, abstractions, and inconsistencies that we find in scientific models". We can therefore talk about surrogates, fictions, plausible worlds, etc., but we cannot be certain that we are in the presence of a "scientific" representation or model until we can identify the appropriate partial isomorphism following the model's success.

Furthermore, Kuorikoski and Lehtinen (2009, p. 121) assert that: "The epistemic problem in modelling arises from the fact that models always include false assumptions, and because of this, even though the derivation within the model is usually deductively valid, we do not know whether our model-based inferences reliably lead to true conclusions". However, since only the *co-exact* premises are used in various heuristic processes, the incorrect premises (also caused by the existence of models of both substantive and auxiliary assumptions) are not used in the cognitive process. Manders (2008) presented the idea of co-exact characteristics in geometrical cognition, and it is worth studying in areas outside of traditional geometry discovery procedures, where it has been beautifully highlighted. In turn, Mumma (2010, p. 264) provides an example of how Euclid's diagrams only add co-exact characteristics to proofs.

In conclusion, I believe it is erroneous to examine scientific models by embracing a foundational confusion of static and dynamic elements of the scientific endeavor. When scientific models are placed in a static context, such as a textbook, they do appear fictional at first because they are immediately compared to the target systems and their intricate experimental apparatuses. However, this also highlights the ideal nature of the models and their explanatory power (cf. Weisberg 2007). On the contrary, scientific models observed within the dynamic processes of scientific creativity—the central theme of epistemology at least since Karl Popper, Thomas Kuhn, and Imre Lakatos—appear to be *explicit* and *reproducible* mechanisms purposefully constructed and altered to further the gnoseological goals of expanding the body of knowledge *not yet available.*

Morrison (2009) makes it clear that models are not fictions, emphasizing that in science they are specifically related to ("finer graded") ways of understanding and explaining "real systems," which go far beyond their approximation benefits and more collateral predictive capabilities. She does, in fact, go on to clarify that because they are "necessary" to arrive at certain results, models that are appropriate to refer to as abstract resist corrections or relaxing of the unrealistic assumptions (as in the case of mathematical abstractions or when models furnish the sudden chance for the applicability of equations) in the so-called process of de-idealization.

According to Cartwright (1989), the main characteristic of these models is not that "relevant features" are removed in order to concentrate on a single, isolated set of properties or laws; rather, what matters is their ability to provide a comprehensively new representation of an empirical (and/or theoretical, as in the case of mathematics or logic) framework: "[...] We have a description of a physically unrealizable situation that is required to explain a physically realizable one" (p. 130). Similarly, Woods (2013) concludes that the development of non-probative premiss-conclusion connections in model-based science plays a major role in empirically forlorn representations, preparing links in ways that set up their conclusions for empirical negotiation at the checkout counter.

Certain other models are more appropriately categorized as *idealizations* since they are simpler to define and permit the inclusion of corrective variables that allow "[...] for the addition of correction factors that bring the model system closer (in representational terms) to the physical system being modeled or described" (Morrison 2009, p. 111). It is, for example, the case of a simple pendulum, where we know how to add corrections to deal with concrete phenomena. Idealizations distort or omit properties, instead, abstractions introduce a specific kind of representation "that is not amenable to correction and is necessary for explanation/prediction of the target system" (p. 112), and which provides information and transfer of knowledge.

Morrison's description of scientific models as abstract aligns with my focus on models as constitutive, going beyond the function of models as idealizations allowing for adjustments and improvements. According to this viewpoint, "abstract" models—whether they have to do with mathematization preparation and support or directly involve mathematical tools—must be conceived of as poietic means of generating fresh insights into the salient characteristics of the phenomena under study, rather than as simple means of making cognitive processes easier. If idealization *resembles* the phenomena to be better understood, abstract models can *constitute* the resemblance itself, as I will illustrate in the following section.

The argument made by Mäki (2009, p. 31) that "It may appear that a fantastically unreal feature is added to the model world, but again, what happens is that one thereby removes a real-world feature from the model world, namely the process of adjustment" is something I must draw attention to because, at least in some creative processes, the adopted model (for instance, in the case of creative thought experiments) is not necessarily implemented through the "removal" or "neutralization" of real-world features.

This is because, ironically, some features of the target system—that is, the supposed real world—have not yet been discovered, so they are the ones that are still "missing." As a result, it is hard to envision that some parts of the model come from the removal of real-world traits; instead, those qualities may come from the cognitive process that created the model in the first place in order to achieve that goal. However, because the systems we wish to subrogate *are mainly unknown*, it is challenging to consistently claim that models represent a "surrogate" system.

4 Resemblance and Feyerabend's counterinduction

In the epistemological context of missing systems (and related subjects, fictions, surrogate systems, credible world, make-believe models, etc.), even the idea of resemblance (similarity, isomorphism, homomorphism, etc.) is debatable. "M resembles, or corresponds to, the target system R in suitable respects and sufficient degrees. This second aspect of representation enables models to serve a useful purpose as representatives: by examining them as surrogate systems one can learn about the systems they represent" (Mäki 2009, p. 32): I argue that resemblance, at least in scientific discovery processes, is inherently partial because it is very hard to suitably resemble things that are not yet known. Actually, it is just the work of models that of creating, in a poietic way, the "resemblance" to the target system. Some discovered properties of the target system resemble the model not because the model resembled them a priori but only post hoc, once discovered thanks to the creative modeling activity itself: the new properties appear well-defined only in the static analysis of the final assessed theory. Morrison also asserts that "To say that fictional models are important sources of knowledge in virtue of a particular kind of similarity that they bear to concrete cases or systems is to say virtually nothing about how they do that. Instead what is required is a careful analysis of the model itself to uncover the kind of information it yields and the ways in which that information can be used to develop physical hypotheses" (Morrison 2009, p. 123).

From this angle, the received view is ironically reversed; we may argue that the newly discovered target system is the one that bears similarities to the model, which is the source of those similarities. Often models are fruitful in discovering new knowledge just because they do not—or narrowly— resemble the target systems to be studied, and are instead built with the aim of finding a new general capacity to make "the world intelligible".[4]

---

[4]I think that a better understanding of ideas like similarity, imaginability, conceivability, plausibility, persuasiveness, and creditworthiness (Mäki 2009, pp. 39–40) would benefit from being examined within the rigorous and multidisciplinary context of abductive cognition, which is overlooked in the studies of the "friends of fiction" except for Sugden (2000, 2009).

Feyerabend (1975) places a strong emphasis on the function of contradiction in contrast to the role of resemblance in his book *Against Method*. He develops a "counterrule" that is the antithesis of the neoposititivistic one according to which "experience" or "experimental results" determine the viability of our theories. This last one is a crucial rule that is at the basis of all theories of confirmation and corroboration. The counterrule suggests that we put out and develop theories that contradict accepted theories and/or accepted facts. Feyerabend emphasizes the importance of "dreaming," but these are Galileo's dreams, not fictions. As I have already mentioned, Feyerabend made a clear distinction between scientific tools (as modeling) and propaganda, which can instead be organized through fictions, inconsistent thought experiments, mistakes, aggressive fallacies, and so on, but that do not play any epistemic role in the specific cognitive process of scientific discovery. I have framed this type of propaganda under the wider concept of "epistemic" warfare.

Returning to the issue of models serving as surrogates, Mäki (2009, p. 35) states: "The model functions as a surrogate system: it is construed and examined with a desire to learn about the secrets of the real world. One yearns for such learning and sets out to build a model in an attempt to satisfy the desire. Surrogate models are intended, or can be employed to serve, as bridges to the world".

First, I would expand on the phrase "secrets of the real world" by adding a few auxiliary remarks. I would warn about the preferability of being post-Kantian by admitting that, through science, we are *constructing* our rational knowledge of the world, which is still objective and apart from us, but it is built. If we say we build surrogate systems to learn about the secret of nature, a debatable realist assumption seems to be presupposed: the models would be surrogates because they are not "reliably reflecting the true reality of the world we are discovering".

In my opinion, the term "surrogate models" should only be applied to models used in some "sciences" that are unable to produce adequate knowledge about the target systems. "There is a long tradition in economics of blaming economists for failing in just this way: giving all their attention to the properties of models and paying none to the relations of the model worlds to the real world" (Mäki 2009, p. 36). Mäki calls the systems described by such models "substitute systems": I will just reserve the term "surrogate systems" for them, as they fake a scientific knowledge that is not satisfactorily attained from a variety of angles.[5]

---

[5]It is important to remember what Morrison says: "Laws are constantly being revised and rejected; consequently, we can never claim that they are true or false"(Morrison 2009, p. 128).

As I mentioned before, there are epistemological issues with the idea of a model as make-believe. In fact, make-believe processes are present in practically all human intersubjective interplay. Here, I may emphasize once again how broad the concept of a credible world is: every cognitive process that seeks to provide information that is both scientific and non-scientific likewise seeks to provide credible worlds. Building scientific models, or the subclass of *epistemologically* credible worlds that effectively lead to scientific ideas, is the dilemma facing science. In this vein, Sugden (2009, p. 10) suggests that an epistemologically "good" credible world would have to be provided by models that are able to trigger hypotheses about the "cause of actual events," that is, in situations where "the fictional world of the model is one that *could* be real". It is beneficial to use Cartwright's classical approach (Cartwright 2009) on capacities:

For her, the function of a model is to *demonstrate the reality* of a capacity by isolating it—just as Galileo's experiment demonstrates the constancy of the vertical component of the acceleration of a body acted on by gravity. Notice how Cartwright speaks of *showing that* C has the capacity to produce E, and of deriving this conclusion from *accepted principles*. A satisfactory isolation, then, allows a real relationship of cause and effect to be demonstrated in an environment in which this relationship is stable. In more natural conditions, this relationship is only a latent capacity which may be switched on or off by other factors; but the capacity itself is stable across a range of possible circumstances. Thus, the model provides a "theoretical grounding" for a general hypothesis about the world (Sugden 2009, p. 20)).

In his cautious analysis, Sugden views these overly optimistic viewpoints on models as instruments for separating the "capacities" of causal factors in reality. He also offers alternative conceptual frameworks to preserve other supposedly weaker aspects of epistemological "sciences," such as certain areas of economics, psychology, or biology, which are never able to achieve the goal of revealing capacities.

In order to rescue these disciplines, he claims that models can only offer "conceptual explorations," which in turn help create plausible counterfactual worlds or really explanatory theories that can lead to inductive (or "abductive") inferences that explain the target systems. Strong methodological claims like those made by Cartwright should, in my opinion, be approached with caution, but there is still an open epistemological question: in the case of models used as conceptual exploration, are they used to depict plausible worlds that can reach a satisfactory theorization of target systems, or are they just providing ambitious but unjustified hypotheses that lack various sound epistemological requirements?

Using Cartwright's strict demarcation criteria, which is restated in "If no capacities then no credible worlds" (Cartwright 2009), it would seem that no more citizenship is allowed to some post-modern exaggeration in attributing the label "scientific" when referring to proliferating fields of academic production of knowledge, from (parts of) psychology to (parts of) economics, and so on, areas which do not—or scarcely—respect the most common accepted epistemological requisites, for example, the *predictivity* of the phenomena that regard the explained systems.

Are we certain that this line is excessively strict, or is it time to call out certain excesses in the abundance of models deemed to be "scientific"? In the "military" framework of the academic struggle between disciplines, which is dominated, at least in my opinion, by a patent proliferation of "scientific" activities that just produce bare "credible" or "surrogate" models, looking aggressively for scientificity, when they are, at best, fragments of "bad philosophy", the epistemological use of the so-called credible worlds appears theoretically suspect but ideologically clear.

The unstable state of several areas of psychological study provides an illustration. Miller (2010, p. 716) examines three claims: "[...] that the dominant discourse in modern cognitive, affective, and clinical neuroscience assumes that we know how psychology/biology causation works when we do not; that there are serious intellectual, clinical, and policy costs to pretending we do know; and that crucial scientific and clinical progress will be stymied as long as we frame psychology, biology, and their relationship in currently dominant ways" He also provides a thorough illustration of the misguided or epistemologically perplexing attempts to localize psychological functions[6] through neuroimaging, as well as the misconceptions surrounding the contribution of genetics to psychopathology, sadly intertwined with untoward constraints on healthcare policy and clinical service delivery.

5 Conclusion

I have argued in this work that scientific models are not fictions. I have maintained that there are serious inadequacies in other related epistemological approaches to model-based scientific cognition (in terms of surrogates, credible worlds, missing systems, and make-believe), which can be identified by utilizing the idea of manipulative abduction and recent cognitive research conducted in scientific labs. The concept of "epistemic warfare," which views scientific enterprise as a complex struggle for rational knowledge in which it is crucial to distinguish between epistemic (such as scientific models) and extra-epistemic (such as fictions, falsities, and propaganda) weapons, has been proposed as a further means of outlining a more satisfactory analysis of fictionalism and its discontents. I come to the conclusion that when models in scientific contexts are fictions, it is because they were merely thrown out as heuristic steps gone wrong, dismissed thanks to a form of negation

---

[6]Cf. for example (Glymour and Hanson 2016).

as failure. By confusing the static and dynamic aspects of the scientific enterprise I have also demonstrated how misleading it is to analyze models in science. In fact, the static perspective overemphasizes the potential fictional nature of models because the creative/active role of modeling is openly or purposefully ignored. I have finally taken a look at Feyerabend's helpful concept of counterinduction, which challenges the significance of resemblance in model-based cognition. This viewpoint has led me to paradoxically arrive at the opposite of the received view: it is the newly known target system that resembles to the model, which itself originated that resemblance.

Acknowledgement. Parts of this chapter are excerpted from my monograph *The Abductive Structure of Scientific Creativity. An Essay on The Ecology of Cognition.* Springer, Cham, Switzerland, 2017, chapters two and four. For the informative critiques and interesting exchanges that assisted me in enriching my analysis of the issues treated in this article, I am obligated to my collaborators Tommaso Bertolotti, Selene Arfini, and Alger Sans Pinillos.

References

Bokulich, A. (2017). Models and explanation. In Magnani, L. and Bertolotti, T., editors, *Handbook of Model-Based Science*, pages 104–118. Springer, Heidelberg/Berlin.

Bueno, O. and French, S. (2011). How theories represent. *The British Journal for the Philosophy of Science*, 62:857–894.

Cartwright, N. (1983). *How the Laws of Physics Lie.* Oxford University Press, Oxford. Cartwright, N. (1989). *Nature's Capacities and Their Measurement.* Oxford University Press, Oxford.

Cartwright, N. (2009). If no capacities then no credible worlds. But can models reveal capacities? *Erkenntnis*, 70:45–58.

Chandrasekharan, S. (2009). Building to discover: A common coding model. *Cognitive Science*, 33:1059–1086.

Clark, K. L. (1978). Negation as failure. In Gallaire, H. and Minker, J., editors, *Logic and Data Bases*, pages 94–114. Plenum, New York.

Contessa, G. (2007). Scientific representation, interpretation, and surrogative reasoning. *Philosophy of Science*, 74:48–68.

Contessa, G. (2010). Scientific models and fictional objects. *Synthese*, 172:215–229.

da Costa, N. C. and French, S. (2003). *Science and Partial Truth. A Unitary Approach to Models and Scientific Reasoning*. Oxford University Press, Oxford/New York.

de Regt, H. W. (2015). Scientific understanding: Truth or dare? *Synthese*, 192(12):3781–3797. Feyerabend, P. (1975). *Against Method*. Verso, London, New York.

Freud, S. (1953–1974). *The Standard Edition of the Complete Psychological Works of Sigmund Freud*. Hogarth Press, London. Translated by J. Strachey in collaboration with A. Freud, et al.

Frigg, R. (2010). Models and fiction. *Synthese*, 172:251–268.

Frigg, R. and Nguyen, J. (2017). Models and representation. In Magnani, L. and Bertolotti, T., editors, *Handbook of Model-Based Science*, pages 49–102. Springer, Heidelberg/Berlin.

Giere, R. (2007). An agent-based conception of models and scientific representation. *Synthese*, 172:269–281.

Glymour, C. and Hanson, C. (2016). Reverse inference in neuropsychology. *British Journal for the Philosophy of Science*, 67(4):1139–1153.

Godfrey-Smith, P. (2009). Models and fictions in science. *Philosophical Studies*, 143:101–116.

Kuorikoski, J. and Lehtinen, A. (2009). Incredible worlds, credible results. *Erkenntnis*, 70:119–131.

Laland, K. N., & Brown, G. R. (2006). Niche construction, human behavior, and the adaptive-lag hypothesis. *Evolutionary Anthropology, 15*, 95–104.

Laland, K. N., & Sterelny, K. (2006). Perspective: Seven reasons (not) to neglect niche construc- tion. *Evolution. International Journal of Organic Evolution, 60* (9), 4757–4779.

Magnani, L. (2001). *Abduction, Reason, and Science. Processes of Discovery and Explanation*. Kluwer Academic/Plenum Publishers, New York.

Magnani, L. (2012). Scientific models are not fictions. Model-based science as epistemic warfare. In Magnani, L. and Li, P., editors, *Philosophy and Cognitive Science. Western and Eastern Studies*, pages 1–38, Heidelberg/Berlin. Springer.

Magnani, L. (2022). *Discoverability. The urgent need of and ecology of human creativity*. Springer, Cham.

Magnani, L. and Bertolotti, T., editors (2017). *Handbook of Model-Based Science*. Springer, Hei- delberg/Berlin.

Mäki, U. (2009). MISSing the world. Models as isolations and credible surrogate systems. *Erkenntnis*, 70:29–43.

Manders, K. (2008). The Euclidean diagram. In Mancosu, P., editor, *Philosophy of Mathematical Practice*, pages 112–183. Clarendon Press, Oxford/New York.

Miller, G. A. (2010). Mistreating psychology in the decades of brain. *Perspectives on Psychological Science*, 5:716–743.

Morrison, M. (2009). Fictions, representations, and reality. In Suárez, M., editor, *Fictions in Science: Philosophical Essays on Modeling and Idealization*, pages 110–135. Routledge, London.

Mumma, J. (2010). Proofs, pictures, and Euclid. *Synthese*, 175:255–287.

Nersessian, N. J. and Chandradekharan, S. (2009). Hybrid analogies in conceptual innovation in science. *Cognitive Systems Research*, 10(3):178–188.

Odling-Smee, F. J., Laland, K. N., & Feldman, M. W. (2003). *Niche construction. The neglected process in evolution*. Princeton, NJ: Princeton University Press.

Sugden, R. (2000). Credible worlds: The status of theoretical models in economics. *Journal of Economic Methodology*, 7:1–31.

Sugden, R. (2009). Credible worlds, capacities and mechanisms. *Erkenntnis*, 70:3–27.

Thom, R. (19_88). *Esquisse d'une sémiophysique*. InterEditions, Paris. Translated by V. Meyer, *Semio Physics: A Sketch*, Addison Wesley, Redwood City, CA, 1990.

Thomson-Jones, M. (2010). Missing systems and the face value practice. *Synthese*, 172:283–299.

Weisberg, M. (2007). Three kinds of idealizations. *Journal of Philosophy*, 104(12):639–659. Woods, J. (2013). Epistemology mathematicized. *Informal Logic*, 33:292–331.

Woods, J. and Rosales, A. (2010). Unifying the fictional. In Woods, J., editor, *Fictions and Models: New Essays*, pages 345–388. Philosophia Verlag, Munich.

Models and representation in science: for a new image of the objectivity of knowledge

Fabio Minazzi

> Knowledge, like the growth of a plant and the movement of the earth, is a mode of interaction; but it is a mode which renders other modes luminous, important, valuable, capable of direction, causes being translated into means and effects into consequences.
>
> John Dewey, *Experience and Nature*

1 Facts and values: the crisis of "Hume's law"?

The following passage by Hume, taken from *A Treatise of Human Nature* is celebrated:

> In every system of morality, which I have hitherto met with, I have always remark'd, that the author proceeds for some time in the ordinary way of reasoning, and establishes the being of a God, or makes observations concerning human affairs; when of a sudden I am surpriz'd to find, that instead of the usual copulations of propositions, *is*, and *is not*, I meet with no proposition that is not connected with an *ought*, or an *ought not*. This change is imperceptible; but is, however, of the last consequence. For as this *ought*, or *ought not*, expresses some new relation or affirmation, 'tis necessary that it shou'd be observ'd and explain'd; and at the same time that a reason should be given, for what seems altogether inconceivable, how this new relation can be a deduction from others, which are entirely different from it. But as authors do not commonly use this precaution, I shall presume to recommend it to the readers; and am persuaded, that this small attention wou'd subvert all the vulgar systems of morality, and let us see, that the distinction of vice and virtue is not founded merely on the relations of objects, nor is perceiv'd by reason.[1]

In this way Hume introduces what is called "Hume's law", which affirms the existence of a clear and drastic distinction between facts and evaluations, between reason and morality, therefore between the dimension of scientific knowledge and the development of human passions and actions. In short, we

---

[1] David Hume, *A Treatise of Human Nature*, reprinted from the Original Edition in three volumes and edited, with an analytical index, by L. A. Selby-Bigge, M.A., Oxford, Clarendon Press, 1896. p. 319, italics in the text; the passage is found in the final part of the first section of the first part of the third book.

could say more briefly, between the world of objective scientific knowledge and the world of values. Which allows us to immediately identify, *à la* Hume indeed, the traditional 'moralistic fallacy', by which what *'is'* is systematically transformed, surreptitiously, into a *'ought to be'*. Hume's empirical point of view thus allows us to critically denounce a widespread model of metaphysical argument which, in general, unduly contaminates the axiological point of view with the ontological one in order to make a *de facto* situation look like *a de jure* one: '*p*' *must be* true because *p* is good' or, and conversely, '*p*' *must be* false, because *p* is bad'. This refers, at least within the established metaphysical tradition of Western philosophy, to a peculiar (fallacious) form of 'general argument' which assumes the following argumentative model as its privileged model of inference: '*p*' implies '*q*' but *q* is bad, *therefore* '*p*' *must be* false' or, and conversely, '*p*' implies '*q*' but *q* is good, *therefore* '*p*' *must be* true'.

In relation to the circumscribed, but certainly eminent, Humean reflection, Mario Dal Pra observed that

> Hume's doctrine of the radical gap between the world of knowledge and the development of the passions is of great importance for the formulation of his ethical doctrine; in fact, on the basis of the basic ambiguity that characterises the Humean construction, and due to the non-rigorous distinction between the descriptive sphere and the critical-philosophical level, on the one hand it gives rise to a complete 'psychological' autonomy of the world of passions, on the other it expresses the principled opposition to intellectualistic-metaphysical ethics; Hume' general opposition to the metaphysical perspective was in fact determined, in the field of ethics, as an aversion to the *a priori* acceptance of 'duties' imposed on the nature of human beings in the name of the metaphysical and religious tradition and of its claimed absolute validity. Hume's ethics therefore assume a general naturalistic orientation, in the sense that it aims at detecting human values in the autonomous mixture of human passions and natural motives. Undoubtedly, through this doctrine, Hume reached a broader understanding of the values that have been revealed in the complex experience of history and led the way to passing from *a moral philosophy* to *a philosophy of morality*, which by renouncing any claim to cognitive determination in relation to the world of values, is better disposed to consider them as autonomous and spontaneous products of human initiative.[2]

This, as mentioned, certainly helps us to better understand, *analytically*, the overall nature of the innovative, decidedly anti-metaphysical Humean reflection as well as its specific development. On the other hand, this

---

[2] M. Dal Pra, *Hume e la scienza della natura umana*, Editori Laterza, Rome-Bari 1973, pp. 242–243.

precious observation, *internal* to Hume's philosophy, must not lead us to forget how this acute and innovative anti-metaphysical and also decidedly anti-spiritualist critical stance, subsequently largely influenced and fertilised the very tradition of critical empiricism of modernity (and also of the neo-positivism that itself originated in the Vienna Circle), by leading to the acceptance, often taken for granted and acquired, of the existence of a clear and drastic distinction between facts and evaluations, between scientific knowledge and the sphere of the will and passions. In this way, at least in the context of the logical empiricism of neo-positivist origin, the prohibition on drawing moral conclusions from factual premises is configured as a widespread 'common sense' especially in the analytic field, which has systematically allowed philosophers to denounce the traditional metaphysical fallacy of claiming to be able to derive what *ought to be* from what *is*. This has led many authors to denounce the parallel philosophical attempt to found ethics within the realm of knowledge, by thus configuring a clear and drastic dichotomy between facts and values.

This significant theoretical outcome is also clearly explained in the light of the effective history of Western modernity. In fact, on a concrete historical basis, the 'moralistic fallacy' as Giulio Preti understood, for example, is 'typical of every metaphysical foundation of ethics, but is specific to naturalism. In 'nature' we already locate what we want to draw from it—the model of 'nature' itself is constituted according to the ethical model that ought to follow from it'.[3] The emblematic and disruptive historical events of the seventeenth-century doctrine of natural law, especially in its innovative reading produced during the Enlightenment, which historically gave rise to the disruptive French Revolution—the authentic turning point in Western history—constitute a significant and truly emblematic 'test bench' for this complex tradition of thought which, precisely in this drastic dichotomy between facts and values, finally revealed its peculiar historical-critical guillotine by which it subverted, *ab imis fundamentis*, the traditional medieval world, to implement, in *the world of praxis*, a revolutionary *civil* entrance to Western modernity (naturally with all its multiple and drastic historical-civil antinomies).

This fundamental and decisive historical context must of course never be disregarded, even when we try to critically understand the *philosophical* nature of this conceptual tradition, by identifying both its intrinsic *values* and its, equally intrinsic, *limits*. Its overall *value* is naturally rooted in the ability to culturally and civilly set free scientific knowledge from any prejudicial metaphysical cage, by releasing all the critical potentialities connected with the objective knowledge of the world. Its *limits* on the other

---

[3] G. Preti, *Alle origini dell'etica contemporanea. Adamo Smith*, Editori Laterza, Bari 1957, p. 184

hand, are to be identified within the historical process of the Enlightenment—also presenting its complexities—which often and willingly ended up by unduly mythologising scientific knowledge itself, by turning particularly its immanent critical nature into a myth, and thus by transforming its inexhaustible criticality (proper and specific to scientific research, which is always open and never concluded), into a dogma and an altogether metaphysical and absolute reality. (In this reconstructive framework post-positivist *scientism* has thus represented, historically speaking, the most widespread cultural and social translation of this myth, which has in fact ended up by elaborating a mythological vision of the scientific enterprise.) It is therefore necessary for us to dig into this subtle, but decisive, and at the same time, cultural, institutional, disciplinary and epistemological 'fissure' using the instruments of criticism in order identify a different perspective, capable of freeing all the immanent critical potential of the scientific and objective knowledge of the world, without, however, falling into an undue dogmatic metaphysical mythologisation of science itself and, therefore, of the immanent critical power of knowledge, which is always open and always revisable.

2 Science and life: *Wertfreiheit* and practical-sensitive activities

If science tends to be—and certainly it cannot but tend to be—*wertfrei*, on the contrary, life can never be *wertfrei*, because living means evaluating. In fact, living always necessarily implies, albeit in a broad sense, the ability to *evaluate*. Better still: it should be said that life always implies the capacity of *being able* to evaluate. In this regard, Preti, in *Retorica e logica*, noted that

> [t]o live is to evaluate—already at the most basic biological level, an organism carries out acts of choice: and these, if we broaden the concept of 'evaluation' are already assessments. And, anyway, a civilisation without axiological instances does not exist, nor is it conceivable. This is why science can hold the central place in a civilization, but it cannot exhaust it or resolve it totally in its own form.[4]

Therefore, the two cultures, namely the rhetorical-axiological culture and the scientific-objective culture, are so intrinsically correlative and are always necessarily interconnected, *with all due respect to* Hume and his famous 'law' (and also to the misleading dichotomy schematically and erroneously

---

[4]G. Preti, *Retorica e logica*, new edition, amended and enriched with Introduction and notes by Fabio Minazzi, Bompiani, Milan 2018, p. 408, while the quotation that immediately follows in the text is taken from p. 407.

conceived by Snow in his famous little volume[5]). On the other hand, however, it is also true that

> [s]cience operates with a decisive, methodical, ἐποχή of all the axiological considerations. Science does not evaluate. Even when it is normative, when it is making technology, it only points out ways to follow, possible operational procedures according to the ends-in-view: but it says nothing about the value of these ends themselves; nor, ultimately, about the value of the operating procedures themselves.

From this perspective—admittedly dichotomous—we are therefore faced with two radically different and tendentially antithetical polarities, since science produces objective knowledge which then allows us to consider different operational procedures, even by providing us with a precise critical evaluation of their intrinsic rationality. However, science can never go beyond this specific field, because when we actually choose to follow a certain procedure, by opting out of other possible ones, in addition to scientific knowledge, an axiological evaluation comes into play, which does not pertain to knowledge as such, but to our decisions which concerns more directly *our* lives. So much so that in this context different and conflicting axiological evaluations can arise, which can also make certain operational procedures appear as 'more rational' which on the contrary turn out to be 'less rational' at the level of pure objective knowledge, because they might even involve a higher 'cost'. (For example when we decide to buy a certain product and/or certain services from a specific provider that charges higher prices than others, but which is more convenient for us or that we choose because it appeals to us more or for various other reasons: personal, historical-biographical, emotional, etc.) Well, in all these cases the 'rationality' of the choice always implies a purely evaluative procedure which systematically goes beyond the level of the mere *Wertfreiheit* of science.

On the other hand, it could also be observed that the very possibility of evaluating always implies, as mentioned, the specific capacity of *being able* to evaluate. In this way the specific relationship between the dimension of knowledge and the dimension of evaluation cannot fail to appear much more problematic and complex than the drastic and controversial dichotomous 'guillotine' of Humean descent could suggest. Conversely, it also seems that we cannot give up on the historical-civil *value*, specific to this empiricist dichotomous guillotine devised by Hume, which, as has also been mentioned, has historically acquired undoubted merits, precisely because, alongside the

---
[5]See Charles P. Snow, *The Two Cultures*, first published in 1959 with multiple reprintings, Cambridge, Cambridge University Press. Italian edition: Charles P. Snow, *Le due culture*, translated by Adriano Carugo, *Preface* by Lodovico Geymonat, Feltrinelli, Milan, 1964 with multiple reprintings. Recently this text has been republished by Marsilio (Venice, 2005), without the historical and emblematic *Preface* by Geymonat.

emotional and concrete historical basis of value, there is also the dimension of objective knowledge. This refers to a demonstrated and argued rational truth, thanks to which a complex patrimony of knowledge has historically been built, which has undoubtedly contributed to improving our overall conditions of life and existence.

How then is it possible to recover all the intrinsic critical value of an objective knowledge of the world without renouncing a critically adequate understanding of the axiological dimension of our own life? The critical link between the axiological dimension and the cognitive one, tendentially *wertfrei*, is therefore configured as much more complex and intrinsically problematic than has ever been suspected by the classical tradition of empiricist descent. Certainly, this connection appears today as worthy of an adequate overall and analytical critical and philosophical rethinking. This was certainly also the intention of various authors, at different time in the history of contemporary reflection. Although it would be impossible here to provide an articulated and exhaustive picture of this interesting critical reflection, nevertheless, I will focus, in particular and with some attention, on the contribution outlined by the great and original American instrumentalist John Dewey.

3 History: which tradition? Herodotus, Hume and Dewey

In *Experience and Nature* Dewey investigated the link between existence and value in detail and in an innovative way, by starting from the awareness both that values 'are what they are' and also from the observation that values are always rooted in the concrete experiences of life, in the world of praxis, thus appearing 'as unstable as the forms of clouds'.[6] Of course, *nihil sub sole novum* (*Ecclesiastes*, 1.10), since already an eminent historian like Herodotus, in the third book of his *Histories* (III, 38, 3–4), reports this famous episode referring to Darius:

> When Darius was king, he summoned the Greeks who were with him and asked them for what price they would eat their fathers' dead bodies. They answered that there was no price for which they would do it. Then Darius summoned those Indians who are called Callatiae, who eat their parents, and asked them (the Greeks being present and understanding through interpreters what was said) what would make them willing to burn their fathers at death. The Indians cried aloud, that he should not speak of so horrid an act. So firmly rooted are

---

[6]See J. Dewey, *Experience and nature*, George Allen & Unwin, London, 1929. The quotations in the text are taken from pp. 396, 399. Italian translation: J. Dewey, *Esperienza e natura*, edited by Piero Bairati, Mursia, Milan 1973, pp. 282–310, quotations which appear in the text are taken from p. 283 and p. 285.

these beliefs; and it is, I think, rightly said in Pindar's poem that custom is lord of all.[7]

A conclusion, however, reached by Herodotus by having anticipated, in this same passage, that 'if it were proposed to all nations to choose which seemed the best of all customs, each, after examination, would place its own first; so well is each convinced that its own are by far the best.' This is also deeply in keeping with Hume's moderate scepticism, for which, as is well known, man is essentially a *habit-forming animal* since *custom* would always be constitutive of our own experience (although in this specific theoretical context Hume then, paradoxically, misses the intrinsic dynamic value of this very constitutive role of *custom*[8]). But if the frank critical recognition of the absolutely central role played by habits certainly does not eliminate the fruitful and intrinsic critical antinomicity of the Humean position (since Hume, as Dal Pra pointed out, 'is a moralist who prefers instinct to reason' but who, the more he prefers instinct, the more he develops the dimension of reason[9]), on the other hand it does not open at all to any holistic-radical relativism (*à la* Feyerabend[10]), precisely to the extent that our being *habit-forming animals* relates historically, in turn, with the articulated and complex technical-cognitive heritage developed by humanity, *step by step*, in the actual course of its history. Indeed, as Dewey rightly points out, with respect to the values rooted in existence,

> [b]ut a brief course in experience enforces reflection; it requires but brief time to teach that some things sweet in the having are bitter in after-taste and in what they lead to. Primitive innocence does not last. Enjoyment ceases to be a datum and becomes a problem.

---

[7]See Herodotus *The Histories*, translated by A. D. Godley, Loeb Classical Library Edition, Heinemann, London, 4 volumes in Greek and English, originally published 1920–1925, pp. 398–399.

[8]In this regard, Dal Pra rightly observed that, 'Hume, therefore, anticipated Kant's Copernican revolution of the relationship between the subject and the object of knowledge, even if the activity carried out by the subject in the constitution of knowledge explicitly assumes a character not cognitive but instinctive. And the fact that there still remains a significant distance between Hume's position and that of Kant also results from the question that in the analysis of habits Hume tends to minimise the initiative of the subject. In fact, habit is a modality of the subject that almost seems to materialise itself in the pure and simple repetition of several moments of observation; it could be said, with a paradox, that the instinctive modality of the subject is the very result of the observation of the object and that for that aspect of it that more directly calls into question the initiative and the activity, it is more the initiative and activity of 'nature' and of the subject in his awareness. As is well known, Kant understood both the innovation of the Humean doctrine and its limits with great clarity; these coincide, moreover, with the insufficient analysis of the cognitive structures, already noted several times' (M. Dal Pra, *Hume e la scienza della natura umana, op. cit.*, pp. 152–153)

[9]M. Dal Pra, *Hume e la scienza della natura umana, op. cit*, p. 392.

[10]See Paul K. Feyerabend, *Science in a free society*, Verso Editions/NLB, London, 1978. Italian translation by Libero Sosio, Feltrinelli, Milan 1981, pp. 106–129.

As a problem, it implies intelligent inquiry into the conditions and consequences of a value-object; that is, criticism. If values were as plentiful as huckleberries, and if the huckleberry-patch were always at hand, the passage of appreciation into criticism would be a senseless procedure. If one thing tired or bored us, we should have only to turn to another. But values are as unstable as the forms of clouds. The things that possess them are exposed to all the contingencies of existence, and they are indifferent to our likings and tastes.[11]

Exactly within this precise context of *lived experiences*, then, *criticism*, namely philosophical reflection, plays its own specific and peculiar role. In this case, according to Dewey, we are in fact in the presence of that rhythm of 'flights and perchings' (*à la* James) with which criticism and critical attitude alternate the emphasis on the immediate and the mediated, on what is enjoyed and consumed and on what, on the other hand, is configured as quite instrumental, by focusing on the different phases of conscious experience. In all these cases

[t]here occurs in every instance a conflict between the immediate value-object and the ulterior value-object: the given good, and that reached and justified by reflection; the now apparent and the eventual. In knowledge, for example there are beliefs *de facto* and beliefs *de jure*. In morals, there are immediate goods, the desired, and reasonable goods, the desirable. In aesthetics, there are the goods of an undeveloped and perverted taste and there are the goods of cultivated taste. With respect to any of these distinctions, the true, real, final, or objective good is no *more* good as an immediate existence than is the contrasting good, called false, specious, illusory, showy, meretricious, *le faux bon*. The difference in adjectives designates a difference instituted in critical judgment; the validity of the difference between good which is approved and that which is good (immediately) but is *judged bad*, depends therefore upon the value of reflection in general, and of a particular reflective operation in especial.

For Dewey, therefore, philosophical reflection can only coincide with this complex operation, and with 'this critical function become aware of itself and its implications, pursued deliberately and systematically'. Not only that: philosophy, starting from evaluative perceptions, behaviours and also from different situations of belief, progressively expands the range of critical reflection precisely to guarantee greater freedom and security to the very acts of direct selection, of rejection or of approval. Thus, Dewey again points out, philosophy

---

[11] J. Dewey, *Experience and nature, op. cit.*, p. 398, while all the quotations that follow in the text are taken, respectively, from the following pages: pp.402–403 (italics in the text), pp. 404–405 (italics in the text); p. 407; p. 410; p. 411; p. 412; p. 414; pp. 420–421; p. 424; p. 428; pp. 428–429; p.429; p. 430 (italics in the text); p. 434; p.435; p. 437.

does not annihilate the difference among beliefs: it does not set up the *fact* that an object believed in is perforce found good as if it were a *reason* for belief. On the contrary: the statement is preliminary. The all-important matter is what lies back of and causes acceptance and rejection; whether or no there is method of discrimination and assessment which makes a difference in what is assented to and denied. Properties and relations that *entitle* an object to be found good in belief are extraneous to the qualities that are its immediate good; they are causal, and hence found only by search into the antecedent and the eventual. The conception that there are some objects or some properties of objects which carry their own adequate credentials upon their face is the snare and delusion of the whole historic tradition regarding knowledge, infecting alike sensational and rational schools, objective realisms and introspective idealisms.

4 Ontological essences or transductive interactions?

Moving within this precise horizon of thought, Dewey therefore seeks to critically overcome all the traditional and multiple 'mental cramps' (*à la* Wittgenstein) specific to the different philosophical traditions (empiricist, rationalistic, realistic and idealistic), to put his eminently *critical* attitude at the centre of philosophical reflection, in order 'to make it clear that there is no such difference as this division assumes between science, morals and aesthetic appreciation'. In this way Dewey wants to underline the critical inadequacy of the traditional dichotomy between facts and values, between knowledge and morals, by aiming at recovering a much more articulated, critical and fruitful horizon of reflection. According to Dewey, it is therefore necessary to be able to critically dismantle the difference, both metaphysical and ontological, which one imagines exists between science, morality and aesthetics, since 'in a moving world solidification is always dangerous'.

In this precise critical context, the role of philosophy consists not so much in competing with science to conquer truth, but in succeeding in 'liberating and clarifying meanings, including those scientifically authenticated'. Operating within this perspective horizon, it is therefore necessary to have the courage to place 'social reform' itself outside an excessively narrow and 'Philistine' context, since it has instead to be reconnected precisely with the 'liberation and expansion of the meanings of which experience is capable'. In short, it is necessary to know how to recapture the concept of 'the richest and fullest experience possible' and then, in this exact perspective, the specific contribution historically provided by philosophy, with its privileged work of conceptual clarification, is rooted precisely in the thorough analyses produced by criticism, in order to be able to recover the complexity and multiplicity of all the interactions that always qualify, structure and characterise human life. Just because 'man needs the earth in order to walk, the sea to swim or sail, the air to fly. Of necessity he acts within the world, and in order to be, he must in some measures adapt himself as one part of nature to other parts.' Through this progressive and always dynamic 'adaptation' it is then possible to discover the *multiplicity of interactions* that human beings build up in the course of their existence, without falling into the metaphysical trap of the ontologisation of the relations codified in the classic tradition of *ens, verum et bonum*, which constituted an absolute metaphysical object, conceived as coincident as a real and existential metaphysical entity. Again for this reason it is necessary, then, *to know how to* critically *rebuild* our own experience, without however, on the one hand, ever expecting to be godlike, and, on the other hand, without becoming disillusioned with a world which would systematically disappoint us. If anything, for Dewey

> a mind that has opened itself to experience and that has ripened through its discipline knows its own littleness and impotencies; it knows that its wishes and acknowledgments are not final measures of the universe whether in knowledge or in conduct, and hence are, in the end, transient. But it also knows that its juvenile assumption of power and achievement is not a dream to be wholly forgotten. It implies a unity with the universe that is to be preserved. The belief, and the effort of thought and struggle which it inspires are also the doing of the universe, and they in some way, however slight, carry the universe forward. A chastened sense of our importance, apprehension that it is not a yard-stick by which to measure the whole, is consistent with the belief that we and our endeavours are significant not only for themselves but in the whole. Fidelity to the nature to which we belong, as parts however weak, demands that we cherish our desires and ideals till we have converted them into intelligence, revised them in terms of the ways and means which nature makes possible. When we have used our thought to its utmost and have thrown into the moving unbalanced balance of things our puny strength, we know that though the universe slay us still we may trust, for our lot is one with whatever is good in existence. We know that such thought and effort is one condition of the coming into existence of the better. As far as we are concerned it is the only condition, for it alone is in our power. To ask more than this is childish; but to ask less is a recreance no less egotistic, involving no less a cutting of ourselves from the universe than does the expectation that it meet and satisfy our every wish. To ask in good faith as much as this from ourselves is to stir into motion every capacity of imagination, and to exact from action every skill and bravery.'

In this way Dewey delineates the median position of human beings, by which, at the very moment in which they assert that their power is limited, as beings that belong entirely to nature, of which they represent a moment and on which they always depend, nevertheless we can also affirm, with a 'chastened sense of our importance' our own *constructive* role which can even push the universe itself forward a little. Human beings must therefore know how to take part, consciously and critically, in the processes of natural reality themselves, by building, in the words of the sociologist Boaventura De Sousa Santos, a sort of articulated 'ecology of knowledges',[12] by means of which we can never forget the *infinite plurality of interactions* within which human beings can perform their actions and develop their critical reflection. This then led Dewey to critically rethink the link between *belief* and *knowledge* by breaking down the traditional empiricist rigidity of this dichotomy. Indeed, if knowledge has generally been conceived as 'pure objectivity' by attributing to it the role of controlling belief through knowledge, science and truth, Dewey, insisted instead that how this dichotomy itself, which is integral to the Western tradition of philosophy, has to be critically rethought, starting from the epistemological awareness that knowledge itself constitutes, in its turn, 'a case of belief'. For this reason it is therefore necessary to decisively turn our backs on the traditional empiricist theory, totally mythological and metaphysical, according to which our knowledge would draw inspiration from 'innocent sensory data, or from pure logical principles, or from both together, as original starting points and material.' Indeed according to Dewey

> [a]ll knowing and effort to know starts from some belief, some received and asserted meaning which is a deposit of prior experience, personal and communal. In every instance, from passing query to elaborate scientific undertaking, the art of knowing criticises a belief which has passed current as genuine coin, with a view to its revision. It terminates when freer, richer and more secure objects of belief are instituted as goods of immediate acceptance. The operation is one of doing and making in the literal sense. Starting from one good, treated as apparent and questionable, and ending in another which is tested and substantiated, the final act of knowing is acceptance and intellectual appreciation of what is significantly conclusive.

But then, Dewey wonders: 'Is there any intrinsic difference between the relation of scientific inquiry to belief-values, of aesthetic criticism to aesthetic values, and of moral judgments to moral goods? Is there any difference in logical method?'

His answer to this question is on the whole negative, precisely because the evaluation of any belief-value always implies a *comparative* judgment, since, when we affirm that an object 'is good' this may perhaps appear as an absolute statement, especially when it is formulated in the context of action and not so much in the context of reflection. However, this affirmation

---

[12]See Boaventura De Sousa Santos, *A cruel pedagogia do vírus*, Boitempo Editorial, São Paulo, 2020. Italian translation: *La crudele pedagogia del virus*, translated by E. Vitello, Castelvecchi, Rome 2020.

about the goodness of a given reality is always the result of a comparative process which, in turn, refers to an evaluative comparison exactly because in these cases 'the issues shift to something comparative, relational, causal, intellectual and objective':

> *Immediately* nothing is better or worse than anything else; it is just what it is. Comparison is comparison of things, things in their efficacies, their promotions and hindrances. The better is that which will do more in the way of security, liberation and fecundity for other likings and values.

From this dynamic, interactive and implicitly *transductive*[13] perspective Dewey is, therefore, able to outline a coherent overall conception of a human being, who no longer qualifies as a sort of 'little god' but who instead fully recognises that humanity belongs to nature as a centre of energy that is always interconnected with multiple other centres of interaction and energy. The Western philosophical tradition from Descartes onwards has considered nature as a kind of *alter ego* in relation to ourselves, which would qualify precisely by its absolute otherness and by its overall intrinsic passivity. On the contrary, from this new instrumentalist and transductive point of view, Dewey re-evaluated Spinoza's position, without ever referring to it explicitly, as well as that of the American Indians, according to whom human beings actually constituted a part, albeit infinitesimal, of nature. It is therefore necessary to start from this 'intrinsicity' between man and nature, an 'intrinsicity' which considers humans as a purely natural element, devoid of any exceptionality in the context of naturality. Dewey wrote:

> When man finds he is not a little god in his active powers and accomplishments, he retains his former conceit by hugging to his bosom the notion that nevertheless in some realm, be it knowledge or aesthetic contemplation, he is still outside of and detached from the ongoing sweep of inter-acting and changing events; and being there alone and irresponsible save to himself, is as a god. When he perceives clearly

---

[13] For the concept of transductivity developed by Dewey it is naturally necessary to refer to the chapter 'Interaction and Transaction' from *The Later Works of John Dewey, 1925-1953*. Volume 16: 1949-1952, *Essays, Typescripts and Knowing and the Known*, written in collaboration with Arthur F. Bentley edited by Jo Ann Boydston, Southern Illinois University Press, Carbondale, 1989/2008, in particular p. 97, where it is specified that 'What we call 'transaction' and what we wish to show as appearing more and more prominently in the recent growth of physics, is, therefore, in technical expression, neither to be understood as if it 'existed' apart from any observation, nor as if it were a manner of observing 'existing in a man's head' in presumed independence of what is observed. The 'transaction' as an object among and along with other objects, is to be understood as unfractured observation—just as it stands, at this era of the world's history, with respect to the observer, the observing, and the observed—and as it is affected by whatever merits or defects it may prove to have when it is judged, as it surely will be in later times, by later manners' (p. 97).

and adequately that he is within nature, a part of its interactions, he sees that the line to be drawn is not between action and thought, or action and appreciation, but between blind, slavish, meaningless action and action that is free, significant, directed and responsible. Knowledge, like the growth of a plant and the movement of the earth, is a mode of interaction; but it is a mode which renders other modes luminous, important, valuable, capable of direction, causes being translated into means and effects int consequences.

In this way the absolute empiricist dichotomy between facts and evaluations, between knowledge and evaluations is undoubtedly overcome critically by elaborating the model of the transductive interaction which, as we have seen, even assumes the growth of a plant as a heuristic-paradigmatic model to analyse critically the complex interaction between human life and the knowledge of the world itself. The model of the biological growth of plants makes it possible to highlight how growth itself takes place through a continuous critical metabolisation that transforms the inorganic into the organic, ensuring that a plant is in fact able to build the environment in which it lives by interactively *building* its own context as well as by interacting with it. Through this fruitful and innovative approach, the traditional way of understanding the function of philosophy itself also changes, since Dewey consequently conceived 'philosophy as the critical method of developing methods of criticism'. On the one hand, this constituted a fecund revival of the tradition of Western criticism already outlined by Socrates in the fifth century BCE; on the other hand, it referred to a new critical-epistemic paradigm in the name of which the increase of objective knowledge must be able to be explained by the interactions of multiple transductive-transactions that also qualify the mode of growth of a plant and a vegetable.

5   The new perspective of Husserlian phenomenology

In the light of Dewey's critical considerations referred to in the previous paragraph, it is clear that what is called Hume's law has undoubtedly lost much of its heuristic éclat and its original methodological absoluteness. Not so much because the distinction between facts and values may appear today 'hopelessly fuzzy, because factual statements themselves, and the practices of scientific inquiry upon which we rely to decide what is and what is not a fact, presuppose values',[14] since this observation constitutes, in reality, a well-known and somewhat discredited critical stance. If anything, because, as Hilary Putnam added, referring to both W. James and A. E. Singer, '*Knowledge of facts presupposes knowledge of values*' and, conversely

---

[14]Hilary Putnam, *Reason, Truth and History*, Cambridge University Press, Cambridge, 1981, p. 128. (Italian translation *Ragione, verità e storia* by Alessandro Nicolò Radicati di Brozolo, edited by Salvatore Veca. Il Saggiatore, Milan 1985, p. 140.)

'*Knowledge of values presupposes knowledge of facts*'.[15] It is therefore necessary to critically investigate this connection by identifying, if possible, a different critical path. To do this, we need to go back to the *moralistic fallacy*, to which we referred earlier by pointing out how the naturalists of the eighteenth century, inspired by the Enlightenment, fell into it precisely to the extent that into their concept of 'nature' they inserted whatever they wanted ... to obtain from it. In this case, as we have seen, the very model of 'nature' is constructed, as Preti pointed out, 'according to the ethical model that should be its consequence'. We are thus faced with an obvious *vicious circle*. The indisputable historical fact that precisely this vicious circularity constituted, through the French Revolution, the historical-civil leaven of modernity certainly does not constitute its philosophical justification. If anything, it is only a very important *de facto* datum which, however, does not nullify the unconvincing logical argument that claims to 'be the foundation' of this same vicious circularity. Precisely in order to overcome this critical impasse, which is both logical and historical, the more mature reflection developed during the Enlightenment by Rousseau and Kant finally developed a philosophically shrewder and more sophisticated naturalism. As Preti further observed, beyond the appeal to 'nature' or to 'reason' what appeared essential in this critically more mature reflection created during the Enlightenment is that

> a pure a priori ideal principle is invoked, which at the same time constitutes the foundation and limit of the historical-empirical variations of morals and of opinions about ethics. This supreme norm of conscience, as universal and necessary, faces contingent manifestations: it is a *critical* principle, in the face of which every norm and empirical evaluation, with its limitation, shows its arbitrariness and historical contingency. No norm stands up to the criterion of reason.[16]

On the other hand, from this supreme *ideal* criterion of reason one can naturally deduce no particular norm, no right and therefore, also no particular system of values, no positive morality, no kind of catechism. If we do it, we fall back into the *moralistic fallacy*. It is therefore definitely crucial to reflect on the role and function of this *ideal* criterion of reason by addressing what has been considered the problem of the place of reason in ethics. But, more generally, it is necessary to question the intrinsic nature of human critical rationality as such. For this reason it is imperative to investigate what human rationality consists of.

In the first place, it could be observed how human reason coincides with *logical coherence*, by thus formulating an answer that refers merely to

---

[15] Hilary Putnam, *The Collapse of the Fact-Value Dichotomy and Other Essays*, Chapter 8 'The Philosophers of Science's Evasion of Values' Harvard University Press, Cambridge, Massachusetts and London, England, 2002, p. 137, italics in the text.

[16] G. Preti, *Le origini dell'etica contemporanea. A. Smith*, op. cit., p. 185.

the *formal* dimension of human rationality. Indeed, logic does not concern only and exclusively the cognitive discourse, but rather it relates, and not only potentially, to any type of possible discourse that can be formulated, in a coherent way, in any field of investigation and reflection. But the formal transversality of this answer reveals its limits, because in this case we are dealing with a purely *formal* rationality, which can certainly make any argument 'rational' (hence also evaluative arguments), but it does not enter into the merits of rationality as such. In fact, this approach, precisely because of its formal limitation, does not make it possible to consider purely evaluative discourse as rational. Indeed, it seems to increase the traditional contrast between the intrinsic rationality of theoretical discourse and the equally intrinsic irrationality of evaluative discourse. However, precisely in relation to this contrast, it would then be worth mentioning an important critical achievement of Hume's, on the basis of which we know that human reason can only *order* the contents on which it reflects, but it can never *create them*. This observation is valid not only for the evaluative field, but also for the theoretical-cognitive field. In every different area of investigation, 'data' are always made available through reason but never produced by it. From this point of view, the ultimate contents of evaluations (attitudes and emotions) are then just as 'irrational' as the 'sensible data' (sensations) that underpin knowledge.

However, if we dismiss this first answer, which insists on the *logical formality* of reason, another sense of rationality can be evoked, which is specific to the typical idea of rationality developed during the Enlightenment and which is related to the logical and methodical reflection concerning what Galilei referred to as 'sensible experiences' i.e., our objective scientific knowledge. As Preti wrote

> [t]he only 'rationality' (in this second sense) of the evaluative discourse lies in the rationality of its cognitive moment, of its motivations. The only disagreements that can be rationally resolved are disagreements of belief. The proof that the accused did not commit the act removes all sense from the discussion about the juridical configuration of the alleged crime.[17]

This has a specific significance, since 'a traditional system of evaluations can be challenged not only by changing attitudes, but also, and more irremediably, if its system of motivations is theoretically false; that is, if science declares it erroneous. The case of witches, although a borderline case, shows very clearly what I mean'.

---

[17]G. Preti, *Retorica e logica*, op. cit., p. 415, from which the immediately following quotation is also taken.

6 Theoretical disciplines as foundations of normative disciplines

Precisely this different approach to the critical understanding of human rationality makes it possible to perform a significant critical overturning of the traditional empiricist approach, which affirms the existence of an irreducible dichotomy between facts and evaluations. Indeed, if the traditional Humean distinction associated with 'Hume's law' leads us to believe that there is no direct link and no possible critical mediation between facts and evaluations, as well as between knowledge and attitudes, the new phenomenological framework outlined by Edmund Husserl enables us, on the contrary, to affirm that, in reality, precisely the opposite is true, since every evaluative judgment is always rooted in a cognitive judgment. In other words, to quote Husserl, every predicate of value, i.e., every evaluative one, must be considered as 'second-order' predicates, or rather as 'predicates of predicates'. In this perspective, to refer directly to the Husserlian *Logical Investigations*, 'theoretical disciplines' are configured 'as the foundation of normative disciplines.'[18] Husserl critically attacked the traditional empiricist (pre-)judgement on the basis of which facts and values do not present any binding relationship, as they are set within an absolute dichotomy, devoid of mediations and, therefore, completely unrelated. On the contrary, Husserl believed that theoretical disciplines themselves constitute the authentic 'foundation' of normative disciplines. In other words, for Husserl every axiological judgment is always rooted in precise, historically determined and configured cognitive assets. To clarify this innovative point of view, Husserl states, first of all,

> [t]he concept of a normative science in relation to that of a theoretical science. The laws of the former tell us (it is usually held) what shall or should be, though perhaps, under the actual circumstances, it neither is nor can be. The laws of the latter, contrariwise, merely tell us what is.

But what is meant by *should be* in comparison to the simple *be*? What is being stated, when it is argued that a 'soldier should be brave' or that a 'teacher should be qualified' or that 'a sportsman must be trained' or that 'parents must look after their children with love and intelligence' or, again, that 'a doctor must be a good clinician'? Well, Husserl observes,

---

[18] E. Husserl, *Logical Investigations*, International Library of Philosophy, edited by Jose Bermudez, Tim Crane and Peter Sullivan, translated by J. L. Findlay from the Second German edition of *Logische Untersuchungen* with a new Preface by Michael Dummett and edited with a new Introduction by Dermot Moran, Routledge, London & New York, 1970/2001, 3 vols. Vol. I, *Prolegomena to Pure Logic*, p. 28 and following quotations appearing in the text are taken from pp. 33–34; p. 35 (italics in the text); p. 36; pp. 36–37 (no italics in the text); p. 37; p. 38 (no italics in the text; texts between both square and round brackets not present in the English text); p. 39.

[i]n all these cases we make our positive evaluation, the attribution of a positive value-predicate, depend on a condition to be fulfilled, whose non-fulfilment entails the corresponding negative predicate.

In short: 'An A should be B' and 'An A that is not B' can only be 'a bad A' precisely because, more generally, 'only an A which is a B is a good A'. This is the general inferential scheme that is used in axiology, which then explains the overall equivalence of the following sentences: 'an A that is B is in general a bad A', 'an A should not be B'; or, again, 'only an A that is not B is a good A'. A cowardly soldier is a bad soldier, just as an unqualified teacher is a bad teacher, as parents unable to take care of their children with love and intelligence are bad parents, as a doctor without clinical knowledge is a bad doctor. To affirm that a soldier should not be cowardly, that a teacher should not be unqualified, that parents should not look after their children without love and intelligence, and that a doctor should not lack a clinical eye, does not, however, imply the falsity of the statement according to which a cowardly soldier is also a bad warrior or that an unqualified teacher is also a bad teacher or, again, that parents unable to take care of their children with love and intelligence are bad parents or that a doctor lacking a clinical eye is a bad doctor. Judgments that relate to *should*, in fact, do not imply any statement about a correspondent *be*, precisely because, logically speaking, a duty and the lack of duty, at least on a logical-formal level, are always mutually exclusive.

We see from these analyses that each normative proposition presupposes a certain sort of valuation or approval through which the concept of a 'good' or 'bad' (a value or a disvalue) arises in connection with a certain class of objects: in conformity with this, objects divide into good and bad ones. To be able to pass the normative judgement 'A soldier should be brave', I must have some conception of a 'good' soldier, and this concept cannot be founded on an arbitrary nominal definition, but on a general valuation, which permits us to value soldiers as good or bad according to these or those properties. Whether or not this valuation is in any sense 'objectively valid', whether we can draw any distinction between the subjectively and objectively 'good', does not enter into our determination of the sense of should-propositions. It is sufficient that something is held valuable, that an *intention* is effected having the content that something is valuable or good.

From Husserl's perspective on the basis of these considerations, a normative proposition can then be defined as that particular proposition which, in relation to a previous general axiological assumption, which stands as its foundation, by determining a correlative pair of value predicates, is capable of expressing the conditions (necessary or sufficient, or also, at the same time, necessary as well as sufficient) for the possession of a given predicate:

If we have once drawn a distinction between 'good' and 'bad' in our valuations in a particular sense, and so in a particular sphere, we are naturally concerned to decide the circumstances, the inner or outer properties that are or are not guarantees that a thing is good or bad in this sense: what properties may not be lacking if an object from that sphere is to be accorded the value of 'good'.

In this way it is possible to construct an articulated hierarchy of axiological judgments which refer to a fundamental norm, by configuring a set of norms that form a closed and independent group, which in the end is determined and qualified precisely by the axiological assumption judged as fundamental. Precisely this general normative proposition will then force, consequently, the entities of a given sphere to adapt as much as possible to the specific and constitutive characteristics of the predicate axiologically assumed as positive and fundamental, which generates, precisely, the general norm of that specific group of norms. In this perspective

[t]he basic norm is the correlate of the definition of 'good' and 'bad' in the sense in question. It tells us on what *basic standard or basic value* all normativisation must be conducted, and does not therefore represent a normative proposition in the strict sense. The relationship of the basic norm to what are, properly speaking, normative propositions, is like the relation between so-called definitions of the number-series and the arithmetical theorems about the relations of numbers which are always referred back to these. The basic norm could also be called a 'definition' of the standard conception of good— e.g. of the morally good—but this would mean departing from the ordinary logical concept of definition.

In any case the idea of a *regulatory discipline* arises just from the totality of the connections existing between different normative propositions. This central and decisive reference for normative disciplines is instead absent in theoretical disciplines, for which the overall unity of their investigations is rooted in the possibility of identifying what arises from the 'inner laws of things' within their 'mutual coherence'. But, as mentioned, for Husserl theoretical disciplines are configured as the authentic foundations of normative disciplines:

Every normative proposition of, e.g., the form 'An A should be B' implies the theoretical proposition 'Only an A which is B has the properties C', in which 'C' serves to indicate the constitutive content of the standard-setting predicate 'good' (e.g. pleasure, knowledge, whatever, in short, is marked down as good by the valuation fundamental to our given sphere). The new proposition is purely theoretical: it contains no trace of the thought of normativity. If, conversely, a proposition of the latter form is *true*, and thereupon a novel valuation of a C

as such emerges, and makes a normative relation to the proposition seem requisite, the theoretical proposition assumes the normative form 'Only an A which is B is a good A', i.e., 'An A should be B'. Normative propositions can therefore make an appearance even in theoretical contexts: our theoretical interest in such contexts attaches value to the being of a state of affairs of a sort—to the equilateral form, e.g., of a triangle about to be determined—and then assesses other states of affairs, e.g. one of equiangularity, in relation to this: If the triangle *is to* [*sollen*] be equilateral, it *must* [*müssen*] be equiangular.

However, in the theoretical sphere, Husserl points out again, this possible reformulation carried out through normative propositions is not essential, because in the cognitive field the ultimate and constitutive intention of theoretical reflection is rooted in the possibility of identification based 'on the theoretical coherence of the things themselves' and for this specific reason 'enduring results are not therefore stated in normative form, but in the forms of this objective coherence, in the form, that is, of a general (*generell*) proposition'. In this way Husserl produces a critical overturning not only of the traditional dichotomy between facts and values, connected with the "law of Hume", but also succeeds in criticising the classic epistemological setting of empiricism itself by overturning its terms of reference. Indeed, if the empiricist believes he can justify a specific axiological judgment by appealing to experience, on the contrary the critical perspective inaugurated by Husserlian phenomenology reminds us how each of our axiological judgments is always rooted within a precise and determined *cognitive assets*. Thus, according to the traditional empiricist approach, a particular class of students will be judged by its teachers as more or less 'good' or as more or less 'bad' in regard to the *experience* of teaching, as gained within this particular group of students. In this way empiricism ends up by discharging the overall responsibility of the axiological judgment on the experiential level, conceived as neutral and, basically, as completely passive: the teacher limits himself to objectively recording the 'good' or 'not-good' quality of a class as such. From this perspective, the teacher, as an evaluator, does not perform any specific role because, in fact, he would limit himself to recording, with objectivity and impartiality, the actual and real condition of that particular class.

On the contrary, the phenomenological perspective makes us notice how teachers, at the very moment when they formulate their axiological judgments in relation to a group of students, in reality do not limit themselves at all to considering their first-hand teaching experience within a class-group in a neutral and passive way, since in formulating their judgments they refer to a precise cognitive model (heuristic and paradigmatic) on the basis of which, even before meeting a specific class, they know very well what 'a good class' is in comparison with 'a bad class'. Therefore, their final axiological judgments do not arise from pure experience, but from a precise comparison of their prejudicial heuristic-cognitive models with the actual experience they make in teaching a specific class.

This is true, more generally, of all our axiological judgments, since all our evaluations are always rooted within a precise and previous theoretical-cognitive horizon. This makes it possible, then, in the first place, to critically highlight the *gnoseological* responsibility itself of all our axiological judgments that do not arise from passive experience, but are the result of an interrelation between our knowledge and our experience. And this is not all: in the second place, this critical horizon configures a much more complex and dynamic relationship, of continuous transductive interrelation, between the evaluative and the cognitive purviews. Knowledge and evaluation are by no means unrelated, rather they affect each other, within the very complexity of experience, which must then be critically unravelled, by understanding the heuristic role exercised by the paradigmatic models of knowledge that we use to construct our experience. Indeed experience, *by itself*, never teaches us anything, if we do not know how to read it, how to interpret it, how to understand it and explain it in the light of a particular theoretical perspective. In the third place and finally, the Husserlian perspective allows us to understand how the development of our technical-cognitive assets necessarily always also have a precise axiological effect, by removing both from human knowledge and from axiology the supposed metaphysical claim that knowledge and axiology can develop in an ahistorical, immutable, absolute dimension, indifferent to the history of human knowledge. On the contrary, it is precisely the intertwining and always changing dynamic between the critical development of our knowledge and the equally mobile and dynamic dimension of our own moral and axiological reflection, which configures a much more articulated and complex life situation, precisely because, as Husserl explicitly writes,

> [e]very normative discipline demands that we know certain non-normative truths: these it takes from certain theoretical sciences, or gets by applying propositions so taken to the constellation of cases determined by its normative interest. This naturally holds, likewise, in the more special case of a technology, and plainly to a greater extent. The theoretical knowledge is there added which will provide a basis for a fruitful realization of ends and means.

From a certain point of view Husserl performed this critical overturning of the traditional empiricist approach by highlighting the *active* critical and epistemological connection, which is also rooted, as already mentioned (see the previous note 8), within repetitiveness itself, apparently neutral and totally passive, triggered by the Humean concept of *custom*. In fact the apparently passive stratification of human experience itself, from which habit ultimately arises, constitutes, *despite itself*, an *active* element through which experience definitely loses that character of total passivity theorised by Hume from the very first pages of *A Treatise of Human Nature*, to configure, albeit *in a nutshell*, precisely that decisive and strategic 'Copernican revolution' that was later theorised and articulated by Kant in his *Critique of Pure Reason*, with the heuristic introduction of the concept of the *transcendental* as a privileged hermeneutic tool, aiming at a better understanding of the inferential deductive nature of human knowledge itself, which was affirmed with the birth of modern science thanks to Galilei and Newton.[19] This is then also related to a similar need with which the more mature reflection developed during the Enlightenment finally emancipated itself from the *moralistic fallacy*, typical of the doctrine of natural law, by directly appealing to a pure *a priori* and ideal principle which constitutes, as has also been mentioned, the limit and the foundation of the historical-empirical variations of the customs and ethos of a specific historical society. This 'parallelism' between the critical maturation of Kantian transcendentality in a purely epistemological context, and the parallel need of being able to identify the role and function of an ideal principle within the continuous historical variability itself of human events (for which see § 3), then confirms precisely the historical existence of the interconnection between theoretical and normative disciplines, with the former as the foundations of the latter.

7 A new image of the objectivity of knowledge

The new Husserlian conception of the relationship existing between theoretical and normative disciplines is based, in turn, on the overall perspective of Husserl's phenomenology, which started from a critical re-evaluation of the correlation between subject and object in order to highlight ideal purely theoretical truths and their heuristic role within knowledge. Again in this case the stance adopted by phenomenology constitutes a radical critique of traditional empiricism. Nor is that all: from his phenomenological perspective, Husserl also started a radical critical discussion of the previous, traditional metaphysical approach, which relied, alternatively, either on a subject conceived as absolute (consider the tradition of ideal realism, from Plato to Hegel), or conversely on an object conceived in an equally absolute and metaphysical way (in accordance with the metaphysical realism specific to materialism, from Democritus to La Mettrie).

Husserl, referring in a completely original and innovative way to Kantian transcendentality, pluralised it, by identifying multiple *planes of reflection* within which and according to which the different disciplines are constituted.

---

[19]In relation to this decisive epistemological theme, I refer to my book, in press, *L'epistemologia storico-evolutiva e il neo-realismo logico. (Historical-evolutionary epistemology and logical neo-realism)*.

In this perspective, Husserl maintained and preserved the structure of *intentionality* specific to the Kantian transcendental, according to which both traditional absolute metaphysical idealism as well as traditional absolute and metaphysical realism were *critically* undermined because, instead of referring to unrelated and absolute ideals, or to realities, equally unrelated and absolute, the focus of the investigation was the specific link established by a correlation between the subjective but empty intentionality with which one addresses the world and the effective capacity that the real world (Kant's empirical reality) possesses in being able to possibly 'saturate' albeit to different degrees of saturation, that prospective intentionality itself. From this transcendentalist phenomenological perspective, the conception of scientific knowledge as well as that of the world of praxis changed profoundly. Indeed, as Preti observed, seen in this perspective,

> the 'world' whose framework is constructed by scientific knowledge is a system of objects—and these objects are *noemata* of the first degree, in whose constitution there are no categories (predicates) of value. The world of science is neither beautiful nor ugly, neither good nor bad: the attitude of scientists, as such (at the moment when they are such, and they remain such) is that of belonging to the ascetic ataraxia of the Stoic-Spinozian wise person. For this reason, Scheler is right to say that a human being (as the being who develops science) 'is the ascetic of life'.

But this is not the attitude of life—of any living being, of any person; it cannot even be the definitive attitude of the scientist, or of the philosopher, as a person-who-lives. Life is praxis, and the world of life is a world of values. It is made up of things that are *noemata* of the second order, they are 'good things' (or 'bad things'; it is made up of actions, and works, which aim at realising values, by turning them into facts and things'.[20]

However, Preti's approach here seems to reaffirm the existence of an underlying dichotomy between the world of knowledge (theoretical truth) and the world of life (evaluation and value). Indeed, Preti himself, in *Retorica e logica*, albeit for many and different reasons, always strongly confirmed this dichotomy, although, as emerges also from this quotation, he did not overlook the strategic importance of the new phenomenological approach to the problem of knowledge and the question itself of the normative disciplines. In fact, from the quotation just given, it emerges that the 'world' in both the theoretical and the practical sphere, always constitutes a universal and complex set of relationships which, in the theoretical sphere, focuses precisely on the elements of knowledge (what we have indicated as the technical-scientific assets available to each specific society), while in the

---

[20]G. Preti, *Retorica e logica*, op. cit., pp. 427–428, while the quotation immediately following in the text is taken from p. 449.

context of praxis the 'world' refers, instead, to a particular and specific set of axiological connections. This should not lead us to forget, as Preti himself never forgets (I will borrow his words again), that

> the axiological culture, by its motivations, by the practical plans themselves that it implies in its tendency to implement values by bringing them into existence, relies on scientific culture: and an axiological picture of the world always presupposes a scientific picture of existence (of nature, history, etc.). The non-coincidence of the picture of the world used by axiological culture with that presented by science produces a historical crisis of civilisation, and therefore represents a dynamic element of change (I always speak within civilisation, that is, on the ground of the reflected cultural life).

It is therefore necessary to focus our attention now on these elements, because these two 'worlds' if they refer to the overall history of the Western tradition, are configured just like the two real 'engines' both privileged and indispensable, *within which* and *thanks to which*, our history has on the whole developed through the centuries. Furthermore, these two different worlds (the theoretical and the axiological) within them present quite peculiar dynamics, which must therefore be studied and comprehended in their specific (albeit relative) autonomy. Thirdly and finally, last but not least, as we have seen, these two 'worlds' also have their own specific and fruitful interrelation, of which a progressive critical awareness has been reached to the extent that the rigid dichotomy between facts and values has been progressively challenged, discussed and criticised, to the point that, by Husserl, its privileged and absolute value was overturned, while this dichotomy was transformed into a flexible heuristic tool for the critical understanding of Western history and of our own human condition. This then also helps us to understand the legitimacy itself with which an author like Preti has in any case decided to hold firm the empiricist dichotomy between theoretical disciplines and the axiological world, by electing it as his privileged heuristic tool to better investigate the developments of the 'two cultures' (the logical-scientific and the axiological) within Western history. As can easily be perceived even from these few considerations, the problem faced is by no means simple and therefore deserves to be analysed critically, with all due caution.

The fundamental point, as I see it, seems to be to recognise, with Husserl, that scientific knowledge constitutes, as we can find again in his *Logical Investigations*, 'purely theoretical truths, ideal in character, rooted in their own semantic content and not straying beyond it. They can accordingly not be affected by any actual or imagined change in the world of *matter of fact*.'[21]

---

[21] E. Husserl, *Logical Investigations*, op. cit., Vol. I, p. 97 (no italics in the text). The quotations that follow in the text are taken from the following pages, again from the first volume: p. 125 (italics in the text); p. 119; p. 113; p. 112; pp. 130–131 ('not' and 'its' in

In which the whole critical distance that exists between the phenomenological and empiricist approaches re-emerges. From this point of view, in fact, the heart of scientific knowledge is not rooted in experience, nor is it possible any longer to conceive scientific knowledge as a product of experience. On the contrary, the value of scientific knowledge is instead rooted in those 'purely theoretical truths, ideal in character' which are formed precisely within the ambit of *meaning* without ever transcending it. If a human being defined by empiricism is a person who learns from experience, for Husserl, on the contrary human beings learn only by virtue of their own critical intelligence, with which they challenge, question and interpret the world, even that of experience, through *open meanings* by means of which *intentionality* strives to identify *ideal laws* capable of pointing out *objective links between things*. This naturally also implies a very different kind of anthropology, since for Husserl it is evident that the superiority of human beings over other living forms is based on their intelligence itself:

> Man's superiority lies in his intelligence. He is not solely a being who brings perception and experience to bear on external situations: he also thinks, employs concepts, to overcome the narrow limits of his intuition. Through conceptual knowledge he penetrates to rigorous causal laws, which permit him to foresee the course of future phenomena, to reconstruct the course of past phenomena, to calculate the possible reactions of environing things in advance, and to dominate them practically, and all this to a vastly greater extent, and with vastly more confidence, than would otherwise be possible. *Science d'ou prevoyance, prevoyance d'ou action*, as Comte tellingly remarks. Whatever misery the one-sidedly overstrained yearning to know may bring to the individual thinker, and that not seldom, the fruits, the treasures of science ultimately accrue to the whole of humanity.

Science, which has ideal truths as its privileged content, therefore originates by an effort of thought and ideas with which we are able to reflect in an innovative—today we would say counterfactual—way on the world of experience itself. This accentuation of the role of ideas, thoughts and intelligence in no way negates the value and function of experience, only it places the function of experience not at the beginning of knowledge, but at the always fundamental moment of its experimental verification. From this perspective, Husserl's vision comes clearly into conflict with the traditional Baconian image of science, according to which scientific knowledge is rooted, *primarily*, in the context of the sense experience of the world. On the other hand, for Husserl, as already for Kant, scientific knowledge cannot even be configured, if we do not understand the fundamental heuristic role played

---

italics in the text, the other italics are mine); p. 132 (no italics in the text); p. 133; p. 149 (italics in the text).

by human intelligence, by our ability to succeed in challenging the world in the light of some ideal truths with which we test our ability to understand the objective links between the things of the world. Of course, due to the phenomenological correlativity that exists between subject and object, it is not possible to "attribute" the cognitive capacity of knowledge to the ideal component alone. In fact, if the latter can actually elaborate, by means of *meanings*, an *ideal* understanding of the world, it is then necessary to submit this merely ideal explanation of the world to a check, to a verification, and also to a possible falsification. But this decisive experimental check is no longer configured *near the source* of science, but *near the conclusion* of scientific inference. Consequently, the constitutive inference of scientific reasoning is no longer the *inductivist* one variously theorised by almost every empiricism of modernity (including the anti-metaphysical verification principle of twentieth-century logical empiricism), but the one of *deductive* inference through which scientific knowledge is configured as an inference capable of making a *computational synthesis of critical integration of reality* which, by constructing virtually and eidetically objective data, makes it possible, in fact, to achieve some *objective knowledge* of the physical world that we can and must subsequently critically test (precisely through verifications and/or falsifications) performed through an accurate and rigorous experimental critical mediation of the different theoretical predictions. This exactly constitutes the decisive innovation of the Kantian transcendentalist stance, which theorised the decisive role of the 'Copernican revolution' precisely to underline how any 'object' of knowledge is such only and solely within a very precise theoretical perspective, within a specific and rigorous conceptual and linguistic universe. The fundamental Kantian swerve, to which Husserl himself refers in a theoretically privileged way—beyond and also *against* his own brief and often reticent explicit acknowledgments—is on a clear collision course with the traditional empiricist image of science that from Hume onwards (but also, and above all, from Francis Bacon onwards) has instead ended up by constituting a sort of widespread common sense for the epistemologists of the last few centuries. Husserl follows exactly the hermeneutic path inaugurated by Kant, by pointing out how, without doubt, animals' actions (which certainly humans share with mammals as a class to which the human species belongs) are largely based on representations and judgments derived inductively and directly from experience (it would suffice to mention—to give just one emblematic example—Aristotelian physics, which constitutes an intelligent rationalisation of the world of common experience). But alongside these fundamental and indispensable actions that put us on a par with animals, there is also an intelligent understanding of the world that requires, instead, a counterfactual reflection, in order to produce original computational syntheses of the critical integration of the experience itself, as human beings have begun to do systematically, from the birth of modern science onwards. In this case we then focus on identifying some certain 'ideal objects ideationally apprehended in the correlates of our acts' precisely because

> [e]ach truth stands as an ideal unit over against an endless, unbounded possibility of correct statements which have its form and its matter in common. Each actual judgement, which belongs to this ideal manifold, will fulfil, either in its mere form or in its matter, the ideal conditions for its own possible inward evidence. The laws of pure logic are truths rooted in the concept of truth, and in concepts essentially related to this concept. They state, in relation to possible acts of judgement, and on the basis of their mere form, the ideal conditions of the possibility or impossibility of their inner evidence. Of these two sorts of conditions of the inwardly evident, the former relates to the special constitution of the sorts of psychical being which the psychology of the period recognizes, psychological induction being limited by experience. The other conditions, however, have the character of ideal laws, and hold generally for every possible consciousness.

There is therefore an evident discrepancy between the psychological-empirical conception of the world and its objective-ideal conception, which in turn refers to the gap existing between the descriptive psychology as defined by empiricist systems and the epistemology of the critical-rationalist system outlined by Husserl:

> The distinction between the psychological mode of treatment, whose terms function as class-terms for mental states, and the objective or ideal mode of treatment where the same terms stand for ideal genera and species, is not a subsidiary, or a merely subjective distinction. It determines the difference between essentially distinct sciences. Pure logic and arithmetic, as sciences dealing with the ideal singulars belonging to certain genera (or of what is founded a priori in the ideal essence of these genera) are separated from psychology, which deals with the individual singulars belonging to certain empirical classes.

Why? Precisely because scientific analyses (and, consequently, also epistemological ones as critical meta-reflections concerning individual disciplines) constitute 'analyses of meaning, and not in any degree psychological ones. Not individual phenomena, but forms of intentional unities are subjected to analysis, not experiences of syllogising, but syllogisms.'

In this way the transcendentalist analysis, inaugurated by Kant and subsequently freely further developed by Husserl from his phenomenological perspective, is placed on a different level of epistemological investigation, which is critically and in a completely original way detached from the traditional plane of the empiricist tradition. Indeed, for Husserl,

> [t]he question is not how experience, whether naive or scientific, arises, but what must be its content if it is to have objective validity: we must ask on what ideal elements and laws such *objective validity of knowledge of the real* is founded—more generally, on what any knowledge is founded—and how the performance involved in knowledge should be properly understood. We are, in other words, *not* interested in the origins and changes of our world-presentation, but in the objective right which the world-presentation of science claims as against any other world-presentation, which leads it to call *its* world the objectively true one. Psychology looks for perspicuous explanations of the formation of world-presentations. World-science (the sum total of the different sciences of the real) wishes to know perspicuously what obtains *in reality*, what makes up the true, the actual world. Epistemology, however, wishes to grasp perspicuously, from an objectively ideal standpoint, in what the possibility of perspicuous knowledge of the real consists, the possibility of science and of knowledge in general.

This then leads Husserl to emphasise the role and function of *objective ideality* through which scientific knowledge is established, since the latter, as it should now be evident, does not arise, *passively*, from experience, but is developed, instead, starting from an *objective ideality* through which it is possible to delineate, counterfactually, a theory by virtue of which one is then able to formulate a deductive computational synthesis that allows us to critically integrate experience itself. As Husserl again points out,

> [b]efore all economising of thought, we must already know our ideal, we must know what science *ideally* aims at, what law-governed connections, what basic laws and derived laws etc., *ideally* are and do, before we can discuss and assess the thought-economical function of knowing them.

Which then helps to better understand the obvious conflict that cannot fail to arise between the intrinsic 'necessity' of scientific knowledge (connected to the very concept of 'scientific law' and the predictability of scientific theories which, precisely, presuppose when something *must necessarily* happen) and the construction of empirical representations and of accidental convictions themselves, which appear to be instead devoid of connections with a binding force, even though they possess an undeniable average utility.

> The errors of this trend toward thought-economics, are due in the end to the fact, that those who go with it, like all psychologistic thinkers, have an interest in knowledge which stops short at the empirical side of science. They fail in a certain manner to see the wood for the mere trees. They concern themselves with science as a biological phenomenon, and do not see that they are touching upon the epistemological problem of science as ideally unified, objective truth.

As Karl Popper often observed, the theory of special relativity, from its first formulation, had always expected the *curvature* of rays of light as they pass through a strong gravitational field. Precisely this prediction, on the basis of which Einstein accurately established—by rigorous merely deductive inference—how a ray of light should necessarily behave in this specific physical situation (by ignoring a common misconception concerning the constantly rectilinear character of the diffusion of light in infinite space) constituted, at the same time, the main challenge to Einstein's theory and its glory. *The challenge*, because by advancing this prediction Einstein actually made, in the words of Imre Lakatos, his theory of relativity stick its 'neck' out to the cleaver of experience, so to speak. As is well known, this prediction was formulated as early as 1905, but was then experimentally verified only in 1919, which accounts for its *glory*. Indeed, only since then, and of course not surprisingly, was Einstein finally proclaimed one of the greatest physicists in the history of mankind. But it is precisely this point connected with the necessity of scientific prediction that has always constituted the concern of empiricism which, with the classic—and certainly glorious and brilliant—Humean analysis of the cause-effect link, nevertheless shows that *ideal ideational role* of scientific theories themselves, which are by no means reduced to the assets of empirical experience, because, if anything, as we have seen, they rather arise from the awareness of the heuristic function of counterfactual ideals that enable us to delineate those deductive computational syntheses with which objective scientific knowledge is developed.

8 The general conditions of the possibility of science according to Husserl

But what are the ideal conditions for the possibility of science? Husserl did not ignore this problem, explicitly investigating the 'conditions of the possibility of science in general' in which he produced some considerations that must be kept in mind, because they provide the most fruitful key to explain the link between the objective knowledge elaborated by science and the world of axiology. As already elucidated previously, for Husserl 'the essential aim of scientific knowledge can only be achieved through theory, in the strict sense of the nomological sciences.' Husserl therefore felt authorised to replace the question concerning the conditions of possibility of science in general with the question concerning the '*conditions of the possibility of theory in general*'. In this regard we have already seen that, for Husserl,

> [a] theory as such consists of truths, and its form of connection is a deductive one. To answer our question is therefore also to answer the

more general question as to the conditions of the possibility of *truth in general*, and again of *deductive unity* in general.²²

Of course, it does not escape Husserl that by investigating this a further question is raised more directly connected with a quite necessary generalisation of the question as to the 'conditions of the possibility of experience'. This is a crucial epistemological challenge that was first identified by Kant in the *Critique of Pure Reason*. Which, if it were still required, confirms that deep underlying connection (often unmentioned by Husserl himself) that exists between Husserlian phenomenology and Kantian criticism, to which I referred earlier. However, Husserl continued, the precise meaning of this question must be further clarified with greater rigor and, in this regard, he added the following:

> It might very well be at first understood *in the subjective sense*, in which case it would be better expressed as a question as to the conditions of the possibility of *theoretical knowledge* in general, or, more generally, of inference in general or knowledge in general, and in the case of any *possible* human being. Such conditions are in part *real*, in part *ideal*. We shall ignore the former, the psychological conditions. Naturally the possibility of knowledge in a psychological regard embraces all the causal conditions on which our thinking depends. *Ideal* conditions for the possibility of knowledge may, as said before, be of two sorts. They are either *noetic* conditions which have their grounds, *a priori*, in the Idea of Knowledge as such, without any regard to the empirical peculiarity of human knowledge as psychologically conditioned, or they are purely *logical* conditions, i.e., they are grounded purely in the 'content' of our knowledge.

It is worth mentioning that this second aspect, which concerns both *noetic* structures and *logical* ones, is at the centre of Husserl's reflection. This appears decisive also for our epistemological reflection. For what reason? Just because, thanks to the *doctrine of intentionality*, a concept (i.e., an *idea*) outlines an objective compass coinciding with its own *noematic* content, which, in fact, determines and qualifies it as that specific idea that becomes part of the different noematic connections that structure the very fabric of objective knowledge, to which we are referring within a specific disciplinary field. Exactly at this point Kant's 'Copernican revolution' comes into play with a fundamental role also in Husserl's reflection.

In the first place, because Kantianism conceives philosophy as a critical meta-reflection that is expressed on previous contents of reflection. This constitutes an important and decisive turning point, also because it annuls philosophy's supposed ability to operate on its own (quite mythical) specific

---

²²E. Husserl, *Logical Investigations*, op. cit., Vol. I, p. 149 (italics in the text); the following citations in the text are taken from pp. 149–150 (italics in the text).

object. By losing the reference to its own specific metaphysical object, philosophical reflection, as a critical meta-reflection, then opens up, with conscious epistemological humility, to every discipline with which it can and must confront itself, in order to learn precisely the infinite complexity of the world, which reveals itself in the actual knowledge constructed by humans through science.[23] But by turning to these disciplines to learn and clarify the multiple and different disciplinary contents, philosophy then brings with it its own particular methodical (indeed, philosophical) habit, with which it exercises its *critical meta-reflection* by investigating the meaning and significance of these various disciplines, by studying their meanings, their categories and universes of discourse, the way to pose problems as well as the way to solve them, models of inference, etc., etc., without however ever recognising and identifying itself, uncritically, with a specific scientific conceptual universe as the object of its study. This makes it possible that philosophy investigates a scientific discipline by fully highlighting, from an *epistemological* perspective, the appropriate specifically *conceptual* dimension (a dimension of thought which is often lost sight of or certainly forgotten or neglected, both by the composite tradition of empiricism as well as by that of positivism, not to then mention all the various and different metaphysical traditions which have often denied to science even the quality of *being able to think*, which they naturally considered as their exclusive prerogative. This happened, just to offer an emblematic example, in relation to Heidegger's ontological metaphysics, clearly influenced by Nazi theories— an influence that is now finally overtly recognised and no longer dismissed with a significant shrug of the shoulders ...). Precisely this meta-reflective critical attitude turns out to be profoundly in tune with the theoretical attitude of Husserlian phenomenology, which always addresses positive knowledge (that of the sciences), by inviting us to suspend just the natural orientation and perform a decisive *epoché* that makes it possible to develop the *analytical* plan of Kant's reflection that we have just mentioned.

In the second place, from the perspective of Kant's 'Copernican revolution' also the way of considering a *concept* changes: now it can be conceived, *à la* Husserl, as a *non-representative and non-ontological ideal unity*, with which the multiple data of empirical intuition can be connected. In this way

---

[23]In *Ideas Pertaining to a Pure Phenomenology and to a Phenomenological Philosophy*, Third Book: *Phenomenology and the Foundation of Sciences*, translated by T. E. Klein and W. E. Pohl, M. Nijhoff Publishers, The Hague, Boston, London, 1980, Husserl wrote: "Treasures of knowledge may lie in the sciences, indeed, they must lie in them, since we cannot doubt that the claim of their statements to validity is a good one, even though within limits still to be defined. But these treasures of knowledge we do not have; we must first obtain them. For knowledge is insight, is truth drawn from Intuition and thereby completely understood. Only through a work of elucidation and making evident, carried out anew on the given sciences, do we bring out the intrinsic values that are hidden in them." (p. 82).

the concept is transformed into a heuristic criterion for understanding the world, which makes it possible for us to realise a computational deduction by means of which we are able to present a critical integration of experience. This makes it viable, as can be immediately comprehended, the elaboration of a much more articulated critical conception of the same experience, since the latter no longer refers to a merely passive function, because, on the contrary, it requires to be always critically fertilised by thoughts, which are capable of reading and understanding it critically, by bringing it back to a unifying function, coinciding with the concept itself. The object-of-knowledge—coinciding with the different disciplinary objects specific to each discipline—therefore refers to a logical-transcendental function of critical integration of experience, by means of which we are able, in fact, to unify, within a determined universe of (purely conceptual) discourse, proper and specific to a particular discipline, all the multiple intuitive contents.

Consequently, and in the third place, the object of knowledge is no longer configured either as a prerequisite for research, or as a totally separate object from the knowledge developed within a specific disciplinary sphere. If anything, once again deeply in tune with Kant's 'Copernican revolution' the object of knowledge is configured—to express it *à la* Sartre—as a specific 'object-of-knowing' that can never be considered by arbitrarily isolating it from the actual field of its scientific discipline. For what reason? Because outside of that theoretical context it no longer has any existence. For this reason, when we speak, for example, of a concept such as that coinciding with an 'element' we are always expected to immediately specify the different disciplinary ambit to which we refer, because the meaning of the concept of 'element' changes, even profoundly, according to the discipline we are referring to (an 'element' in physics is very different from an element in medicine, biology, maths, music, geometry, etc.). Why are we faced with this multiplicity of elements? Exactly because the object-of-knowing can no longer be imagined as *external* to the act of knowing itself (for example as an 'internal' or 'external' element), because for Husserl it is configured as *a content of the act of knowing itself*, i.e., as a *constitutive polarity of the very objectivity of the ideal unity* through which we objectively study a specific area of the world (physical, biological, mathematical, algebraic, medical, etc.).

From this innovative epistemological and hermeneutic perspective, 'reality', 'existence' and 'truth' itself can no longer be conceived as a sort of archetypal form of reality, presupposed in relation to knowledge, because, if anything, each of them is configured instead, as a *specific modality within the very structures of objective knowledge*, which is constituted by always taking *primarily* into account the specific conditions of a scientific discipline concerning the constitution of the object itself in a specific theoretical and experimental field. But these constitutive conditions of the object-of-knowledge, conceived as an internal moment of the specific structures of the knowledge developed by the discipline taken into consideration, at the same time provide the conditions of our own experience, which is no longer configured as a neutral and passive dimension, precisely because our experience is formed instead within the ideal tension, with which the world is understood according to its objective necessity.

In this way it seems that Husserlian phenomenology, as an insightful development of the 'Copernican revolution' outlined by Kant, is then able to critically re-establish empiricism itself, by freeing it from all its traditional psychological (and sceptical) limits to inaugurate a new and fruitful perspective and epistemological horizon. In fact, if we assume, with Husserl, the traditional doctrine of *intentionality* as a fundamental structure of human knowledge, then the object-of-knowing can only be configured as a *noema*, that is, as an object that turns out to exist *inside* the act of knowing, precisely because it constitutes the *thought content of that act*, or a content *targeted by intentionality*. Moreover, this decisive Husserlian consideration must also be kept in mind:

> Talk about recognising objects, and talk about fulfilling a meaning-intention, therefore express the same fact, merely from different standpoints. The former adopts the standpoint of the object meant, while the latter has the two acts as its foci of interest. Phenomenologically the acts are always present, while the objects are sometimes non-existent. Talk of fulfilment therefore characterises the *phenomenological* essence of the recognitive relation more satisfactorily. It is a primitive phenomenological fact, that acts of signification [*Signifikation*] and acts of intuition [*Intuition*] can enter into this peculiar relation. Where they do so, where some act of meaning-intention fulfils itself in an intuition, we also say: 'The object of intuition is known through its concept' or 'The correct name has been applied to the object appearing before us.[24]

Indeed, in Husserl's phenomenology the *noema* is configured as the critical synthesis of two different moments: the intentional *morphé* (a function of the critical integration of experience) that addresses the world with a specific intention of significance and the sensory material, the *hyle*, specific to hyletic data, which is precisely targeted by the intentionality of *morphé*, and, however, has the potential ability to saturate (or not) just that specific *project of signification* through which intentionality tries to conceptually

---

[24]E. Husserl, *Logical Investigations*, op. cit., Vol. II, p. 206, text between square brackets and italics not in the English text. In this regard, see also the Italian translation with German parallel text of the important volume by Husserl, *La teoria del significato*. Introduction, translation, notes and apparatus by Anselmo Caputo, Bompiani, Milan, 2008, with my *Preface* published on pp. 5–21.

understand the world. It is the functions of critical integration of experience which make hyletic data intentional; these, without the presence of *morphé* would be completely 'deaf' and impenetrable. Indeed experience, *by itself*, is always 'deaf' if we are not able to read it as a unity, in the light of some specific theoretical intentionality, as Galileo Galilei, the acknowledged father of modern science, already knew. Galileo observed, in fact, that nature, although the 'observant executrix of God's commands' is nevertheless always 'inexorable and deaf to our entreaties, will not alter or change the course of her effects.'[25] In short, nature for Galileo is 'deaf and inexorable' in relation to human beings, who should then be able, on their own, to critically probe the deafness of matter, in order to understand it *conceptually* with the aim of identifying within it that cogent necessity capable of tracing the multiple 'passions' of a given phenomenon back to a physical law (as argued on the third day of *The Discourses and Mathematical Demonstrations Relating to Two New Sciences*). To achieve this cognitive end, human beings can only count on their intelligence and critical abilities (always connected with a specific force of will as well as with a certain necessary physiological well-being). After all, Galileo's treatment of naturally accelerated motion opens with the following consideration:

> Et prima, definitionem ei, quo utitur natura, oppresses congruentem investigare atque explicare convenit. Quamvis enim aliquam lationis speciem ex arbitrio confinare, et consequentes eius passiones contemplari, non sit inconveniens [...], tamen, whenquidem quidam accelerationis specie graveum descendentium utitur natura, eroundem speculari passiones decrevimus, si eam, quam allaturi sumus de our motu accelerato definitionem, cum essentia motus naturaliter accelerati congruere contigerit. Quod tandem, post diuturnas mentis agitationes, repperisse confidimus; ea potissimum ducti ratione, quia symtomatis, deinceps a nobis demonstratis, first respond to atque congruere videntur ea, qua naturalia experimenta sensi repraesant (VIII, 197)

> And first of all it seems desirable to find and explain a definition best fitting natural phenomena. For anyone may invent an arbitrary type of motion and discuss its properties; [...] but we have decided to consider the phenomena of bodies falling with an acceleration such as actually occurs in nature and to make this definition of accelerated motion exhibit the essential features of observed accelerated motions.

---

[25]The quotes from Galileo are taken from *Letter to the Grand Duchess Christina of Tuscany* (1615) and *Third Letter on the Sunspots* (1613). Italian edition: New reprint of Edizione Nazionale *Le opere di Galileo Galilei*, edited by Antonio Favaro, G. Barbera Editore, Florence 1968 (first edition 1890–1909), 20 volumes in 21 tomes. The first quotation in the text is taken from Volume V, p.316, the second quotation from Volume V, p.218 and the third from Volume VIII, p.197).

> And this, at last, after repeated efforts we trust we have succeeded in doing. In this belief we are confirmed mainly by the consideration that experimental results are seen to agree with and exactly correspond with those properties which have been, one after another, demonstrated by us.[26]

This significant link of congruence that Galileo identified as existing between his innovative physical theory, *ex suppositione*, of naturally accelerated motion and the actual physical properties of this motion, experimentally controlled in the laboratory,[27] is precisely related to the Husserlian problem concerning the possibility that every science has of *being able* to identify objective links existing between the objects within the scope of its analysis. Indeed, it is precisely on this level that the more or less complete 'saturation' of a particular project of giving meaning to the world takes place. This project is originated by the specific intentionality of a scientific theory, by virtue of which a specific functional *morphé* formulates computational syntheses of hyletic data, thus configuring a discipline-specific knowledge, which, as we have seen, always arises from a specific critical integration of our experience. In this perspective, 'nature' can therefore only be configured as a 'correlate of consciousness: Nature *is* only as being constituted in regular concatenations of consciousness.'[28] Which, in fact, allows Husserl to distinguish, within the intentionality, as mentioned, 'between the *components proper* of intentive mental processes and their *intentional correlates*' since 'corresponding in every case to the multiplicity of Data pertaining to the really inherent noetic content, there is a multiplicity of Data, demonstrable in actual pure intuition, in a correlative '*noematic content*' or, in short, in the '*noema*'.' Consequently, for Husserl,

> the 'parenthesis' undergone by perception prevents any judgment about perceived actuality (i.e., any 'judgment' having its basis in unmodified perception, thus taking up into itself its positing). But it does not prevent the judgment about the fact that perception is consciousness *of* an actuality (the positing of which, however, should not be 'effected'; and it does not prevent any description of this perceptually appearing 'actuality' as appearing with the particular

---

[26] Galileo Galilei, *Dialogues Concerning Two New Sciences*. Translated from the Italian and Latin into English by Henry Crew and Alfonso de Salvio. With an Introduction by Antonio Favaro, Macmillan, New York, 1914. For further analysis of Galileo's epistemological stance see F. Minazzi, *Galileo 'filosofo geometra'*, Rusconi, Milan 1994.

[27] On this theme of the analysis of Galileo's epistemological stance see F. Minazzi, *Galileo 'filosofo geometra'* op. cit. passim.

[28] E. Husserl, *Ideas Pertaining to a Pure Phenomenology and to a Phenomenological Philosophy*, First Book *General Introduction to a Pure Phenomenology*, Translated by F Kersten, Martinus Nijhoff Publishers, The Hague/Boston/Lancaster, 1983; p.116; p. 213 (italics in the text); p. 214 (italics in the text); pp. 220–221 (italics in the text).

ways in which it is here intended to, appearing only 'one-sidedly' in this or that orientation; and so forth.

9 The influence of objective scientific knowledge on axiology

Precisely the correlation between the noetic moment and the noematic moment allows us to better investigate not only the overall nature of scientific knowledge, but also the links themselves that can be established, historically, between the 'world' of science and the 'world' of axiology. In truth, many thinkers, from Plato to the present, have variously underlined the fruitful connection that is always established between *life* and *culture*, between *Geist* and *Leben*, between the drives of life and the dimension of rational reflection. In this regard, Preti, a thinker mentored by Banfi[29], took into account, in particular, the reflection of the German philosopher Georg Simmel, whom he came into contact with above all thanks to the mediation of his mentor Banfi. Therefore, in *Retorica e logica* Preti writes:

> Culture, any culture, is born out of life: but, once it has arisen, it exercises a kind of asceticism with respect to life, keeps it in suspension, 'turns its back on it' and elaborates ideal forms of validity that obey immanent criteria, no longer that of their immediate vitality. This is true for the specific and distinct value of truth, as for any other value. But, at this point, the forms of culture put life itself in crisis: they disconcert it at the very moment that they tend to reorganise it within broader, richer, more comprehensive horizons. So they come back to life as 'more life'.[30]

Preti, as a faithful follower of Banfi, thus stresses the rich fundamentally antinomic tension which always arises between *Geist* and *Leben*: if in fact life, as a set of vital drives, requires, in the first place, indeed, to be *lived*, on the other hand, thought performs a sort of radical *epoché* compared to the world of praxis or *Lebenswelt*, by placing it, in fact, in parentheses in order to apparently unfold in a dimension which, while taking root in lived experience, nevertheless is presumed to be configured independently of the experience itself. In this perspective *to live* a given reality (whatever it is) turns out to be fundamentally different from *reflecting* on this reality. Reflection must inevitably move away from life—and its blind impulses—in order to create its own 'critical lenses' in the light of which it addresses

---

[29]For an overall picture of Banfi's mentoring of Preti and of all the intertwining connections within the 'School of Milan' see, in particular, the following volumes: *Sul bios theoretikós di Giulio Preti*, edited by F. Minazzi, Mimesis, Milan-Udine 2015, 2 Vols.; *Mario Dal Pra nella 'scuola di Milano'*, edited by F. Minazzi, therein 2018 and *Sulla scuola di Milano*, edited by F. Minazzi, Giunti, Florence, 2019.

[30]G. Preti, *Retorica e logica*, op. cit., p. 448, while the quotation that immediately follows in the text is taken from p. 449.

the world as if observing it from a distance. However, the undoubted critical gain that thought cannot fail to acquire in this way, by evading the drives and constraints of experience as such, involves a price: that of abstraction and detachment from the body, flesh and blood, and from *lived experiences* themselves. Ultimately, philosophical reflection itself, precisely in its aspiration to universal criticism, is fuelled by this antinomy and is thus configured as a universal reflection that intends to prescind from time while being unable to do anything but operate in the midst of time ...

As we have seen, for Husserl theoretical disciplines always constituted the foundation of normative disciplines. With the consequence that it can then be deduced that every axiological 'world' always presupposes, as its basis (often unmentioned and hidden) an essential reference to the 'world' of scientific culture. Of course, between these two different 'worlds' or, if you prefer, levels of reflection, multiple relationships can always be established because the axiological culture can be in profound harmony with the scientific knowledge of its time, or it can instead create a discord—more or less serious, more or less profound—between scientific culture and the axiological world. When such a discord occurs, we may be faced with a historical crisis of civilisation that can lead to a catastrophic outcome, or to a revolutionary solution, through which a complete reshuffling of cards is performed in order to shape a new society and new prospects for growth and dynamic development. In this regard, Preti still observes that,

> [a]xiological culture, insofar as it is organised in a system of ethical institutions, tends to close itself in its substantial immutability, in its immanence—as we have seen. And by closing itself it becomes not only extra-vital ('more than life'), but anti-vital ('less life'). And this happens when its real presuppositions have changed, that is when an erroneous image of existence is developed—erroneous precisely from the point of view of knowledge.

Naturally, both of these different worlds have their own specific degrees of 'stickiness' and are also characterised by the specific way in which they are structured and organised. The axiological dimension is thus characterised by a basic contrast which, generally, is established between the dimension of the *Moralität* (which basically refers to the moral conscience of the individual) and its more strictly ethical dimension (the *Sittlichkeit*, to use the Hegelian terminology again, in its turn influenced by the Kantian one) which is recognised, indeed, in the ethical customs of a specific historical society. Generally, at least on the axiological level, the growth and spread of a new specific need for morality constitutes the leaven of a historical society, because this new *Moralität* seeks precisely to establish itself as a hegemonic element by opposing in this way the traditional *ethos* now rooted in a custom perceived as completely 'natural' and, as such, 'unchangeable' (while it is itself a historical product). The new morality intends precisely to undermine the old ethics in order to be able to establish itself as new ethics that is the expression of a different morality: by subverting the traditional customs, the new morality in fact aims to take their place. In this way morality ends up by historically transforming itself into an ethic which, sooner or later, inevitably, in turn, will be challenged by a new and unexpected morality that will oppose it as an ethical form at that point outdated, obsolete and inadequate for a world which, in the meantime, has changed profoundly. This does not at all open the way to any form of absolute relativism (in itself contradictory) because, if anything, by accepting an interesting critical suggestion of Ludovico Geymonat, expressed in *Scienza e realismo* (1977), it can be observed that, in the course of history, this dialectical relationship between morality and ethos constitutes an interesting series of different cognitive assets specific and peculiar to the civil institutions within which human history unfolds. But in this respect, it is better to quote Geymonat directly. He writes and argues as follows:

> in the first chapter we explained, however, that science cannot be reduced to a collection of theories, each one enclosed in itself; that is, we have said that, to understand the whole meaning of these theories, it is not enough to examine them in isolation one from the other, but it is necessary to place them in what we have called the 'scientific-technical cultural heritage' in continuous evolution, which includes, besides individual theories considered in their completeness, a vast field of non-axiomatisable investigations (investigations ranging: from first explorations of a group of phenomena to attempts to frame them in this or that theory, from the most subtle methodological debates to the analysis of the philosophical implications of axioms assumed on the basis of our deductions, etc.). Well, something similar can be repeated, in our opinion, also for legal systems; that is, if we want to understand their full meaning, we cannot limit ourselves to examining them in isolation one from the other, but we must consider them in a wider framework that includes, in addition to the legal systems themselves, a complex of institutions, of unwritten laws, customs, etc.; therefore, the consideration of the time parameter is essential (as understood by the historical disciplines). We can call this the 'cultural heritage of civil institutions' in order to underline the analogy with the 'scientific-technical cultural heritage.' And just as in order to understand the dynamics of science, we should refer to this kind cultural heritage, so to understand the dynamics of legal systems it seems obvious that we will have to refer, not only to the individual systems considered in their entirety, but to that highly articulated and

variable framework, to which we have given the name of the 'cultural heritage of civil institutions'.[31]

To adequately understand the complex historical dynamics of this specific 'cultural heritage of civil institutions' it will be necessary to resort to its dialectical analysis, which, of course, can also be employed to understand the specific dynamics of the 'scientific-technical cultural heritage'. In any case, the world of science and that of axiology certainly present a different and specific 'stickiness' precisely because the scientific enterprise has as its vital, main and indispensable fulcrum, precisely *criticism* (while in the axiological ambit, as mentioned above, criticism constitutes, if anything, a moment which, in general, occurs mainly within the traditional dialectic between morality and ethics).

In this regard, Preti, by reflecting on the notions of 'truth' specific to the scientific world and the axiological world—or by analysing their respective 'souls' since the 'soul' that is the form of a culture, constitutes its notion of 'truth'[32]—offered the following, valuable, definition of scientific truth:

> while humanistic-literary truth is a value linked to universal concrete historically determined events/experiences, scientific truth is a value that refers to a *free ideal human universality in general*. 'Free' in the sense that it does not recognise any authority as such—neither of men, nor of scholars, nor of tradition: since even a single scientist can recognise it and assert it against even the most venerable and accredited opinions. 'Ideal' because it is, in a certain sense, abstract, that is (rather) formal: its criteria are formal criteria, in a certain sense a priori with respect to every possible experience and every possible discourse. It is not to the concrete (social) human being that it addresses itself, but to an ideal universally human audience, defined only and exclusively by operating and judging according to these criteria.

The criticism that science appeals to is, therefore, an essentially immanent and radical criticism, whose 'foundation' is provided solely by its own arguments, because it can never appeal to any other authority (either person, institution, or tradition). If, in fact, science appeals to an *auctoritas* it ends up by irremediably crippling its own critical spirit, which can only be fulfilled as a 'free ideal human universality in general'. Precisely for this reason scientific knowledge can never generate an absolute and non-transcendable

---

[31] L. Geymonat, *Scienza e realismo*, Feltrinelli, Milan 1977[1], 1982[2] (new revised and enlarged edition), pp. 124–125. On the more mature thought of Geymonat, see my third and most recent monograph about Geymonat: F. Minazzi, *Geymonat epistemologo*, Mimesis, Milan-Udine 2010.

[32] G. Preti, *Retorica e logica*, op.cit., p. 379, while the quotations that immediately follow in the text are taken, respectively, from pp. 386–387 (italics in the text) and from pp. 449–450 (italics in the text).

truth, because it can always radically question its own cognitive results. On the other hand, by working in this way, science does not fall into any contradictory absolute relativism, precisely because its knowledge is actually such as it is, or rather it constitutes a kind of *objective knowledge*, which is developed and established within a particular 'regional ontology' determined by the discipline itself whose scientific cognitive assets are possibly being examined.[33] This allows us to better understand the dynamic role that science and its objective knowledge can always exercise in relation to the world of axiology. As Preti further wrote,

> knowledge, as regulated by the autovalue of truth alone, is less sticky than *ethos*: of course, it also tends to be preserved, but the law of truth, with the accentuated asceticism it requires, neutralises most of the reasons for stickiness. Science is more 'unprejudiced' and therefore, by its own office, more responsive to the changes that occur in reality. Therefore, by operating critically against the old pseudo-theoretical basis that supports an archaic system of ethical institutions (and therefore of values), it forces it to change, thereby forcing the entire system to re-motivate itself, and therefore to reorganise itself: with the result that different ethical institutions will arise, and will often be *very* different from the previous ones. And so scientific ascesis is a tool for readjusting *ethos* to the demands of life: it restores its foundation to the world of values, the very condition of its effectiveness—it keeps open the ways of its own self-transcendence. This, and no other, is the primary function of scientific knowledge, *as knowledge*, within the historical dialectic of civilisation.

This then configures the eminently dynamic, critical and *liberating* function of the objective knowledge elaborated by science, precisely in relation to the world of values. It is significant that the objection of 'immorality' towards science and scientific knowledge itself has often been raised in the course of history. To the extent that the 'sacred' values of a society are threatened or vacillate on the verge of an epochal meltdown, then it is precisely science, which is *indifferent to values*, that has been variously judged (and condemned) as materialistic, atheist, mechanistic, anti-social and as socially dangerous. Moreover, there have been scientists and epistemologists who have belittled these criticisms by affirming that science is instead deeply sensitive to values and even intrinsically religious, precisely because there is also an intrinsic religiosity of scientificity itself ... But, as we have seen,

---

[33]For an original examination of the *L'oggettività e i suoi contesti* I refer both to the exhaustive analysis developed in the homonymous volume by Evandro Agazzi (Bompiani, Milan, 2018) and to my previous monographic study on the epistemological problem of objective knowledge: F. Minazzi, *Le saette dei tartari*, Franco Angeli, Milan, 2004. English version: Evandro Agazzi, *Scientific Objectivity and its Contexts*, Springer International Publishing, Cham, 2014.

science does not constitute a world of values, but rather it is configured, if anything, as a complex form of the objective spirit that is organized and forged around an immanent value such as that of scientific truth and immanent criticism, or rather of the objective knowledge of the world achieved by scientific thought through some arguments that can always be improved and made increasingly rigorous and critical. In this precise sense, then science knows only the concepts of true and false, while it completely ignores the concepts of good, bad, ugly, beautiful, adversable and desirable, as the seventeenth-century philosopher Spinoza already stated with great clarity. He elucidated, with undoubted in-depth analysis and clarity, precisely the pure theoretical ideal value of scientific knowledge. But then Spinoza himself paradoxically ended up by unduly overloading this right and correct image of objective scientific knowledge, by transforming it into an *amor intellectualis* which contrasts with the very 'soul' of scientific research. But the 'square circle' outlined by Spinoza was then actually realised also in subsequent human history whenever either an axiological value was wrongly attributed to science or this was attacked precisely because of its lack of values. Faced with this paradoxical situation, if we return to Husserl's approach, it appears clear that the founding noema of a world is precisely the cognitive and theoretical one, whose propositions are either true or false. In this perspective, as we have seen, the axiological dimension exists only on the condition that the primary object exists. Consider the history of witchcraft: witches were variously persecuted as long as it was believed that a discipline such as witchcraft actually existed and also to the extent that an effective cognitive significance was attributed to this discipline. But when the impossibility of witchcraft was finally realised, the persecution of witches gradually disappeared, precisely because its founding proposition—the theoretical-cognitive one concerning the existence of witches—had lost any possible objective value. Similarly, when the physiological pathological nature of epilepsy was finally recognised, the traditional and widespread belief in the 'sacred disease' gradually disappeared from the cultural horizon and epileptics were no longer persecuted as forces of evil or revered as diviners, because an attempt had finally been made to treat them as sick people.

From all these considerations then follows the *well-argued* consequence that we can express by sharing an insightful conclusive remark by an epistemologist like Geymonat:

> what the masses spontaneously but firmly oppose to those who, on the basis of these findings, set themselves up as a severe critic of scientific-technical progress, to which they would like to oppose a culture 'free' from any scientific contamination, can be summarised in a few lines: to stop this progress by invoking purely moralistic arguments or by trying to counteract old ideas of the world with an idealistic background, is the fruit of mere fantasy and is therefore doomed to failure. The real main

contradiction of our culture is not between scientific-technical progress and the romantic aspiration to a kind of life that belonged to the pre-scientific era (it might be that it can appear worthy of regret only to those who have not realistically examined all of its aspects, including the most cruel and repugnant ones). The main contradiction of our culture is the contradiction itself (between labour and capital) inherent in the societies within which our culture (the scientific-technical one as well as the humanistic one) takes root and develops. It follows that the means to which one must resort to eradicate the evils generated, within this society, by scientific-technical progress are very different and far more serious than those often proposed by the romantic denigrators of scientific rationality and, with it, of the whole modern world. [In this perspective it is necessary] to initiate a truly new civilisation, which dialectically moves beyond the current one, starting precisely from its contradictions: contradictions that cannot be simplistically denied or veiled as if they were a figment of our imagination, but, on the contrary, should be investigated in depth, exasperated, taken to their extreme consequences, until an authentic solution emerges, which can only consist in a real, courageous, revolutionary process.[34]

From this perspective of a much called-for radical social change on a global level, we can then conclude our brief reflection by affirming, paradoxically, this time with Spinoza, that the authentic value of a scientific truth that is *wertfrei* is rooted precisely in its *critical liberating force*. This is its undoubted historical value, which we cannot renounce, since it is this that has historically helped us to emerge from barbarism ...

---

[34]L. Geymonat, *Scienza e realismo*, op. cit., pp. 142–143.

Scientific worldviews and models in Hermann von Helmholtz and Werner Heisenberg

Gregor Schiemann

Fakultät für Geistes- und Kulturwissenschaften, Fachgruppe Philosophie, Bergische Universität Wuppertal, Gaußstraße 20, 42119 Wuppertal, Germany

By scientific worldviews I mean conceptions that contain assumptions about and descriptions of the world. They are based on scientific knowledge and aim to increase this knowledge. They also serve in part to make scientific findings popular in society, and in part they take up non-scientific ideas. Their content need not be limited to theoretical discussions, but can include ethical principles, practical instructions for action, or also aesthetic evaluations. Scientific worldviews have accompanied modern science since its inception and continue to play an important role in the development of knowledge and the self-understanding of science.

Scientific worldviews and models may be related to each other in a variety of ways. I make a basic distinction between two relations, and I will discuss an example of each of them. On the one hand, models were and still are developed within the framework of scientific worldviews. For example, worldviews are the starting point for formulating models for phenomena that these conceptions do not as yet sufficiently capture. On the other hand, however, scientific worldviews can themselves take the form of a model. For example, worldviews must make simplifications in order to grasp the complexity of the world even approximately. Presumably, the two relations need not be mutually exclusive. In the two examples I discuss, however, the two relations are contrasted.

Hermann von Helmholtz, from whose work I take the first example, played an active role in the increase in use of models in natural science during the nineteenth century. This growing relevance, which paved the way for the current position of models, still unfolded essentially within the framework of the mechanistic worldview that can be traced back to the early modern transformation of science. Helmholtz was considered the leading exponent of this view. I will discuss one of the last of his mechanical models, that of so-called monocyclic systems. His aim in developing this model was to establish the similarity between the structures and representations of mechanical and thermodynamic phenomena in order to contribute to the understanding of the latter. Helmholtz's approach, which from our present-day perspective was misguided, led him to the limits of mechanistic model construction. Olivier Darrigol has proposed a Wittgensteinian image to capture this: Helmholtz climbed the ladder of model construction to the highest rung and then threw it away, in order, on the level thus reached, to make the transition to a description of the world from general principles.[1]

The collapse of the mechanistic worldview, the foundation of modern physics and further advances in science provided starting points for the second example, the one developed by Werner Heisenberg. Heisenberg took up a conception whose origins go back to antiquity—namely, that reality is organised in levels in accordance with superior principles. He formulated his approach as a model that systematically related scientific knowledge and his own life experience to phenomena of the respective levels. The application of mechanics is assigned to just one level in his model. Whereas Helmholtz had still mistakenly assumed that his worldview was true, but gave his model at best hypothetical validity, Heisenberg presented his worldview as a whole only as a hypothesis. For Heisenberg, it was not the only possible conception of the world and it was potentially subject to historical change that could affect all components of the model. However, the change that has occurred since then has not undermined the plausibility of the model.

In what follows, I will discuss the two models and conclude with a comparison and evaluation. Beforehand, I would like to note that neither Helmholtz nor Heisenberg described the representations that I have selected as models. This may be due to linguistic conventions of the time or to systematic reasons that still apply today. I assume a broad conception of models that covers both examples and understands by a model an interpretative representation of an object or system. Applying this conception to Helmholtz's monocyclic systems seems to me to be unproblematic, but there are alternative ways of characterising Heisenberg's conception of levels, as I will explain.

1 Hermann von Helmholtz's monocyclic systems

Hermann von Helmholtz's mechanism was based on the successful application of physical mechanics and was limited to natural phenomena, which he contrasted with mental phenomena. I situate him in a mechanistic tradition that considered matter and motion to be the only causes of all natural phenomena and claimed that it could grasp the forms of motion completely through the concepts and laws of physical mechanics. Within this tradition, Helmholtz defended a conception that placed the mechanical concept of force on an equal footing with that of matter. Helmholtz regarded his own mathematical formulation of the law of conservation of energy as the most successful application of mechanics and the most important confirmation of mechanism. He took the fact that mechanical energy could be converted into other forms of energy as proof that all natural phenomena have a mechanical foundation.[2] Analogies subsequently contributed to the mechanistic

---
[1] Cf. Darrigol 1994: 237.
[2] Cf. Schiemann 2009: 90–98 and Caneva 2021: 141–152.

understanding of electromagnetic phenomena. Thermodynamic phenomena represented one of the last unsolved problems of the mechanistic account of nature in the second half of the nineteenth century. How could it be explained that the whole energy of a thermal engine could not be transformed into mechanical work? What mechanical natural processes could be responsible for the inexorable increase in this no longer usable portion of heat in closed systems?

To improve the understanding of reversible processes, Helmholtz created the so-called monocyclic systems in the mid-1880s.[3] These were mechanical models whose internal structure was known entirely and whose concrete form did not necessarily have anything to do with the submicroscopic processes that mechanism regarded as the basis of thermal phenomena. The models applied concepts and laws of the physical theory of mechanics, so that only conservative—i.e., location-dependent—forces acted within the system, while the additional external forces did not necessarily have to be conservative. The coordinates of the moving or moved parts fell into two kinds. The one kind affected the physical state of the system only by its velocity. Helmholtz conceived of its motion as cyclic, i.e., each of the moving elements returned to the same place after a certain time. Systems in which the cyclical motions only depended on one parameter were called 'monocyclic'. With the second kind of coordinates, only the position had an effect on the state of the system, and the changes in position were thought to be negligibly slow.

With this division of coordinates, Helmholtz wanted to draw an analogy to the difference between the amount of heat in a system and the work done in it. The coordinates that produced effects through velocity were supposed to determine the thermodynamic properties, whereas those that produced effects through position determine the work done in the system. As examples of realisations of his monocyclic systems he offered technical constructions, such as a frictionlessly spinning top on which external forces act. That natural systems corresponding to the monocyclic constructions actually exist in nature would only be demonstrated later (by Boltzmann). Insofar as Helmholtz's intention in developing his models did not depend on realisations, they can also be described as fictional. Moreover, they did not contain any information about the material properties of the moving elements.

Helmholtz's model did not aim at a material but instead at a formal analogy between mechanics and thermodynamics, although the formal analogy was not free from material presuppositions. In formal terms, the mathematical representation of changes in the energy of the monocyclic system had the same structure as the change in the quantity of heat of a thermodynamic

---

[3]Cf. Helmholtz 1884. For the following compare Schiemann 2009: 388–397 and Bierhalter 1994.

system. Here, temperature corresponded to kinetic energy and entropy to a function of the mechanical impulses. The entropy equation for reversible systems was thus formally identical to the energy equation of a mechanical system. Helmholtz used the term 'analogy' in a way that corresponds to how it is understood today. Accordingly, analogies contain structural similarities between two different object domains.

Alisa Bokulich has pointed out that, in the context of nineteenth-century mechanism, formal analogies can also be understood in terms of a conception of levels.[4] Taking this as a starting point, the pure mathematical equations employed by Helmholtz can be interpreted as an upper level, beneath which is a level in which these equations are applied with different variables. The phenomena represented by these equations are then situated a further level down. Helmholtz's mechanical analogy thus included two types of relations of representation: the just mentioned representation of the real phenomena by the equations of the middle level and, within this level, the representation of the thermodynamic equation by the mechanical equation of the model. Finally, mechanism still assumed the fundamental level of mechanically moved matter, which was supposed to generate the phenomena—in this case, those of the heat. This layer was beyond the testimony of direct perception and, as Helmholtz believed, was at best accessible to science.

Helmholtz explicitly did not claim that his analogy could explain mathematical relations of thermodynamics. His purpose in constructing the model only becomes clear against the background of his mechanistic worldview: within the framework of this worldview, the motion of heat appears—I quote Helmholtz—'as a motion of an unknown kind'. He continues:

> Under such circumstances it seems to me entirely rational to investigate under which most general conditions the [...] distinctive features of the motion of heat might occur in other well-known classes of motions.[5]

The monocyclic systems fell under the 'well-known classes' and thus served to elucidate what is unknown in terms of what is known. They mediated between the theory of mechanics and a domain of phenomena which could not yet be clearly situated among the objects of mechanics. This procedure for extending knowledge is typical of models involving analogical relations. They are not equipped to produce knowledge of something new that cannot be explained in terms of what is already known.

Helmholtz's attempt must be judged a failure because he started from false presuppositions. He could only establish the formal analogy based on arbitrary assumptions that satisfied his mechanism. Instead of using the statistical velocity distributions considered indispensable today, he calculated with

---

[4]Cf. Bokulich 2015.
[5]Helmholtz 1884: 176. Translation by Ciaran Cronin.

average values of the velocities. Moreover, his analogy permitted processes whose existence was excluded within the framework of the phenomenological laws of thermodynamics.[6] The most serious shortcoming, however, was that his analogy did not cover irreversible processes, as Helmholtz himself realised.

In an effort to integrate irreversibility into his worldview, Helmholtz shifted the focus of his reflections in his later years from mechanical models to general mechanical principles. In deriving the mechanical equations for monocyclic systems, he had already assumed the principle of least action as universally valid. His work in connection with the application of the principle to several physical phenomena also failed to capture irreversible processes, but made an essential contribution to the spread of variational principles in physics.[7]

2 Werner Heisenberg's order of reality

This brings me to the second example, Heisenberg's model of a scientific worldview. While Helmholtz's entire scientific work can be situated in the context of his mechanism, no particular worldview seems to have consistently influenced Heisenberg's work in a comparable way. It fits with this abstinence that the thoughts he nevertheless formulated concerning a worldview are to be found in a separate manuscript that was presumably written in 1943, but was only published posthumously in 1984. In a handful of public lectures from the 1940s one can find hints of this worldview. However, they provide no indication of the differentiated presentation in his substantial text, comprising around 150 book pages. The editors gave the book the fitting german title 'Ordnung der Wirklichkeit' (Order of Reality).[8] Since 2019, it has also been available in an English translation.[9]

Heisenberg's model of levels divides the world into six superimposed 'domains of reality', which are labelled in part according to the scientific disciplines that deal with them, in part according to the concepts that characterise them. In ascending order, these are the physical domain, the chemical domain, the domain of life, the domain of consciousness, the domain of symbols, and finally the domain of the so-called creative forces. According to Heisenberg, the physical domain includes the objects of classical physics and those of the two theories of relativity; the chemical domain, in his opinion, is formed by the objects of thermodynamics and quantum mechanics. While he describes these areas using the concepts and law-governed regularities of the associated theories, he does not assign the domains above them to

---

[6]See Franz Richarz's critique, discussed by Bierhalter 1994: 440 f.
[7]Cf. Schiemann 2024.
[8]Heisenberg 1942. Cf. Schiemann 2008: 84–113.
[9]Heisenberg 2019.

particular theories or disciplines and confines himself to characterising them in terms of their distinctive concepts. He relies on scientific knowledge as far as it seems possible to him and, in addition, sometimes brings in his own life experience. Presumably, the latter also enters into the uppermost level, which results from influences acting on beliefs and cognitive processes of individuals or groups. As phenomena to which this level refers, Heisenberg discusses religious myth and intellectual enlightenment, to which he attributes excellence in science and art.[10]

Heisenberg derives the basic determinants of the relationship between the concepts constitutive of the model and the areas of reality assigned to them from the child's acquisition of language in the lifeworld.[11] The concepts do not summarise sensory impressions, but instead represent states of affairs or thoughts. The more specifically they are determined and the better they have proved, the more precise their representational function becomes. Scientific language, to which Heisenberg attributed a partly static, partly dynamic character, is more precise than everyday language. Concepts of static language, as they are typically used by the mathematical sciences and jurisprudence, clearly refer to particular realities; the concepts of dynamic languages, which are found primarily in the humanities, are less concerned with representing phenomena than with the relationship to other concepts, with creating new concepts and with producing conceptual networks which, in their complexity, stand in interpretive relations to reality.

According to Heisenberg, static and dynamic languages each contain objective and subjective elements of representation. A fact is objective if it can be 'detached from ... its representation', subjective if 'in a complete description ... it may perhaps not be possible to ignore that we ourselves are interwoven in that web of connections'.[12] Objective and subjective aspects are found in every level, but in specifically different relations. Heisenberg arranges his levels between the ideal poles of the purely objective and the purely subjective. The lowest level, that of classical physics, is closest to the objective pole. Its idealisation can refrain to the largest extent from subjective aspects. The uppermost level is closest to the subjective pole. Although the knowledge acquired on this level is objective in character, it owes its existence to individual subjects. The model prescribes an ascent of the levels from the lowest to the highest, with a gradual increase in the subjective element. Heisenberg sees the scientific character of his model in its departure from objectivity. In addition, he justifies the systematic arrangement of his levels through the sequence of the ratios of objective and subjective elements.

---

[10] Loc. cit. 53ff.
[11] Loc. cit. 20ff.
[12] Loc. cit. 33 and 46.

Finally, he intimates that this level structure is proposed as a solution to the problem of overcoming the separation between objective nature and subjective mind that goes back to René Descartes. He wants to replace this simplification of the world, which he considers far too crude, through a successive transformation of the relationship between objective and subjective aspects.[13] The question, however, is whether the separation between object and subject or between nature and mind can be sublated if we uphold the associated concepts. Won't the separation then be imported into each layer?

Despite the affinity between the levels achieved by successively lowering or raising the ratio of objective and subjective elements, there remain sharp conceptual distinctions between the levels. Separate boundary case relationships are defined for exceptional transitions that nevertheless exist between the levels. There are no relationships of reduction between the levels. The concepts of one level cannot be explained in terms of those of another level. Each neighbouring level exhibits something new that Heisenberg describes, but without clarifying its origin. The demarcation between the levels give the model a plural character. The model is only formally unified. But, the fact that the levels are separated from one another and transitions between them are only possible in exceptional cases does not mean that the phenomena assigned to them cannot occur together. In the lower area, the levels are completely contained within the neighbouring upper levels. The physical concepts are also valid in the context of their application in the domain assigned to chemistry, and the chemical terms are also valid in the context of their application in the domain assigned to biology.

Heisenberg's model of the order of reality does not raise any claim to exclusive validity. One of the characteristic features of his order is that the possibility of alternative worldviews is already built into it, both systematically and historically. A remarkable feature of his model is that it can also be read in reverse, leading to a quasi reverse order.[14] If one started from the uppermost level of the creative forces, the worldview would not have a scientific, but potentially a religious character. On Heisenberg's conception, the question of the meaning of life, which is excluded by science, would thus stand at the beginning and continue to serve as a guide in the gradual descent to objectivity. Presumably, the determinations of the layers and, consequently the phenomena represented by them, would change fundamentally. In particular, objectivity would appear, in Heisenberg's words, as an 'infinitely remote singularity that even though it is indeed decisive for order in the finite sphere ... can never be reached'.[15]

---

[13] Loc. cit. 34.
[14] Cf. Schiemann 2008: 91 f.
[15] Heisenberg 2019: 33.

Historically speaking, Heisenberg points to the transformation of worldviews in human history.[16] He situates the order he drafted in the series of these transformations, which is open towards the future. Heisenberg's order uses new natural scientific findings and relies on the knowledge of other disciplines, which has in part been known for some time. Although it does not explicitly distance itself from the mechanistic worldview, it can be understood as an alternative successor worldview that assigns mechanics only to a limited level. According to Heisenberg, not only the representations, but reality is also subject to change. In this way, social upheavals can also influence how the levels are represented. Heisenberg saw National Socialist rule and the beginning of the Second World War as a profound cultural break that could affect the scientific worldview.[17]

Heisenberg's order of reality can also be called a theory. There is little consensus on the concepts of model and theory. Moreover, often they are not sharply distinguished. In favour of the use of certain meanings of the notion of theory would be that Heisenberg's reflections employ independent structural principles and aim to unify various descriptions. However, Heisenberg himself seems to have believed that he was still far away from a theory. At times he speaks not so much of an existing order as of the search for an order. His remarks are fractured, incomplete and are not systematic in their structure. For example, he does not justify differences between the conceptual definitions of the levels and sometimes fails to provide adequate clarification of relationships between neighbouring levels. Against this background, the use of the expression 'model' can also be understood as designating a pragmatic substitute for a theory that is perhaps yet to be formulated.

A similar world model was developed around the same time by the philosopher Nicolai Hartmann, but Heisenberg was probably unaware of it. Although Hartman's outline is conceptually and systemically more elaborate, it contains a problematic critique of modern physics.[18] '[A]s a model for the order modern science is searching for', Heisenberg refers to a brief remark in the supplements to Johann Wolfgang von Goethe's theory of colours, where a comparable division of the world can also be found.[19]

3 Concluding remarks

Helmholtz's model is located between scientific worldview and reality. The scientific worldview claims that physical mechanics is applicable to all natural phenomena. The example discussed concerns a structural analogy between

---

[16] Loc. cit. 29ff.
[17] Loc. cit. 20 and 118f.
[18] Cf. Schiemann 2019.
[19] Heisenberg 2019: 35, cf. Goethe 1989: 788.

the mathematical representations of a model derived from physical mechanics and a natural phenomenon that has not yet been explained, namely, heat. The model has a descriptive character and is completely intelligible. It is supposed to demonstrate that thermal phenomena could be produced by mechanical motions. It becomes apparent, however, that these would have to be motions whose natural appearance is difficult to imagine, since the mechanical model is a tricky technical construct. Moreover, the model does not correspond to mathematical descriptions of other heat phenomena.

Even the assumptions of the mechanistic conception of the world have proven to be wrong, elements of the conception of levels it advocated have retained their importance for scientific research to the present day. Among them is the assumption of a level of processes that generate the phenomena, as this has become established in contemporary philosophy of biology under the heading of a 'mechanical philosophy', as well as the assumption of a layer of mathematical relations detached from the phenomena and their representations.

The notion of a model as an interpretative representation of an object or system I presuppose can be applied to Helmholtz's monocyclic systems, but not to his mechanism. The monocyclic systems represent an object of 'an unknown kind' and have interpretative content in their descriptive and analogical properties. His mechanism, however, is not intended to be a representation, but as the true mirror of natural phenomena. In contrast, Heisenberg stresses the interpretative and representational character of his worldview in different respects. The elements that enter into the representation of the world as subjective parts of the levels are to be mentioned as interpretive. Moreover, the possibility of alternative representations of the world gives his order an interpretative quality.

Conceptions of levels have been formulated since antiquity and remain relevant in contemporary science, as exemplified by emergence theory and the critiques of reductionism. They are scientific worldviews and share with them the good reasons for being called models. Scientific conceptions of the world will probably remain interpretative representations for at least as long as we lack a scientific theory that encompasses the world as a whole. As models, they can confine themselves to generating unity through formal structural elements, examples of which are provided by Heisenberg's model.

References

Bierhalter, Günter (1994): Helmholtz's Mechanical Foundation of Thermodynamics. In: David Cahan (Ed.), *Hermann von Helmholtz and the Foundation of Nineteenth-Century Science*. Berkeley, Los Angeles, London: University of California Press, p. 432–458.

Bokulich, Alisa (2015): Maxwell, Helmholtz, and the Unreasonable Effectiveness of the Method of Physical Analogy. In: *Studies in History and Philosophy of Science Part A,* Vol. 50, p. 28–37.

Caneva, Kenneth L. (2021): *Helmholtz and the Conservation of Energy. Contexts of Creation and Reception.* Cambridge: MIT Press.

Darrigol, Olivier (1994): Helmholtz's Electrodynamics and the Comprehensibility of Nature. In: Lorenz Krüger (Ed.), *Universalgenie Helmholtz. Rückblick nach 100 Jahren.* Berlin: Akademie Verlag, p. 216–242.

Goethe, Johann Wolfgang von (1989): *Schriften zur allgemeinen Naturlehre, Geologie und Mineralogie.* Hg. Wolf von Engelhardt und Manfred Wenzel. Sämtliche Werke Bd. 25. Frankfurt a.M.: Deutscher Klassiker Verlag.

Heisenberg, Werner (1942): Die Ordnung der Wirklichkeit. In: Werner Heisenberg, *Gesammelte Werke.* Vol. CI: Physik und Erkenntnis: 1927–1955. München, Zürich: Piper 1984, p. 217–306.

Heisenberg, Werner (2019): *Reality and Its Order.* Transl. by Martin B. Runscheidt et al. Cham: Springer.

Helmholtz, Hermann von (1884): Studien zur Statik monocyklischer Systeme. In: Hermann von Helmholtz, *Wissenschaftliche Abhandlungen.* Bd. 3, Leipzig: Johann Ambrosius Barth 1885, p. 119ff., 163ff. and 173ff.

Schiemann, Gregor (2008): *Werner Heisenberg.* München: Verlag C.H. Beck.

Schiemann, Gregor (2009): *Hermann von Helmholtz's Mechanism: The Loss of Certainty. A Study on the Transition from Classical to Modern Philosophy of Nature.* Dordrecht: Springer.

Schiemann, Gregor (2019): Levels of the World. Limits and Extensions of Nicolai Hartmann's and Werner Heisenberg's Conceptions of Levels. In: *Horizon, Studies in Phenomenology.* Vol. 8, Issue 1 (Philosophy of Nicolai Hartmann), p. 103–122.

Schiemann, Gregor (2024): Hermann von Helmholtz on the Unification of Science. In: Helmut Pulte, Jan Baedke, Daniel Koenig, Gregor Nickel (Eds.), *New Perspectives on Neo-Kantianism and the Sciences New Perspectives on Neo-Kantianism and the Sciences.* London: Routledge.

The requirement of total evidence: epistemic optimality and political relevance

Gerhard Schurz

Institut für Philosophie, Heinrich Heine University Düsseldorf, Universitätsstr. 1, 40225 Düsseldorf, Germany

Abstract. The requirement of total evidence says that one should conditionalize one's degrees of belief on one's total evidence. In the first part I propose a justification of this principle in terms of its epistemic *optimality*. The justification is based on a proof of I. J. Good and embedded into a new account of epistemology based on optimality-justifications. In the second part I discuss an apparent conflict between the requirement of total evidence and political demands of *anti-discrimination*. These demands require, for example, that information about the sex of the applicant for a job should not be included in the relevant evidence. I argue that if one assesses the applicant's qualification in terms of those properties that are directly causally relevant for the job performance, then properties that are merely indirectly relevant, such as sex, race or age, are screened off, i.e., become irrelevant. So, the apparent conflict disappears.

1 Introduction

The requirement of total evidence—henceforth abbreviated as RTE—says the following:

> In order to rationally estimate the epistemic probability (P) of a hypothesis, one should conditionalize this probability on one's total evidence, i.e., all 'relevant' evidence that is available to the epistemic subject. Thus, if E is the subject's total evidence, then $P_{\text{actual}}(H) = P(H|E)$. (RTE)

Thereby the evidence E is assumed to be 'approximately certain'.[1] Among others, the RTE was introduced by Carnap (1950, 211f.). If the hypothesis is a singular prediction, Fa, the RTE coincides with Reichenbach's principle of the narrowest reference class, which says that we should conditionalize Fa's probability on its membership in the narrowest (relevant) reference class for which we possess evidence (Reichenbach 1949, sec. 72). That the evidence can be restricted to relevant evidence is obvious, since irrelevant evidence does not change the probability and can be omitted, i.e., $P(H|E_{\text{rel}} \wedge E_{\text{irr}}) = P(H|E_{\text{rel}})$.

---

[1] For uncertain evidence, Jeffrey conditionalization has to be applied:

$$P_{\text{actual}}(H) = \Sigma_{\pm E} P(H|\pm E) \cdot P_{\text{actual}}(\pm E).$$

(The notion "$\Sigma_{\pm E}$" is explained in the text.)

Why is the RTE reasonable? It is certainly necessary to *fix* the evidence on which we conditionalize somehow, because otherwise we may end up in contradictions.[2] But why should this be the most comprehensive evidence? Why is it not better to leave evidence out if we do not like it? In what follows we illustrate our problem at hand of a simple *weather* example, as follows:

1. R denotes the prediction that it will rain tomorrow in my area.

2. The probability of R, $P(R)$, is assumed to be implicitly conditionalized on given the general background evidence that we live in a sunny area with a 20% rain chance. So we assume $P(R) = 0.20$ and $P(\neg R) = 0.80$.

3. F denotes the additional evidence that the barometer has fallen, indicating a rain-chance of 95%, even for areas that are normally sunny.

Our assumptions entail that $P(R) = 0.20$, but $P(R|F) = 0.95$. So we must fix the evidence on which we conditionalize our probability of the hypothesis, R, in order to avoid probabilistic incoherence. But why should we conditionalize our prediction on the total or *most specific* evidence, F? Why should we not rather be coherentists and stick with conditionalizing our belief about tomorrow's weather on our general background evidence that we live in an overwhelmingly sunny area, *ignoring* the additional evidence F, so that we are not forced to give up the friendly-weather-belief that we like?

Hempel (1960, 453f.) and Suppes (1966) argued that for a Bayesian probabilist, who identifies her or his degrees of belief with rationally estimated probabilities, the RTE follows already from the probability axioms, or equivalently, from the requirement of probabilistic coherence. For $P(A) = 1$ implies $P(B) = P(B|A)$ (since $P(A) = P(A|B) \cdot P(B) + P(A|\neg B) \cdot P(\neg B) = P(A|B) \cdot 1 + P(A|\neg B) \cdot 0 = P(A|B)$). So given the evidence F is taken as certain, then $P(R) = P(R|F)$; so our coherent degree of belief in the hypothesis R must already be conditionalized on all evidence that is taken as certain. Likewise, if F is almost certain, then provided $P(R|F)$ is not close to zero, $P(R)$ must be approximately equal to $P(R|F)$. Roush (forthcoming, 31, fn. 47) considers this argument as an advantage of Bayesian probabilism. From the viewpoint of *applied* epistemology, however, I think this argument is insufficient, since real epistemic agents are far from being probabilistically omniscient. What people really do when estimating the probability of a future events, such as the possibility of tomorrow's rainfall, is retrieving from their memory some known facts that are regarded as relevant cues for this prediction, and then estimating the predicted probability conditional on the conjunction of these cues. For this epistemic practice the RTE is

---

[2]In application to explanations, Hempel (1965, sec. 3.4) spoke of the "ambiguity of statistical explanations".

highly important, because it requires that instead of confining oneself with just one or a few cues, one should actively retrieve all relevant cues that one knows. For example, if you base your prediction on a weather forecaster on the Internet, but there is a second forecaster that predicts differently (a situation that does not occur unfrequently), then the RTE tells you that you should not just rely on one forecaster and ignore the other. Even for rational Bayesians, the RTE is not self-evident, because Bayesianism does not prescribe how an epistemic agent should mold her or his probabilities. For coherentist Bayesians, ignoring a piece of evidence F when estimating the actual probability of a prediction R just means that they change their probability of F from a value close to 1 to some lower value. Why should such a 'probabilistic suppression' of an unwanted fact not be a legitimate epistemic practice, for the mutual sake of increasing the coherence of our beliefs and desires? Why are we *worse off* if we follow this practice rather than follow the RTE? Moreover, why is searching for new (cheap) evidence better than applying the ostrich-method of avoiding the acquirement of new evidence (putting one's hat in the sand)?

To obtain a positive answer to these questions, we need an explicit *justification* of the RTE. Moreover, recall that according to Reichenbach's ingenious idea the justification of the RTE would at the same time tell us how the statistical (or frequentist) probabilities of repeatable events should be connected with the epistemic probabilities of single instances of these events. The above weather example is nothing but such a connection: the statistical chance of rain (Rx) in some reference class (Cx), abbreviated as $p(Rx|Cx)$, is transferred to a particular day, namely *tomorrow* (a), as the epistemic probability of a rainfall tomorrow: $P(Ra) = p(Rx|Cx)$ (where "Cx" is a condition that refers to the past of x, logically expressed by a functor, $Cx = Gfx$). The reason why we *want* a connection between epistemic and statistical probabilities is simple: only if there is such a connection, will the probabilistically *expected utilities*—which are the central guide for rational decisions—agree with our actually experienced *average utilities* (in the long run); otherwise maximization of expected utilities could fail to be actually utility-increasing. However, there are different possible reference classes Cx—in our example that I live in a sunny area, that the barometer fell yesterday, etc. Which reference class should we choose? According to Reichenbach's "principle of narrowest reference class", we should identify the epistemic probability of a single case hypothesis with its statistical probability conditional on the total (relevant) evidence about the respective individual a; in our example: $P(Ra) = p(Rx|Fx)$.[3] Therefore, a justification

---

[3] The transfer of $p(Rx|Fx)$ to $P(Fa)$ is also called "direct inference" and is related to the so-called statistical principal principle; thereby "P" must be prior in regard to the involved individual a (see Schurz 2014, 160 and 2024, 58f.).

of the RTE would give us at the same time a justification of transferring statistical probabilities to single cases by means of the RTE.

In the next section, we offer such a justification of the RTE, based on a reconstruction of a seminal proof of Good (1966). The proof demonstrates that for practical as well as predictive success, the best what we can do is to conditionalize on the total available evidence. The proof is an instance of what is called an *optimality justification*. It is part of the account of epistemology based on optimality-justifications developed in Schurz (2024) that grew out from work on the optimality of meta-induction (Schurz 2019).

2 An optimality justification of the requirement of total evidence

In what follows I explain the proof for the simplest case of binary partitions, illustrated at hand of our weather example. So we are interested in predicting the binary variable $\pm R$, where "$\pm$" stands for "unnegated" or "negated", i.e., $\pm R \in \{R, \neg R\}$, in our example, that it will rain (R) or not rain ($\neg R$) = tomorrow. Note that strictly speaking we have to represent the prediction R by the atomic formula Ra_{n+1}, where $a_1, a_2, \ldots$ stands for a sequence of days, a_{n+1} for the day tomorrow and a_n for today. We dispense with this formal complication since the meaning is obvious.

Preceding each day we obtain additional evidence about whether the barometer reading has fallen or not, $\pm F$, where according to our estimation $P(R|F) = 0.95$ and $P(R|\neg F) = 0.15$.

Good's proof of the optimality of the RTE is devised for *success in actions*, whose utility depends on the unknown utility-determining circumstances or predictive targets, in our example $\pm R$. We assume that in our example the possible actions are:

the action(s) of taking an umbrella with us or not, abbreviated as $\pm U$.

The decision concerning $\pm U$ must be made today, for example because we leave today for a mountain tour tomorrow. Concerning the utilities, $u(A|C)$ denotes the utility of action A given the circumstance C.[4] In our example, we assume the following utility values:

$$u(\neg U|R) = 0, \quad u(\neg U|\neg R) = 0, \quad u(U|R) = 3, \quad \text{and} \quad u(U|\neg R) = -1.$$

---

[4] In causal decision theory (Weirich 2020) one often writes $u(A \wedge C)$ instead of $u(A|C)$. This indicates that also C may contribute to the total utility outcome. This notation is appropriate if the circumstances includes factors that are *effects* of the actions, but we do not assume this (see below). Our utilities express the utility-effect of the action relative to the total utility of the action-independent circumstances; this is reflected in the notation "$u(A|C)$", which is close to Savage's notation (Steele and Stefanson 2020, sec. 3.1). For action-independent circumstances both notations are equivalent, because in this case the decision matrix can be rescaled by adding to each row a row-specific constant without changing the Eu-ordering of the actions (see Jeffrey 1983, 35–37).

Utilities and probabilities are assumed to be reliably estimated.

According to decision theory the *expected utility*, Eu, of the actions $\pm U$ are given as:

$$\begin{aligned} \text{Eu}(U) &= P(R) \cdot u(U|R) + P(\neg R) \cdot u(U|\neg R) \\ &=_{\text{def}} \Sigma_{\pm R} P(\pm R) \cdot u(U|\pm R). \\ \text{Eu}(\neg U) &= P(R) \cdot u(\neg U|R) + P(\neg R) \cdot u(\neg U|\neg R) \\ &=_{\text{def}} \Sigma_{\pm R} P(\pm R) \cdot u(\neg U|\pm R). \end{aligned} \quad (1)$$

In informal words: The Eu of action U is the sum of U's utilities under the different circumstances $\{R, \neg R\}$ multiplied with their probabilities. (Similarly for $\neg U$.)

So in our example, without additional evidence we get:

$$\text{Eu}(U) = 0.2 \cdot 3 - 0.8 \cdot 1 = -0.2 < \text{Eu}(\neg U) = 0.2 \cdot 0 + 0.8 \cdot 0 = 0.$$

So with the above utilities, if all what I know is $P(R) = 0.2$, then my wisest action is not to take an umbrella.

The philosophical assumption behind the decision-theoretic formula (1) is that the choice of action is *free* in the sense of being probabilistically *independent* from those utility-determining circumstances that are *not causally influenced* by the actions. In the formula (1), the cells of the partition of circumstances range over those circumstances, in our example $\pm R$. This assumption justifies that we write $P(\pm R)$ instead of $P(\pm R|\pm U)$, since $\pm U$ has no causal influence on tomorrow's rain. We will defend this assumption below. Here we merely point out that we may include action-dependent circumstances by expanding in equation (1) the term $u(U|\pm R)$ as follows:

$$u(U|\pm R) = \Sigma_i P(D_i|U) \cdot u(U \wedge D_i|\pm R),$$

where $\{D_1, \ldots, D_n\}$ is an additional partition of action-dependent facts. Inserting this equation into (1) gives us

$$\text{Eu}(U) = \Sigma_{\pm R} P(\pm R) \cdot \Sigma_i P(D_i|U) \cdot u(U \wedge D_i|\pm R),$$

which is a version of Skyrms' causal decision theory (Skyrms 1980, sec. IIC; Weirich 2020, sec. 2.3).

The argument of Good's proof in my reconstruction consists of two steps:

Step 1 of Good's proof: The expected utility Eu of a *fixed* action—one that is independent of which additional evidence you observe—is provably *preserved* under conditionalization of the probabilities of the circumstances on new evidence $\pm F$. In other words: the Eu does not change under *refinements* of the partition of action-independent circumstances. In our example this means the following:

$$\mathrm{Eu}(\neg U) = \mathrm{Eu}(\neg U|\{F, \neg F\}), \qquad (2)$$

where

$$\mathrm{Eu}(\neg U|\{F, \neg F\}) = P(F) \cdot \mathrm{Eu}(\neg U|F) + P(\neg F) \cdot \mathrm{Eu}(\neg U|\neg F),$$

and

$$\mathrm{Eu}(\neg U|F) = \Sigma_{\pm R} P(\pm R|F) \cdot u(U| \pm R)$$
$$= \text{the Eu of } \neg U \text{ updated with } P(\pm R|F),$$

and similarly,

$$\mathrm{Eu}(\neg U|\neg F) = \text{the Eu of } \neg U \text{ updated with } P(\pm R|\neg F).$$

Similarly for $\mathrm{Eu}(U)$.

The proof of (2) is as follows. Analytically it holds that

$$\mathrm{Eu}(U|\{F, \neg F\}) = P(F) \cdot \Sigma_{\pm R} P(\pm R|F) \cdot u(U| \pm R \wedge F) + $$
$$P(\neg F) \cdot \Sigma_{\pm R} P(\pm R|\neg F) \cdot u(U| \pm R \wedge \neg F). \quad (3)$$

We assume, however, that

$$u(\pm U| \pm R \wedge \pm F) = u(\pm U| \pm R) \quad \text{(utility-neutral additional evidence)}. \quad (4)$$

This holds because the circumstances $\pm R$ determine the utilities of the actions. So the fact expressed by the evidence, $\pm F$, has no further influence on their utility.[5] From (3) and (4) we obtain:

(5) *Proof of (2):*

$\mathrm{Eu}(U|\{F, \neg F\})$
$= P(F) \cdot \Sigma_R P(\pm R|F) \cdot u(U| \pm R) + P(\neg F) \cdot \Sigma_R P(\pm R|\neg F) \cdot u(U| \pm R)$
$= \Sigma_R [P(\pm R \wedge F) \cdot u(U| \pm R) + P(\pm R \wedge \neg F) \cdot u(U| \pm R)]$
$= \Sigma_R [P(\pm R \wedge F) + P(\pm R \wedge \neg F)] \cdot u(U| \pm R)$
$= \Sigma_R P(\pm R) \cdot u(U| \pm R) = \mathrm{Eu}(U).$ \hfill Q.E.D.

Step 2 of Good's proof: Now, the point of conditionalization is that the new evidence may *change* the optimal action under a particular observational

---

[5]It is also possible to prove (2) without assumption (4), by assuming Jeffrey's framework that identifies utilities and expected utilities; his "desirability axiom" (1983, 80, (5–2)) implies for our example that (2) holds. However, Jeffrey's axiom is rather strong.

outcome $\pm F$. If F is observed, this indicates a high chance of rain, and so the F-conditional Eu of U is much higher than that of $\neg U$. In our example we get

$$\mathrm{Eu}(U|F) = 0.95 \cdot 3 - 0.05 \cdot 1 = 2.8 > \mathrm{Eu}(\neg U|F) = 0.95 \cdot 0 + 0.15 \cdot 0 = 0.$$

If $\neg F$ is observed, we should not change the best evidence-independent action $\neg U$; in this case, the surplus of $\neg U$ over U even increases. In our example we get

$$\mathrm{Eu}(U|\neg F) = 0.15 \cdot 3 - 0.85 \cdot 1 = -0,4 < \mathrm{Eu}(\neg U|\neg F) = 0.15 \cdot 0 + 0.15 \cdot 0 = 0.$$

In conclusion, after conditionalization the rational subject performs the conditionalized or *evidence-dependent action*

$$U^* =_{\mathrm{def}} \text{``}U \text{ if } F \text{ and } \neg U \text{ if } \neg F\text{''}.$$

For U^* the Eu is computed as follows:

$$\mathrm{Eu}(U^*|\{F, \neg F\}) = P(F) \cdot \mathrm{Eu}(U|F) + P(\neg F) \cdot \mathrm{Eu}(\neg U|\neg F). \quad (6)$$

$\mathrm{Eu}(U^*|\{F, \neg F\})$ is greater than the Eu of the best fixed action, $\mathrm{Eu}(\neg U|\{F, \neg F\})$, since $\mathrm{Eu}(U|F) > \mathrm{Eu}(\neg U|F)$. To see this, compare equation (6) with the equation below the equation (2): the two equations differ only in the terms $\mathrm{Eu}(U|F)$ respectively $\mathrm{Eu}(\neg U|F)$, and since $\mathrm{Eu}(U|F) > \mathrm{Eu}(\neg U|F)$, $\mathrm{Eu}(U^*|\{F, \neg F\}) > \mathrm{Eu}(\neg U|\{F, \neg F\})$ follows, where $\mathrm{Eu}(\neg U|\{F, \neg F\}) = \mathrm{Eu}(\neg U)$ (as proved in (5)) and $\neg U$ is the best fixed action.

The basic argument is entirely independent of the assumed utilities. Even if the utility of taking an umbrella given rain would be much smaller than given not-rain (for example because of a dictator who punishes people who are taking an umbrella while it rains), the theorem would go through. Either under one of the two evidential outcomes $\pm F$ the evidence-dependent Eu of one of the two actions, say A', becomes greater than the best evidence-independent action, call it A_{ind}, then we switch from A_{ind} to A' under this outcome and this will increase the Eu, or under both evidential outcomes A_{ind} has still maximal Eu, in which case we stay with A_{ind} and (by the proof in (5)) the Eu will be preserved.

This proof generalizes to arbitrary finite partitions of possible actions, circumstances and evidence, leading to the following result:

Theorem (Optimality of the RTE). Assume a partition $\mathbf{C}$ of possible circumstances and a partition of possible actions $\mathbf{A}$ whose Eu is governed by the decision-theoretic formula (1). Then:

(i) Conditionalization of the probabilities of the circumstances $C \in \mathbf{C}$ of the agent's possible actions $A \in \mathbf{A}$ on the cells of a partition $\mathbf{F}$ of additional evidence can only increase but not decrease the Eu of the agent's evidence-dependent action A^* defined as follows:

(U^*) "For all cells $F \in \mathbf{F}$, if F is observed, then choose action A_F", where A_F is the action with the highest F-conditional Eu.

(ii) Moreover: Let A_{ind} be the fixed (evidence-independent) action with highest Eu. Then: If for all $F \in \mathbf{F}$, $A_F = A_{\text{ind}}$, then A^* has the same Eu as A_{ind}, but if for at least one $F \in \mathbf{F}$, $A_F \neq A_{\text{ind}}$, then the Eu of A^* increases.

The general mathematical fact behind this theorem is expressed by Schwartz (2021) as follows: The maximum of a weighted average (which is $\text{Eu}(\neg U|\{F, \neg F\})$) is always smaller than or at most equal to the corresponding average of the maxima (which is $\text{Eu}(U^*|\{F, \neg F\})$) (see also Bradley and Steel 2016, 4).

Three features of this general result are remarkable:

First: The argument holds for *every* utility function. This result is astonishing, in particular in the domain of predictions (see below).

Second: The only essential assumption of the optimality result is that the costs of *acquiring* new information are negligible.[6] If these costs are too high, they could of course offset the benefits gained. Some counterexamples to the RTE are of this sort—for example, the first counterexample in Schwarz (2021).

Third: The result implies two things: (i) That you should take into account all the (relevant) evidence that you actually possess, but also (ii) that you should try to gather new evidence whenever this is easily possible, because by doing so you cannot decrease and will in most cases increase the Eu of your actions.

Horwich (1982, 125–128) objected against Good's proof that it would apply only to practical (non-epistemic) actions. But this is not true: the possible actions in Good's proof may also be purely epistemic actions, for example, *predictions* whose utility is given by a predictive scoring measure. In our example, the actions would be predictions of tomorrow's weather, abbreviated as "pred($\pm R$)" for predicting R or $\neg R$. The optimal fixed prediction in our weather example would be pred($\neg R$). But conditional on observing F the optimal prediction is not $\neg R$ but R. So the rational forecaster predicts R if F was observed and $\neg R$ if $\neg F$ was observed, and this increases the predictive score. Let us designate this evidence-dependent prediction as pred*. Good's proof applies in precisely the same way and our theorem applies: the Eu of pred* can only increase but not decrease the Eu of the best evidence-independent prediction, and this results holds for every scoring function (for details cf. Schurz 2024, sec. 7.3).

---

[6]Note that the utility of the *acquirement* of evidence is a different matter than the utility of the fact expressed by the evidence.

We have illustrated Good's argument for *qualitative* predictions (predictions of events), but a related argument applies to the predictions of *probabilities* (cf. Thorn 2017). In this case the possible predictions are P-distributions $P : \{e_1, \ldots, e_n\} \to [0,1]$, where $\{e_1, \ldots, e_n\}$ are the possible events (in our example $\pm R$). The prediction is scored against the truth-value "1" of the true event, e_{true}, among the partition of predicted events, i.e., score(pred) $= 1 - \text{loss}(P(e_{\text{true}}), 1)$, where "loss" is a loss function (cf. Cesa-Bianchi and Lugosi 2006, ch. 9). For probabilistic predictions the scoring function is usually assumed to be proper (e.g., quadratic), because only for proper scoring functions is it optimal for the forecaster to predict her (rationally estimated) probabilities of the events (cf. Brier 1950; Maher 1990, 113). In contrast, for linear scoring (loss(pred, 1) $= 1 - $ pred), it is optimal to predict the roundings of the event's probabilities to 0 or 1 (the so-called "maximum rule"; cf. Schurz 2019, 103). However, Good's optimality argument for the RTE generalizes also to non-proper scorings, provided the predictions pred $\in [0, 1]$ are allowed to deviate from one's actual probabilities that are used to compute the Eu.[7]

Let me finally note that the optimality of the RTE has an important consequence for the *externalism-internalism* debate, in the justificational sense of externalism/internalism (cf. Schurz 2024, sec. 3.2). In epistemological externalism, the question of choosing the right reference class in which the reliability of a belief-generating method should be determined is part of what is called the *generality problem* (Conee and Feldman 1998, Matheson 2015). Within externalism this question is largely undecided or at least hard to answer. But within justification-internalism, the question has a straightforward and unique solution: the reliability should be evaluated with regard to the agent's total relevant evidence for the belief in question.

At the end of this section let me return to the presupposition of our decision-theoretic formula (1): that the choice of action is *free* in the sense of being probabilistically *independent* from those utility-determining circumstances C_i that are not causally influenced by the actions. First, note that if we conditionalize our decision on the available evidence E, this independence condition has to be formulated conditionally: C_i and the chosen action A should be independent conditional on E, i.e., $P(C_i|E) = P(C_i|E \wedge A)$. *Second*, the independence condition excludes various versions of Newcomb's

---

[7] It may happen that conditionalizing on one cell of $\pm E$, say on E, brings the old actual probabilities close to 0.5 (e.g., of $P(R) = 0.2$ and $P(R|E) = 0.3$). In this case Good's strategy with linear scoring would require to predict the old non-actual probabilities conditional on E (and the new conditionalized probabilities conditional on $\neg E$), which is not allowed if one must allows predict one's actual probabilities. Horwich (1982, 128f.) proved that the RTE maximizes the Eu of one's actual probabilities even under linear scoring, which is a second important result. But his proof is specially designed for linear scorings and does not generalize to arbitrary scorings.

paradox, in which some past event X (in Newcomb's paradox the prediction of a perfect or nearly perfect forecaster) determines which action you will choose, or the probability with which you will choose it, already in advance, so that there is a probabilistic dependence between the circumstances C_i (that incorporate $\pm X$) and your choice of action. Newcomb's paradox in its various versions forms a second line of purported counterexamples against Good's proof of the universal rationality of the RTE (the 2nd, 3rd and 4th counterexample in Schwarz 2021 falls under this category). I am inclined to think, however, that the assumption of Newcomb's paradox is in conflict with the fact that decision theory delivers a normative recommendation. It is not possible for me here to go into the extensive literature on the Newcomb paradox[8] and I content myself here with a brief statement of my main argument. Decision theory gives the normative recommendation that you should *always* choose the action with highest expected utility, conditional on the total evidence E. But in in typical Newcomb-type situations, the normatively recommended action is different from that action that is determined or predicted by the past event X. This implies that in many cases it will be *impossible* for you to follow the decision-theoretic recommendation. But this means that the decision-theoretic recommendation will itself be itself unreasonable, because according to the famous *Ought-Can* principle (Ought implies Can), a normative recommendation can only be reasonable if the recommended action *can be* done. But in Newcomb-type situations you know that with considerable probability the recommended action cannot be done, because a past event forces the agent to choose an action different from the recommended one. On the other hand, if the recommended action luckily agrees with the action the agent is forced to do, then the normative recommendation becomes superfluous.

In conclusion, if actions are determined by past circumstances, then normative recommendation either violate the Ought-Can principle or become superfluous. Therefore the freedom assumption seems to be an implicit presupposition of decision-theoretic recommendations.

3 The political relevance of the requirement of total evidence

In the concluding section we discuss an apparent *conflict* of the RTE with political requirements of *anti-discrimination*. Consider the example of sex discrimination in job hiring (Birkelund et al. 2022):

1. According to the RTE, information about the sex (or biological gender) of the applicant should be included in the qualification-relevant evidence *iff* it is statistically relevant.

---

[8]Cf., e.g., Nozick (1969), Eells (1981), Lewis (1981), Skyrms (1982), Horwich (1985), Weirich (2020).

2. In contrast, politicians of anti-discrimination often require sex to be ignored despite of its statistical relevance, because it would lead to discrimination.

Of course, if the belief about a correlation between sex and job qualification is not statistically supported, but is based on *prejudice* or some other sort of *cognitive bias*, then the RTE does *not* demand sex to be included. Then we should leave out the male/female information simply because the job assigner's beliefs about properties correlated with biological sex is biased, i.e., wrong. There is a rich literature about cognitive prejudice and bias, but here we will not enter these topics. Rather, we make the idealizing assumption that our statistical beliefs are well supported by the statistical evidence. In other words, the assessment procedure of the job assigner is not biased but well calibrated. Then it seems that we have a conflict: For the job assigner, conditionalizing on the additional information about sex *increases the expected qualification* of the chosen candidate(s). But at least for some candidates this seems to be *unfair*, given that fairness means that the job assignment corresponds to the candidates' objective job-relevant qualifications. This understanding of fairness is also called the *meritocratic* understanding (cf. Barocas et al. 2023, ch. 4).

Let us give an *example*: A woodworking factory has to hire a person for a wood chipper job that requires a lot of physical strength. According to statistical evidence, males are physically stronger on average than females. So if sex is a criterion for job hiring, then a female applicant will have less chances *even if* she is physically very strong. If statistics is correct, these cases of unfairness will be in the minority, but they will unavoidably occur, and with significant frequency. Similar examples may be given with sexes switched. For example, assume a nursery school hires a person for early childhood care. According to statistical evidence, females caregivers are better accepted by young children than males. So if sex is used as a criterion, a male person will have less chances to be hired even if children would like him most (cf. Birkelund et al 2022, 347).

The only solution which I see is the following: One should base the decision about the job assignment solely on information about the *directly relevant* properties of the applicants. With this I mean those properties that are most direct causes of the job performance of the candidate (if the candidate would be hired), within the set of evidentially accessible variables. If we do this, then the merely indirectly relevant properties such as sex, race or age are *screened off*, which means that after conditionalization on the directly relevant properties, they become irrelevant. In our example: The wood factory should directly test the candidates for their physical strength and other directly relevant properties, such as social skills, reliability, etc. Given this information, additional information about sex or other merely indirectly relevant properties of the applicants becomes irrelevant. This is an implication of the so-called *causal Markov* condition, according to which conditionalization on the direct causes screens off indirect causes from their effects, and likewise, conditionalization on the common causes screens off their effects from each other.[9] This means in terms of probabilities:

$$P(\text{qualification} \mid \text{physical strength \& sex}) =$$
$$P(\text{qualification} \mid \text{physical strength}). \quad (7)$$

Let us generalize this idea. Assume the following variables (or partitions of their possible values) designated by bold-face letters:

1. **Q** is a partition of degrees of qualification of candidate (e.g., from 1 (best) to 5 (worst), understood as expressions of their *future job performance* which is to be *predicted*.

2. **D** is a partition of evidentially accessible properties of the candidates that are (supposedly) directly causally relevant for **Q** and measured by a score **S** on which the decision is based.

3. **A** is a partition of additional information, for example about sex, race or age (etc.), that is merely indirectly relevant, by being correlated with **S**. In the literature on fairness in machine learning, **A** is often called the (partition of) *sensitive attributes* (Barocas et al. 2023, ch. 3; Mitchell et al. 2021, 149).

Then I propose the following

> *Fairness criterion:* If score is fair, then $\text{Indep}(\mathbf{Q}, \mathbf{A}|\mathbf{S})$ should hold (where "$\text{Indep}(\mathbf{X}, \mathbf{Y}|\mathbf{Z})$" means that if we fix the variable **Z** to a particular value, then the values of **X** and **Y**, respectively, are mutually probabilistically independent). (F)

In the literature on fairness in machine learning, (F) corresponds to an important anti-discrimination criterion that has been called *sufficiency* (Barocas et al. 2023, ch. 3) or *predictive parity* (Mitchell et al. 2021, 154).

The causal model behind the above fairness criterion is illustrated in Figure 1 below. Causal arrows are distinguished into required ones (marked with "r"), admissible but not required ones (marked with an "a"), and excluded ones (marked with a backslash "\"). Thus, the sensitive attribute **A** may (but need not) be relevant for **Q**, the job qualification, but if **A** is relevant for **Q**, then merely indirectly, via the path over the directly relevant

---

[9]Cf. Lauritzen et al. (1990), 50; Spirtes et al. (2000), sec. 3.4.1–2; Pearl (2009), 16–19; Schurz and Gebharter (2016), sec. 2.3, conditions (6) and (8).

properties **D**, whence **A** is screened off by conditionalization on **D**. This requires that the variable **D** must be complete, in the sense of covering all or almost all properties of the job candidate that are direct causes for **Q**. Moreover, the score **S** must be accurate in the sense of measuring the values of **D** precisely; if this is the case, then not only **D** but also **S** screens off *A* from **Q**—which is the required condition because **S** determines the decision who will get the job. What is excluded is that information about **A** directly influences the score **S** or the decision (independent from **D**), or that **A** has a direct influence on **Q** (relative to the model), which would mean that the scoring variable **S** leaves out important causal information and, thus, fails to screen off indirect causes of **Q**.

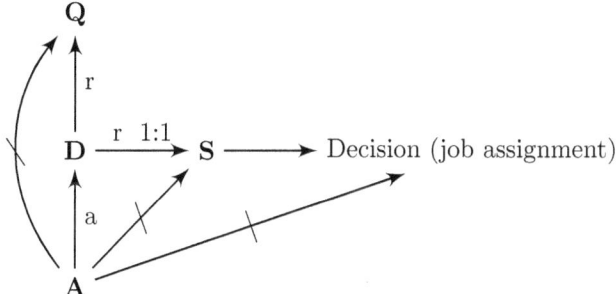

FIGURE 1. The causal model behind the fairness criterion of sufficiency (or predictive parity). Causal arrows are distinguished onto required ones ("r"), allowed ones ("a") and excluded ones ("\").

Summarizing, it seems that by conditionalizing on the directly relevant properties, unfairness can be avoided. Moreover, if we are not sure which of the evidentially accessible variables are the directly relevant ones, then conditionalization on *more* information can reveal possibly discriminating variables that are merely indirectly relevant—by detecting screening-off relations. So it seems that the RTE 'wins': it is not really in conflict with anti-discrimination. Is this true?

I conclude this paper with a brief discussion of three objections to the above fairness criterion.

Objection 1: In the literature on fairness in machine learning, there is a hot controversy about the "right" criterion of fairness (Barocas et al. 2023, ch. 3 & 4). In my view the above criterion is the right one, given the causal model of Figure 1. Let me mention two rival criteria of fairness:

The first rival fairness criterion is called *independence* or *statistical parity* and requires Indep(**S**, **A**) (Barocas et al. 2023, ch. 3). This means that on average all **A**-members—in our example both sexes—should achieve the same qualification score. Obviously, this can only be compatible with meritocratic fairness if on average all **A**-members—in our example both sexes—are equally qualified. Otherwise this criterion leads to some sort of "affirmative action" that is discussed below.

A second rival is called the criterion of *separation* (ibid., ch. 3) which requires Indep(**S**, **A**|**Q**). In this criterion, the roles of the variables **S** and **Q** are switched, compared to our preferred criterion (F). Thus in the causal model on which the separation criterion is based, **S** is assumed not to express causes but the effects of **Q**. This implies a rather different understanding of **Q** and **S**. It makes sense if **Q** takes the role of **D**, i.e., is identified with actually measurable properties of the candidates that are supposedly relevant for its job qualification, while **S** is a possibly inaccurate score of **Q**.

Objection 2: Some people, politically mainly left-wing oriented, argue for so-called *affirmative action*. This is based on the idea that members of an underrepresented or even discriminated group should be preferred even if they are on average less qualified, because this kind of "compensatory unfairness" is necessary for breaking up historically or socially anchored injustice. An example would be the university policy to hire 50% males and 50% females for a professor job in theoretical philosophy, which is a discipline where we typically have 75% males and 25% females among students, researchers and applicants for the professor job. Affirmative action is controversial—how much unfairness (in the meritocratic sense) is tolerable in this attempt to encourage women's engagement with theoretical philosophy? I do not want to discuss this question here. Rather, I want to emphasize that *even if* one supports affirmative action, the general optimality proof of the RTE stays intact, since RTE's optimality holds for *all* utility functions. All what changes for a selection criterion based on affirmative action is the relevant utility function of the available actions and the partition of utility-determining circumstances. In our example, the utility of the of hired applicant is then not only based on the candidates merits, but also on other desired properties such as the sex of the candidate. So "sex" is no longer merely "indirectly relevant", but becomes a directly relevant property.

Objection 3: In my view this is the hardest objection. It objects that our claims hold only under the idealizing assumption that we possess sufficient information about the directly relevant qualification properties of the candidates. If the job recruiter is uncertain about these properties of the candidates, then the RTE recommends conditionalization of the estimated qualification on evidence about merely indirectly relevant evidence properties. This will increases the expected qualification of the hired candidate, since now his or her qualification is no longer screened off from these indirectly relevant properties. However, the so achieved increase of the average qualification has the cost that it will produces a certain amount of unfairness. This unfairness can be measured in terms of the numbers of pairs of candidates A, B in which A is preferred over B although A is less competent than B.

In conclusion, in such a situation there is a trade-off between maximizing the expected qualification of the chosen candidate and maximizing meritocratic fairness. What policy would be reasonably fair in such a situation? I cannot go into the details of this question but confine myself with a remark concerning a frequently heard suggestion, namely that without knowledge about the directly job-relevant properties, one should choose the candidate *randomly*. Remarkably, many people find such a random choice as fair. However, if we use our measure of unfairness—the numbers of pairs of candidates A, B in which A is preferred over B although A is less competent than B—then a random choice will in most cases both decrease the expected qualification of the chosen candidate *and* increase the amount of unfairness. So the random-choice strategy is not a truly satisfying solution. I conclude that a true dissolution of the conflict is not possible by the suppression of information, but only by its magnification, by trying to achieve as much information as possible about those properties that are directly relevant for the decision one has to make.

Acknowledgement. Work on this paper was supported by the DFG Grant SCHU1566/9-1 as part of the priority program "New Frameworks of Rationality" (SPP 1516). For valuable comments and inspirations I am indebted to Mario Günther, Johan van Benthem, David Papineau, Otavia Bueno, Michael Rescorla, Corina Strößner, Gila Sher and Sherilyn Roush.

References

Barocas, S., Hardt, M., & Narayanan, A. (2023). *Fairness and Machine Learning*. Cambridge/M.: MIT Press.

Birkelund, G. E., Lancee, B., Nergard Larsen, E., Polavieja. J. G., Radl, J., & Yemane, R. (2022). Gender discrimination in hiring: Evidence from a cross-national harmonized field experiment. *European Sociological Review*, 38, 337–354.

Bradley, S., & Steele, K. (2016). Can free evidence be bad? Value of information for the imprecise probabilist. *Philosophy of Science*, 83, 1–28.

Brier, G. (1950). Verification of forecasts expressed in terms of probability. *Monthly Weather Review*, 78, 1–3.

Carnap, R. (1950). *Logical Foundations of Probability*. University of Chicago Press.

Cesa-Bianchi, N., and Lugosi, G. (2006): *Prediction, Learning, and Games*. Cambridge: Cambridge University Press.

Conee, E., & Feldman, R. (1998). The generality problem for reliabilism. *Philosophical Studies*, 89, 1–29.

Eells, E. (1981). Causality, utility, and decision. *Synthese*, 48, 295–329.

Good, I. J. (1967). On the principle of total evidence. *British Journal for the Philosophy of Science*, 17, 319-321. Reprinted in Good, I. J. (1983), *Good thinking* (pp. 178–180). Minneapolis: University of Minnesota Press.

Hempel, C. G. (1960). Inductive inconsistencies. *Synthese*, 12(4), 439–469.

Hempel, C. G. (1965): *Aspects of Scientific Explanation and Other Essays in the Philosophy of Science*. New York-London: Free Press.

Horwich, P. (1982). *Probability and Evidence*. Cambridge: Cambridge Univ. Press.

Horwich, P. (1985). Decision theory in light of Newcomb's problem. *Philosophy of Science*, 52, 431–450.

Jeffrey, R. (1983): *The Logic of Decision* (2nd ed.). University of Chicago Press.

Lauritzen, S. L., Dawid, A. P., Larsen, B. N., & Leimer, H.-G. (1990). Independence properties of directed Markov-fields. *Networks*, 20, 491–505.

Lewis, D. (1981). Causal decision theory. *Australasian Journal of Philosophy*, 59, 5–30.

Maher, P. (1990). Why scientists gather evidence. *British Journal for the Philosophy of Science*, 41, 103–119.

Matheson, J. D. (2015). Is there a well-founded solution to the generality problem? *Philosophical Studies*, 172, 459–468.

Mitchell, S., Potash, E., Barocas, S., Amour, A., & Lum, H. (2021). Algorithmic fairness: Choices, assumptions, and definitions. *Annual Review of Statistics and Its Application*, 8, 141–63.

Nozick, R. (1969). Newcomb's problem and two principles of choice. In N. Rescher (Ed.), *Essays in Honor of Carl G. Hempel* (pp. 114–146). Dordrecht: Reidel.

Pearl, J. (2009). *Causality*. Cambridge: Cambridge University Press.

Reichenbach, H. (1949). *The theory of probability.* Los Angeles: University of California Press.

Roush, S. (forthcoming). Epistemic justice and the principle of total evidence.

Schurz, G. (2014): *Philosophy of Science. A Unified Approach.* New York: Routledge.

Schurz, G. (2019). *Hume's Problem Solved: The Optimality of Meta-Induction.* Cambridge/M.: MIT Press.

Schurz, G. (2024). *Optimality Justifications: New Foundations for Epistemology.* Oxford and New York: Oxford University Press.

Schurz, G., & Gebharter, A. (2016). Causality as a theoretical concept: Explanatory warrant and empirical content of the theory of causal nets. *Synthese*, 193, 1071–1103.

Schwarz, W. (2021): Counterexamples to Good's theorem. https://www.umsu.de/blog/2021/740.

Skyrms, B. (1980). *Causal Necessity: A Pragmatic Investigation of the Necessity of Laws.* New Haven, CT: Yale University Press.

Skyrms, B. (1982). Causal decision theory. *Journal of Philosophy*, 79, 695–711.

Spirtes, P., Glymour, C., and Scheines, R. (2000). *Causation, Prediction, and Search.* Cambridge: MIT Press.

Steele, K., & Stefánsson, H. O. (2020). Decision theory. In *Stanford Encyclopedia of Philosophy* (Winter 2020).

Suppes, P. (1966). Probabilistic inference and the concept of total evidence. In J. Hintikka and P. Suppes (Eds.), *Aspects of Inductive Logic* (pp. 49–65). North-Holland, Amsterdam.

Thorn, P. (2017). On the preference for more specific reference Classes. *Synthese*, 194, 2025–2051.

Weirich, P. (2020). Causal decision theory. In *Stanford Encyclopedia of Philosophy* (winter 2020).

What logic represents

Johan van Benthem

Institute for Logic, Language and Computation, University of Amsterdam, P.O. Box 94242, 1090 GE Amsterdam, The Netherlands & Department of Philosophy, Stanford University, 450 Jane Stanford Way, Blg 90, Stanford CA 94305, United States of America & Joint Research Center for Logic, Tsinghua University, Beijing, 100084, P.R. China

> **Abstract.** In this short note, we discuss a few senses in which logic represents natural language and natural reasoning and then fan out to a broader perspective on applied logical analysis.

1 Introduction

The discipline of logic started when thinkers in Antiquity noticed recurrent patterns in valid and invalid inferences occurring in reasoning practices and found that these could be studied as such. Since reasoning usually takes place couched in natural language, a medium whose syntax serves many further functions, these reasoning patterns were made explicit using special notations for logical forms. In modern logic, logical forms live in formal languages with a complete syntax and semantics that start looking like full-fledged alternatives to natural language, a line taken in the famous 'equality in principle' thesis for natural and formal languages in Montague 1974. This raises the issue of what logical systems model or represent, and we will phrase the following discussion in these terms, though we will also question the full-language methodology in the end. Our light discussion will gradually draw in the choice of semantic structures and other basic themes in the design of logical systems.

2 Logical syntax and representing natural language

Patterns. The emphasis on discovery of *patterns* is a common theme in studies of the historical origins of logic and other academic disciplines, cf. Bod 2022. And one might think that these patterns are linguistic, since they were presumably extracted from natural language, our common medium of expression and communication. But how should we think of the matching of natural language 'in the wild' with designed logical patterns?

Syntax. Consider the common didactic practice of training students in 'translations' of inferences stated in natural language in some formalism such as first-order predicate logic. We can think of this as projecting natural language into a simpler language of forms that highlight just the structure that is relevant to inferences. The Latin diminutive 'formula' is particularly apt here in its literal meaning of 'little form', as we are aiming for simplicity.

Grammar and simplicity. Yet, what simplicity means is a vexed issue, and at the level of syntax alone, not that much comes to mind. One might compare the length or other measures of *syntactic complexity* of natural language sentences with that of their formula translations, though I am not aware of significant results in this direction. Indeed, logical syntax can even add space-consuming devices that do not occur overtly in natural language expressions, such as scope indications and variable binding. On the positive side one could see these extras as logical syntax modeling not just expressions, but broader linguistic mechanisms. Variable binding offers a simple model for anaphora and discourse coherence, and thus its more intricate structure beyond natural language surface syntax comes with its own benefits.

Another angle on syntactic simplicity places the focus on *grammatical complexity*. Grammars for formal languages are usually context-free: cf. van Benthem 1988, a study of logical syntax, for details—and exceptions. In contrast, grammars for natural languages are often context-sensitive, that is, higher up in the grammatical Chomsky Hierarchy of complexity.

But arguably, the simplicity and utility of logical formulas rather has to do with their *uses*, namely, their function in analyzing or recognizing inferences. We now turn to this angle.

Proof systems and text grammar. In the above reconstruction of historical origins, the point of logical formulas is their role in making the structure of inferences explicit. Formal notations such as, say, "A or B, not-$A \Rightarrow B$" do just this, with sentential variables A, B for parts of a possibly much more complex linguistic expression whose precise nature does not matter, and a focus on the specific logical expressions of disjunction and negation that do matter to the validity of the given inference, cf. Bolzano 2014, Bonnay & Westerståhl 2016.

In doing so, we extend the above view of sentence grammar to one of *text grammar*: the logical structure of sequences of sentences involved in an inference. When chaining individual inferences into more complex proofs, this text grammar also brings its own technical notions that may go beyond natural language texts, such as long-distance dependency management of conclusions on assumptions in natural deduction, cf. Prawitz 1965.

Variety. One striking feature of the logical study of proofs is the *variety of available systems*, from Hilbert-style axiomatic to many styles of natural deduction. One can think of these as different computational implementations of deduction for practical purposes, but one can also take them more realistically. They are then proposals for representing a particular style of reasoning, a claim suggested by the terminology 'natural deduction'. I am inclined to the latter view, but the criterion of success for such claims is not always clear, since logical proof systems are also meant as a tool to be learnt, and *improve* a given reasoning practice. Thus they exhibit the same two faces as the discipline of logic itself, harboring both descriptive and normative aspects in its ambitions, a tension that I will mostly ignore here.

Digression: natural logic. The idea that formal languages are indispensable for analyzing inference in natural language has not gone unchallenged. The program of *'natural logic'*, van Benthem 2008, Moss 2015, uses natural language syntax as is to represent some inference practices in ways that are simpler than the usual logical representations. The issue then shifts to *when* it becomes more profitable to make the transition to formal logical modeling.

Meanings: inferential and semantic. The discussion so far may suffice for an inferentialist who holds that proof rules determine the meanings of logical expressions. But I myself think semantically and want an independent analysis of meanings, if only, to judge whether a proposed proof system makes sense. What follows will be a semantic perspective bringing to light further plurality of representation in logic. Even so, many of the following themes may also make sense in a purely proof-theoretic treatment which I do not pursue here.

3 Logical semantics and representing natural language

The usual translation exercises in logic courses do not seem to be purely syntactic, as the first-order language used comes with an intended semantics that involves two features.

Semantics 1: Conceptual frameworks. One component of a semantics is a structured view of what the described reality looks like. In a common view of predicate logic, these are models with a domain of individual objects and predicates and functions over these. This can be seen as a proposal for a *conceptual framework* for natural language and inference. And as such, it is a choice of representation since natural language does not force us to think in just this way. In fact, some philosophers and linguists have rejected an ontology with individual objects as primary citizens, cf. Keenan & Faltz 1986. And even for formal languages, logic itself has an alternative in the long-standing algebraic tradition, Sanchez Valencia 2004, that works with, one might say, domains of concepts with various interrelations, and only admits underlying objects for the algebras if these can be introduced through representation theorems.

Variety is the rule in logic. The preceding is not a criticism of the standard Tarski semantics for predicate logic. The latter has proved a widely useful representation for human inference, for automating reasoning, and for proving results stating deep insights into the metatheory of reasoning with predicates and quantifiers. The point is just that, as with any proposed representation, there can be attractive alternatives. There are many further examples of such framework options in logic, especially when we turn to modal expressions that go beyond the static here and now. For instance, many formats exist for representing the pervasive temporal reasoning in natural language: tense logic with Past and Future operators, interpreted on points or alternatively on intervals, but also different logical forms provided by a two-sorted predicate logic over points in time, or yet other structures, cf. van Benthem 1995.

Semantics 2: Mechanisms of interpretation. The second fundamental aspect of a semantics is how it makes the connection between the syntax of a language and the intended models. Famously, for predicate logic, this *interpretation mechanism* is compositional and based on Tarski's notion of satisfaction which involves assignments of objects to variables as 'states' of the interpretation process. And yet again, there are alternatives to such a package of type of models plus type of interpretation mechanism. For instance, dynamic semantics, cf. the survey Nouwen, Brasoveanu, van Eijck & Visser 2016, has an alternative more procedural view of what happens when we interpret expressions with anaphora, and there are yet other attractive formats, such as discourse representation theory, Kamp & Reyle 1993, or game-theoretic semantics, Hintikka & Sandu 1997. What all these examples make abundantly clear is that logic can also model many different views of the semantic interpretation process.

Compositionality. These options also illustrate another virtue of logical modeling. A general analysis and design principle for semantic interpretation of all the above kinds is *compositionality*, Baltag, van Benthem & Westerståhl 2023. Logical languages are both the origin and the most perspicuous illustration of how this methodology works. Moreover, it is their abstract simplicity that helps us develop a range of compositional interpretation procedures.

4 Task dependent representation: Functions of natural language

Our discussion so far has left out an important parameter. Representation is usually there for some *purpose*, and its adequacy can depend on that purpose. Now natural language has many different functions, and so far we have only encountered two of these.

World description. Natural language is a medium for *describing* what the world is like, or what the language users take the world to be like. Predicate logic offers a model for that function: its language represents the structure of natural language sentences describing situations in the world, while its models are a way of representing those situations.

Theoretical terms. The simple term 'description' quickly gets more complex when we move away from simple situations in the world and look at the many theoretical terms in language. When we call a person "friendly", we do not assign an observable property, but express a complex expectation about behavior of that person over time. And explicit modal expressions like "believe" even populate the physical world with 'constructs': unobservable mental attitudes that serve as postulated theoretical terms to make sense of human behavior, van Benthem 1983, just as physicists postulate forces or fields in their theories to make sense of observable reality. Thus, the conceptual framework of a semantics may also include quite complex abstract notions that shape our perspective of, and expectations about the world.

Inference. However, this note started with another function of natural language, namely, as a vehicle for *inferences*. It is not obvious that the same logical forms that help analyze inference are also optimal for describing the world. Already van Benthem 1987 asked why it is that the same representation in formulas of predicate logic works so well for such different purposes. Even so, divergences do exist in logic, for instance, with the use of Skolem forms in resolution theorem proving, which are not easily humanly interpretable, Robinson 1965.

Communication and coordination. A third crucial function of natural language that has attracted attention from logicians is *communication*. Again it is not obvious why the logical forms that serve description or inference would also serve this further purpose. And indeed, current dynamic-epistemic logics for communication employ additional logical operators for information updates that have no direct counterparts in natural language, Baltag & Renne 2016. We will not discuss the representational role of the latter logical forms here.

Beyond information. Communication is a way of *coordinating behavior* which involves more than the informational focus of logical modeling. Successful communication is at the same time a way of agenda management, achieving goal alignment, and even of achieving the emotional resonance that is crucial to understanding, learning, and shared agency.

5 Connecting representations to what they represent

From natural to formal languages. What is the connection between natural language and logical formalisms designed for functions like those discussed above? One might think that this is just an art of modeling based on experience, but sometimes more can be said.

Translation. Logic texts often use the term *'translation'* from natural into formal languages, but this may suggest too much. A predicate-logical formula is seldom a faithful rendering of a natural language sentence, except for the simple type of discourse of the "Mary knows John" type one finds, for instance, in factual data bases, or in simple natural language processing.

Paraphrase. For many other purposes, one can view a logical formula as a *paraphrase* of a natural language sentence, geared toward representing the essentials needed for a particular task. Examples of this abound in work on 'logical AI', McCarthy 2001, where the logical text describing the relevant content of a problem to be solved may diverge considerably from what the natural language version says, both qua formula structure and qua arrangement of the text. This paraphrasing ability is much more widespread and useful than translation skills, and while it cannot be made algorithmic like translation, it can be trained and honed.

Maintaining harmony. One can also juxtapose natural language and representing logical formulas without any claim of intrinsic adequacy except for demanding that actions in the two realms should stay in step. The latter view is made more precise in the analysis of logical modeling in Moss & Westerståhl 2023. The authors assume that natural language sentences describe 'situations' or 'scenarios', seen as parts of the world, or as empirically real mental pictures that we form of the world. We are then free to connect sentences with formulas and situations with models in any way we like, but the criterion of adequacy is the harmony expressed in the following diagram, whose arrow structure should commute:

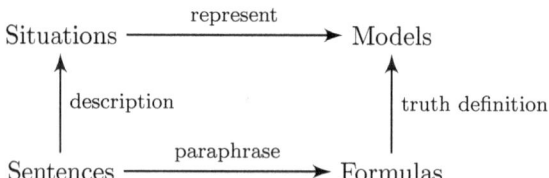

Starting with a sentence or text, if we first move to logical formulas at the bottom and then, staying in the logical realm, follow the formal truth definition in logical models upward, we should get the same effect as first following the informal description upward in the empirical realm, and only then follow the representation into logical models. Here the arrows can also stand for relations rather than functions, with 'truth in a model' as an obvious example. This leaves much more freedom for how the logical theorist decides to make connections.

Note that a commuting diagram for just one concrete sentence and formula can be constructed entirely ad-hoc. To make the analysis do real work, we will want to demand commutation for all representation pairs in some family to be specified in the intended application.

Similar attunement diagrams make sense for inference, where logical inferences between formulas should track actual reasoning steps in natural language. And they can also be used to check whether proposed formal update mechanisms track real information flow.

General tracking. Now this perspective might be considered 'behaviorist' since we do not apply any criterion of intrinsic resemblance, but only demand that representations stay attuned to the empirical practice they are modeling. But this generality is also a virtue. Indeed, the preceding methodology, which can be made precise in a general category-theoretic setting, applies to a wide range of forms of 'tracking' one system with the aid of another.

Connecting situations and models. The preceding diagram raises a further question: what connects real structures like situations or scenarios with the models in a logical semantics? There are many candidates in the literature, from isomorphism to weaker simulations or embeddings. We will discuss these later under the heading of transformations and invariants. But as with the above paraphrasing, assigning formal models to real-world scenarios may be something of an art based on experience, rather than an algorithmic procedure.

6 Equivalences within the logical language

Next we move to representation *inside logic itself*, as there are also substantial issues here.

From formulas to propositions. Once inside the realm of logic, perhaps the major theme for a logical system is exploring the *valid laws* governing reasoning in the domain under study. This adds a complication to our earlier discussion. We may have suggested so far that the representing object for a sentence is literally the logical formula associated with it, in any of the manners outlined in the preceding section. However, the valid laws of a logical system induce a notion of *equivalence* between formulas, and thus, the real logical object doing the representing is the structure underlying that equivalence class. In common philosophical parlance, we are after the *proposition* expressed by these equivalent formulas.

Alternative logics. This perspective raises deep issues that run through the logical literature. Which notion of equivalence is appropriate to the external domain being represented? For instance, does a sentence of the form not-not-S express the same proposition as sentence S? The answer is positive in a classical truth-oriented perspective, but negative when representing a constructive mathematical practice where negation means refutation. One can construe logical proposals for dealing with constructivity, or in recent years: hyper-intensionality, as offering different, less or more fine-grained, views of what one takes to be the relevant structure of propositions. These alternatives may arise with different choices of semantic frameworks, when e.g., truth gets replaced in favor of 'support', or they could have more proof-theoretic motivations, as is the case for various constructive logics.

A landscape of levels. The resulting variety forms a landscape where different systems focus on *different 'levels of grain'* in representing their object of study. This variety can even arise when we fix one particular formal language, say the standard one of propositional logic. At one extreme one can find coarse representations of propositions as sets of worlds, at another, the very syntax of the logical formulas themselves. This landscape is not linearly ordered, and has many gradients: sets versus topologies, qualitative versus quantitative, and so on.

The above is just a very brief summary of some well-known facts about logic. I stated them merely to emphasize their relevance to how we can represent empirical practices, and as background for the following points that are sometimes neglected.

Freedom in language design. A multi-level landscape of options is entangled with the *design of logical languages*. More fine-grained representing structures can interpret richer logical languages, so the issue should not just be strength of identification but also the medium of representation. Some literature on alternative logics ignores this point, focusing on one standard language, say, of propositional logic, without raising the question whether this formal language is the best medium for the semantic picture one is advocating.

To me there is a serious conceptual desideratum of *expressive harmony* between a semantic framework and the logical language one chooses to access it with. And this harmony is also important technically: infelicitous language design can make proof systems for validities opaque and completeness extremely hard to prove, merely by self-imposed restrictions.

Co-existence instead of competition: translations. A next point to note is that there need not be a 'right' representation for a given reasoning practice in this landscape of options Many languages and models may make sense, and what logic then offers is a total systematic picture. But there is a force for coherence in logic, in terms of a web of systematic *translations* and other forms of correlation that run across and facilitate commensurability for many logical systems.

No preferred direction. Next, there is *no preferred direction* for design in the landscape. In the history of science, coarsenings have proven just as fruitful as refinements. Compare the coarser qualitative perspective of Topology with the detailed quantitative level of Analysis. Coarser levels can highlight essentials that were invisible down below, such as the simplicity of continuous maps in Topology versus the epsilon-delta definitions in Analysis. For a more philosophical example, a 'hyper-intensional' logic is not automatically better than a 'standard modal' one: each may offer insights at its own level. I myself would even say that, if hyper-intensional logics had come first in history, there would have been a later major discovery that it also makes sense to throw away detail and introduce the standard modal logics.

Syntax from 'what' to 'how'. My third and final point concerns *pure syntax*, usually seen as a non-contender for the structure of propositions. However this may be, syntax represents something essential, even when logical equivalence identifies different formulas. Despite such validities, say, "not-(P or Q)" and "not-P and not-Q" are *different ways of getting to* the same denoted proposition. This 'how' can be seen clearly in the evaluation games associated with different formulas in game-theoretic semantics, and the various strategies that players have in these, which give different reasons for the truth of a formula in a given model. This combination of 'how' and 'what' seems crucial to our use of language.

Aside: computing. Syntax is also essential to *computation*, which needs code. While the algebraic terms $x + x^2$ and $x^2 + x$ always denote the same number, they correspond to different procedures for producing that number, and in general some procedures can be more perspicuous or efficient than others. It has even been suggested that such algorithmic differences are crucial to an algorithmic understanding of the Fregean notion of 'sense', Moschovakis 1993.

7 Invariances among logical models

Having discussed equivalence in logical syntax, let us now turn to equivalence in logical semantics. Formal models as they stand are seldom the true structures one has in mind. Models usually come with *invariance relations* that leave 'the same structure' intact. The standard example is isomorphism, which says that it is immaterial to the structure which actual objects do the representing. Accordingly, logical formulas will be true for objects in one model iff they are true for the images of those objects under an isomorphic map to another model. This requirement is even part of the definition of a logic in Abstract Model Theory.

Invariance relations. But as with logical equivalence, there are many options for invariance relations between models, depending on what underlying structure is the focus of interest. Isomorphism is a very fine sieve, but, say, in modal logic, a much coarser identification is often taken to represent the crucial accessibility structure of patterns of possible worlds or process states, namely, some form of bisimulation, Blackburn, de Rijke & Venema 2001.

Erlanger Program. This variety matches practice in mathematics, in a tradition going back to the Erlanger Program, Klein 1872. A mathematical theory describes structures that come with a *group of designated transformations* that define when two different manifestations of that structure are 'the same' from the perspective of the theory. For instance, Euclidean Geometry looks at spaces under the standard transformations of translation, rotation and reflection, while Topology identifies spatial structures under the much coarser notion of homeomorphism. Both perspectives have their uses, neither is 'better' than the other.

Systematic attention to the role of transformations and invariance is less common in the philosophical or linguistic literature. But it does occur implicitly when we realize that an ontology needs to come with a 'criterion of identity' between objects, Noonan & Curtis 2022, or perhaps better: between different semantic ways of getting to the same structure.

8 Connecting logical languages and logical models

Invariants and the emergence of language. The two main perspectives in the preceding discussion, formal language and semantic models, are intimately connected. Given any notion of transformation between structures, there will be *invariants*: predicates whose truth is not affected by moving from objects in one model to those in another model related by a transformation. Already Helmholtz 1883 saw such invariances as crucial to *the genesis of languages*, since languages will tend to express patterns that we reuse in different manifestations of the same empirical situation or scenario. This theme underlies the above Erlanger Program and the ubiquity of invariance in physics and other disciplines, Suppes 2003. In philosophy, the theme also occurs occasionally, as in the situation theory of Barwise & Perry 1983 with its emphasis on the informational constraints that structure our world.

Logical languages and invariance. The harmony of semantic invariance relations between models and language design is especially clear when we analyze, not just deductive power, but expressive power of logical languages. We can think of these languages as designed to describe invariant properties and predicates in one's semantics. One part of this match is the persistence of truth or satisfiability of logical formulas under the relevant invariance relations between models, the other, usually deeper, direction is 'expressive completeness' results showing when the logical language can define all invariant predicates. We will not elaborate this theme, but refer to the model-theoretic literature, cf. Hodges 2020.

Once more, we conclude that in logic, language design and choice of semantics go together.

Caveat: Two senses of representation. The preceding sections moved away from the original issue in this note. We started with a practice of language use and reasoning, and how logic-internal notions represented these external empirical ones. But then we shifted to internal issues such as whether a given logical formula represents its underlying proposition, or whether a concrete model represents the equivalence class defining its structure. We believe that these issues still form a whole by *composing* the two senses of representation. Logical formulas represent natural language sentences, but at the same time they represent logical propositions, so they are a connecting locus between sentences and propositions. And likewise, specific models mediate between actual situations and abstract structure.

This concludes our brief discussion of modeling and representation in logic. What follows is an afterthought questioning the standard 'formal language package' view we took for this.

9 Coda: piecemeal merging versus global juxtaposition

In this paper, we have mainly compared complete natural languages or reasoning practices with the architecture of entire logical languages, semantics, and proof systems for modeling these empirical phenomena. In this final section, we briefly outline an alternative view.

For a start, we could also see the task of logical analysis as *piecemeal problem solving*, which comes with a range of formal solutions as required by the occasion.

Reasoning challenges. Here is a well-known example from the psychology of reasoning:

> Fifteen farmers own at most thirteen cows each. Does it follow that at least two farmers own the same number of cows? (Mercier, Politzer & Sperber 2017)

Experimental subjects turn out to be hard-pressed to justify an answer. What definitely does not work is transcribing the sentence and the putative conclusion into straightforward logical formulas as we suggested above and then applying formal deduction. The key to solving this problem is finding the right way of thinking, or more concretely, a good representation which makes us see the answer in a simple manner. In this particular case, we need to see the problem as an instance of the Pigeon Hole Principle that, if we put k objects into n boxes, where $k > n$, at least one box will get two objects. In the given case, there are 14 boxes, the number of cows a farmer can own, ranging from 0 to 13, and we place 15 farmers in them.

First representation, then calculus. This example is typical for actual reasoning problems. The difficulty is usually not applying the deduction or computation rules of some calculus, but the prior step of representing the given problem in a way that makes its solution via that calculus easy or at least feasible. And such a representation may work for some but not all problems, so uniform approaches via logical languages and proof systems seem off the mark. What we need then is a repertoire of different representations that help piecemeal with actual scenarios, an ability we can train by just learning and understanding more examples.

Aside: logic and counting. In this piecemeal view, logic still makes sense. Inference patterns codified in logic do occur widely, witness the literature on philosophical or computational logic. But what the preceding example suggests is that reasoning patterns involving counting may be just as basic, a thesis developed in much more detail in van Benthem & Icard 2023. There does not seem to be an obvious priority for logic over arithmetic here.

Hybrids and merges. But there is also a further issue. Problem solving is local in that only a few well-chosen formulas are needed as paraphrases, and only a few relevant inferences need to be drawn. And we do not move entirely into a formal world of derivation and computation with these, leaving the natural language formulation of the problem behind. Indeed, instead of complete and separate natural and formal languages, we can also think of illuminating paraphrases for a problem as *hybrids* of natural language and logical formulas, in the same way as the language of mathematical research is a hybrid of the two.

Dynamic interactions. Well-understood, even the earlier diagram from Moss & Westerståhl 2023 fits this view. While the diagram suggests a strict separation of empirical and logical realms, it can also be seen as making a *methodological distinction*. In reality, there may be a dynamic. A successful formal analysis may influence natural language practice, and some of its notions and notations may make their way into our ordinary linguistic repertoire.

The virtues of hybridity. Perhaps the term 'representation' is then no longer appropriate, as this suggests a separation between what represents and what is represented. The question rather becomes if logic can help *improve* our linguistic and reasoning practices, just as mathematics does. I believe that the looser *hybrid view* is much closer to how logic is used in both mathematical and philosophical practice. The hybrid language of mathematical research and for that matter, of philosophy papers using logic, is a fascinating flexible medium which combines the virtues of both formal and natural languages. The formal components provide precision as needed, but the embedding in natural language makes sure that texts build up interest and *shared purpose*. The natural language also allows for *paraphrasing* and explaining formal proofs at higher less detailed levels increasing our understanding of what makes the formal level tick. I believe that the study of the fascinating mixtures of natural and formal has been neglected in contemporary logic, semantics, and philosophy of language.

10 Conclusion

We have discussed the basic senses in which logic can be said to represent natural language and natural reasoning, involving both syntax and semantics. We then moved to the role of representation inside logic in one picture of semantic invariance and logical language design. We did not present any grand conclusion from all this. Our discussion was rather meant to highlight the variety of representations available in logic, which fits well with the variety of tasks that logic can be applied to. A multi-thread narrative like this seems closer to the realities of applied logic, and if nothing else, it may create awareness of the debatable presuppositions in innocent-looking terminology such as 'the logical form' of sentences.

One theme has been ignored in this paper. Logic is not just meant to faithfully *describe* reasoning as humans perform it, it is also a *normative* discipline offering standards. Without the driving force of correction, human intellectual progress would be unimaginable. The latter theme has been ignored in my discussion, but logical representation also has the potential, and perhaps even ambition, to enlighten and where needed, improve practice.

Acknowledgement. I thank Dag Westerståhl for his comments on a draft of this paper.

References

A. Baltag, J. van Benthem & D. Westerståhl, 2023, Compositionality in Context, in A. Palmigiano & M. Sadrzaheh, eds., *Samson Abramsky on Logic and Structure in Computer Science and Beyond*, Springer Science, Dordrecht, 773–812.

A. Baltag & B. Renne, 2016, Dynamic-Epistemic Logic, *Stanford Encyclopedia of Philosophy*.

J. Barwise & J. Perry, 1983, *Situations and Attitudes*, The MIT Press, Cambridge MA.

J. van Benthem, 1983, Logical Semantics as an Empirical Science, *Studia Logica* 42, 299–313.

J. van Benthem, 1987, Meaning: Interpretation and Inference, *Synthese* 73:3, 451–470.

J. van Benthem, 1988, Logical Syntax, *Theoretical Linguistics* 14, 119–142.

J. van Benthem, 1995, Temporal Logic, in D. Gabbay et al., eds., *Handbook of Logic in Artificial Intelligence and Logic Programming*, 4, Oxford University Press, 241–350.

J. van Benthem, 2008, A Brief History of Natural Logic, in M. Chakraborty et al. eds., *Logic, Navya–Nyaya & Applications*, College Publications, London 2008, 21–42.

J. van Benthem, 2021, Semantic Perspectives in Logic, in G. Sagi and J. Woods, eds., *The Semantic Conception of Logic*, Cambridge University Press, Cambridge UK, 117–141.

J. van Benthem & Th. Icard, 2023, Interfacing Logic and Counting, *Bulletin of Symbolic Logic* 29:4, 503–587.

P. Blackburn, M. de Rijke & Y. Venema, 2001, *Modal Logic*, Cambridge University Press, Cambridge.

R. Bod, 2022, *A World of Patterns*, Johns Hopkins University Press, Baltimore.

B. Bolzano, 2014, *Theory of Science*, Translation of the 1837 German original by R. George and P. Rusnock, Oxford University Press, Oxford.

D. Bonnay & D. Westerståhl, 2016, Compositionality Solves Carnap's Problem, *Erkenntnis* 81:4, 721–739.

S. de Haro & J. Butterfield, 2024, *The Philosophy and Physics of Duality*, Oxford University Press, Oxford.

H. von Helmholtz, 1878, Ueber die Thatsachen welche der Geometrie zu Grunde liegen, *Nachrichten von der Königlichen Gesellschaft der Wissenschaften zu Göttingen*, 9.

J. Hintikka & G. Sandu, 1997, Game-Theoretic Semantics, in J. van Benthem & A. ter Meulen, eds., *Handbook of Logic and Language*, Elsevier, Amsterdam, 361–410.

W. Hodges, 2020, Model Theory, *Stanford Encyclopedia of Philosophy*.

H. Kamp & U. Reyle, 1993, *From Discourse to Logic*, Springer, Dordrecht.

E. Keenan & L. Faltz, 1986, *Boolean Semantics for Natural Language*, Reidel, Dordrecht.

F. Klein, 1872, *Vergleichende Betrachtungen über neuere geometrische Forschungen*, Deichert, Erlangen.

J. McCarthy, 2001, Concepts of Logical AI, *Logic-Based Artificial Intelligence*, Kluwer, 37–52.

H. Mercier, G. Politzer & D. and Sperber, 2017, What Causes Failure to Apply the Pigeonhole Principle in Simple Reasoning Problems? *Thinking & Reasoning*, 23(2), 184–189.

R. Montague, 1974, *Formal Philosophy*, Yale University Press, New Haven.

Y. Moschovakis, 1993, Sense and Denotation as Algorithm and Value, in J. Oikonen & J. Väänänen, eds., *Logic Colloquium Helsinki 1990*, Lecture Notes in Logic, 2, Springer, Dordrecht, 210–249.

L. Moss, 2015, Natural Logic, in S. Lappin & Ch. Fox, eds., *The Handbook of Contemporary Semantic Theory*, John Wiley & Sons.

L. Moss & D. Westerståhl, 2023, *Modeling as Commuting Diagrams*, Department of Mathematics, Indiana University Bloomington & Institute of Philosophy, University of Stockholm.

H. Noonan & B. Curtis, 2022, Identity, *Stanford Encyclopedia of Philosophy*.

R. Nouwen, A. Brasoveanu, J. van Eijck & A. Visser, 2016, Dynamic Semantics, *Stanford Encyclopedia of Philosophy*.

D. Prawitz, 1965, *Natural Deduction*, Almqvist and Wiksell, Stockholm.

J. A. Robinson, 1965, A Machine-Oriented Logic Based on the Resolution Principle, *Journal of the ACM*, 12, 23–41.

V. Sanchez Valencia, 2004, The Algebra of Logic, in D. Gabbay et al., eds., *Handbook of the History of Logic*, Elsevier, Amsterdam, 389–544.

P. Suppes, 2003, *Representation and Invariance of Scientific Structures*, CSLI Publications, Stanford.

H. Weyl, 1963, *Philosophy of Mathematics and Natural Science*, Atheneum, New York, reprint from 1927 German edition.

Models, representation, and idealization
Revisiting the inferentialism debate

Jesús Zamora Bonilla

Lógica, Historia y Filosofía de la Ciencia, Facultad de Fliosofía, C. de Bravo Murillo, 38, Chamberí, 28015 Madrid, Spain

Abstract. The view of scientific models as 'inferential prostheses' is defended against some recent criticisms. In particular, I argue how the view can offer a reasonable answer to the problems of a general theory of scientific representation, and how it does not depend on ontological assumptions about denotation. A defense of the idea that models do actually represent the world, and that they can give us representations of the world increasingly closer to the truth, is offered against the radical artifactualism of Sanches de Oliveira and the anti-veritism of Potochnik.

> Ordo et connectio idearum idem est, ac ordo et connectio rerum.
>
> Spinoza

> God writes straight with crooked lines.
>
> Teresa of Ávila

1 Introduction: models as inferential prostheses

The Conference on 'Models and Representations in Science', held at the University of Münster in September 2023 under the auspices of the *Académie Internationale de Philosophie des Sciences*, was a perfect occasion for revisiting one topic which, though deeply essential in the evolution of my philosophical ideas, I had only discussed it in an explicit and detailed way in a couple of papers, co-authored with my colleague and friend Xavier de Donato, papers that already were more than one decade old. In preparing my participation in that conference, I realised that these papers, especially the one that had appeared in *Erkenntnis* in 2009, had received a number of interesting comments by other authors since its publication, but the fact was that we, due to the pressure of other tasks and projects in the meantime, had not had until then the chance of answering any of those comments. Of course, the following pages contain only my own opinions, and they must not necessarily coincide with Xavier's views on the topics I will discuss.

The most important claim of "Credibility, Idealization, and Model Building" was that scientific models have to be seen fundamentally as *'inferential prostheses'*. This idea fits rather coherently both with the views of scientific models as artifacts (e.g., Knuuttila 2011), since protheses are after all a kind of manmade tools, and with the inferentialist approaches to scientific models and representations (e.g., Suarez 2015), according to which the essential role of models is to facilitate surrogate inferences to their 'real world' targets.

We can summarise these similarities by saying that our approach combines Knuutila's *artifactualism* about scientific models' *nature* with Suarez's *inferentialism* about scientific models' *function*. In this respect, we do not claim that our view is an especially original one, of course; what was most innovative in our papers was the framing of the different abstract modelling strategies and functions (like idealization, optimisation, approximation, representation, understanding, etc.) within a more comprehensive inferentialist philosophical view, in particular, the normative-pragmatic-expressivist brand of inferentialism famously championed by Robert Brandom (e.g., Brandom 1994), as an extension of Wilfried Sellars (1963) idea of knowledge as the ability of "playing the game of giving and asking for reasons". It is reasonable, hence, that some of the comments our view has received have to do with the approach not being 'Brandomian' (or, as we shall explain, deflationist) enough, or with such an approach being able of answering the questions levelled to an inferentialist theory of scientific representation. The main goal of this new paper will be precisely to answer those criticisms, and spell out how the project fits with a deflationary view of scientific knowledge in general, and of scientific representations and idealizations in particular.

2 Brandomising scientific models

A possible way of putting the problem our approach attempted to tackle is offered by the following text from a recent book on scientific models as representations (Frigg and Nguyen 2020):

> Rather than attempting to investigate the conditions of epistemic representation by investigating the representational practices that establish it in every instance, one could instead take those conditions as foundational, and investigate how they give rise to representational practices, practices which themselves are explained by the inferentialist's conditions (rather than explaining them). Such an approach is inspired by Brandom's (...) inferentialism in the philosophy of language, where the central idea is to reverse the order of explanation from representational notions—like truth and reference—to inferential notions—such as the validity of argument. We are urged to begin from the inferential role of sentences (or propositions, or concepts, and so on)—that is, from the role that they play in providing reasons for other sentences (or propositions, etc.), and having such reasons provided for them—and from this reconstruct their representational aspects. So by analogy, rather than taking the representational practices (analogues of truth and reference) to explain the inferential capacity of carriers (the analogue of validity), we reconstruct the practices by taking the notion of surrogative reasoning as conceptually basic (...) Such an approach is outlined by de Donato Rodríguez and Zamora Bonilla (2009) and seems like a fruitful route for future research.[1]

---

[1] Frigg and Nguyen (2020), p. 92.

One of the main goals of an inferentialist conception of scientific models is, exactly, that of changing the typical order of explanation in philosophy of science, so that, instead of giving an account of how scientific inferences are possible thanks to the representational properties of the scientific models (or theories) that are employed in those inferences, what we do is to explain what scientific representations are, how they function, and how they are evaluated, in terms mainly of their inferential virtues. The fundamental idea of this inferentialist view is, indeed, the one captured by the expression *surrogative (or surrogate) reasoning*: scientists (and non-scientists alike, by the way) employ models as tools *on which* to perform some inferences that would be much more difficult (or directly impossible) to carry out 'directly on', or 'explicitly about', the real-world systems the models attempt to correctly represent (whatever this 'directness' actually may mean in each particular case). A model is a physical or mathematical system (or 'structure') some of whose properties and connections amongst its elements we know how to manipulate in order to perform some inferences within it, and we take profit of this inferential capacity by interpreting some of the model-system elements as 'representing' some analogue elements in the real-system that is our 'target'. The main difference with a 'representationalist' (and hence, non-inferentialist) account would be that the 'representing' part mentioned in the previous sentence is in itself explained in inferential terms: the fact that some elements in the model-system 'represent' some elements in the target-system reduces to the fact that model-users know how to perform some *inferences* from sentences that talk about the target-system to sentences about the model-system, and vice versa. This basically replicates Hughes (1997) famous "DDI-account", where the initials stand respectively for "denotation" (the inference from target to model), "demonstration" (inference within the model), and "interpretation" (inference from model to target), but the idea is at least as old a the German physicist Heinrich Hertz's (1894) description of how scientific reasoning is performed with the help of our "images in thought", and, if we allow ourselves a little bit of hermeneutical freedom, it may also be glimpsed in Baruch Spinoza's famous dicto according to which "the order and connection among ideas is the same as the order and connection among things" (*Ethics*, II.7), only that, as we shall see below, contemporary people cannot be as optimistic about that 'sameness' as the old rationalist philosopher was, because that equivalence has often to be seen as just a matter of more or less lucky *conjecture* and of bigger or smaller *approximation*.

Instead, according to representationalist approaches, like that of Frigg and Nguyen, an essential aspect of scientific models is their being a *representation* of some real systems, a notion that (besides creating some conceptual difficulties—to which we shall refer later—about models that do not have a specific real system as their target) presupposes the existence of some kind of *ontological* relation of correspondence between the model and the system. This relation can be interpreted both as the semantic relation of *reference* (the target being the Fregean 'reference' of the model, i.e., the object the model—as a symbol—'points to'), and as the also semantic property of *truth* (or 'accuracy': how well the model describes the target). But, contrarily to how it is at times (mis)understood, Brandomian inferentialism does not *deny* that we may reasonably talk about a model's reference or about a model's truth (or lack thereof); what this approach allows to do is to understand the meaning of the ideas of reference and truth in terms of their *expressive role*, i.e., in terms of what having those concepts permits to *say* to users of a language that contain the corresponding terms (as contrasting to users of some imaginary language that lacked any terms analogous to the concepts of truth and reference). According to Brandom, this expressive role is basically what he calls an *anaphoric* function ('anaphora' being the technical grammatical term for the function of *pronouns*). For example, the idea of 'reference' serves mainly to help speakers to determine when two expressions are co-referential, in the sense that one of them can substitute the other (as the pronoun 'substitutes' the name), and hence, when an inference from a sentence containing a name or description to a sentence containing another name or description is valid (if both names or descriptions are co-referential). Similarly, the expressive role of the concept of 'truth' is allowing speakers to assert, to deny, to question, to express doubts about, etc., some propositions that do not need to be repeated, or that are only indirectly or abstractly identified in the speech (as when I say "what this report contains is not totally true", or "everything that logically follows from true premises is true"). Hence, truth and reference are not primarily a kind of deep ontological stuff for the *philosopher* to discern, but a couple of mundane expressions that *ordinary speakers* employ in order to clarify to other ordinary speakers what they are saying or what they are talking about. I insist: this does not mean at all that a scientific proposition 'cannot be objectively true', or that typical scientific models 'do not refer to something in the world'. It only means that what the *philosopher* can say about it is not essentially different, nor more ontologically profound, than what *ordinary scientific speakers* tell when they say, for example, that the Crick-Watson model of DNA is a 'right' description of DNA molecules, or that its wires 'represented' electronic chemical bonds. All this makes sense of Frigg and Nguyen's correct description of the inferentialist approach as one not intrinsically *contrary* to the representationalist *claims* about which are the representational virtues and properties of scientific models, but only different in the *type of explanation* we offer of those properties and virtues: a good model is not good *primarily* in the sense that it 'rightly depicts the world', but is good primarily in the sense that it allows to carry out numerous, interesting and successful inferences about the world, and it is *because of this* that we *infer* that the model must probably be an accurate description or representation of the (relevant fragment of the) world ... an inference that, after all, it will be real practicing scientists (rather than philosophers) who will have to say if it is valid, or by how much it is, and under which circumstances.

Naturally, representationalist philosophers like Frigg and Nguyen are rightly entitled to ask how well inferentialist views of models, such as our own, responds to what they see as the main questions a philosophical theory of scientific representations has to answer, and also how it overcomes some possible general difficulties they see in other inferentialist approaches.[2] This is what I shall try to do in the section 4. Before that, it is relevant to consider other comments our approach has received, in particular from Khalifa, Millson and Risjord (2022). These authors have developed what they call "a thoroughgoing inferentialism", or a "thoroughly deflationary account of scientific representation", and (as I mentioned) criticise our own view for not being 'deflationary enough'. By 'thoroughgoing inferentialism', Khalifa *et al.* understand a view that "makes no appeal to denotation nor to any non-linguistic representation relationship in its account of surrogative inference". Our approach, instead, would—according to them—suffer from what they call "the smuggling objection", i.e., from necessarily presupposing some 'substantive' *denotation* relation in order to explain how our explanation of the representational capacity of models works. I confess it is difficult for me to discern how Khalifa *et al.* reach exactly this diagnosis of our approach, for Donato and myself said basically nothing about denotation in our paper. My guess is that their diagnosis arises from our use of something similar to the already mentioned Hughes' DDI-account, though we called "immersion" the first of the three inferential steps (instead of "denotation", as Hughes does), i.e., the inference from target to model. But my view is that it is not right to interpret that first 'D' (or our 'immersion' step) in a representationalist way, i.e., as an (ontologically) 'substantive relation' that needs to be presupposed *by the philosopher* in order to make her explanatory account to work. Rather on the contrary, in my own view at least (I cannot speak for other inferentialists), that first 'step' *is intrinsically and primarily an inferential step*, an essential part of the inferential practice of the model users; in particular, it corresponds to the inferences they make from *claims about the target system* to their presumed equivalents *in the model system*. All the full DDI cycle (inference from target to model, from model to model, and from model to target) has to be seen, in our *surrogative* account, as an indirect way of constructing inferences *from target to target*, like, for

---

[2]Frigg (2023), p. 275.

example, in the case of prediction making: we obtain some empirical data *about the real material system*, transform them into the language of the model system, and perform some model-based calculations whose results are in their turn translated as (still unchecked) claims about the material system; hence, what we do with the help of the model is an inference from the available empirical data to new testable predictions. All of the steps of this process are *inferences*, even the steps from the material system to the scientific model. If there is something here like a 'substantive denotation *relation*', it is just the (scientific, not philosophical) *conjecture* that the model will be useful in allowing successful predictions by following those kind of operations (i.e, of *inferences*). Hence, I do not think that our approach 'smuggles' in any non-inferentialist-enough kind of elements. But perhaps a clearer and more explicit argument by Khalifa *et al.* could make me see the objection in some more positive view.[3]

Related to this, I find something problematic in Khalifa *et al.*'s attempt to explicate the surrogative inferential use of models with something like (what they call) an *inferential pedigree*. As they formulate the issue, the question is *how to justify inferences from the model to the target*, i.e., how to justify that a conclusion we reach within the model can be applied to the target. The 'inferential pedigree' would consist in the set of all reasons that make *this kind of inference* a legitimate one. But this applies only to the *third* step in the surrogate inference machinery (Hughes' 'interpretation', or the 'I' in the 'DDI-account'), whereas, as far as I understand the very idea of surrogate reasoning, it is rather the *second* D (Hughes 'demonstration', or what Donato and I called 'derivation') which is a literal surrogate or *substitute* of the inference (much more difficult to do without the help of the model) from the target to the target itself (or, more precisely, from *some* claims about the target to *other* claims about the target).[4] The other two types of inferences in the DDI-account serve, obviously, to operate the 'translation' from claims about the target to claims about the model,

---

[3]A related criticism has been recently leveled by Suárez (2024), in which our application of Brandom's inferentialism is, rather surprisingly, described as "a study of science through its linguistic categories and syntax, which was valuable prior to the semantic conception and mediating models revolution in the late 1990s, (but) looks too restrictive now". This is particularly shocking because our interentialist view of models' function and functioning is essentially *the same one* as Suarez's, only that embedded into a Brandomian inferentialist framework. It goes without saying that Brandom's own theory is immensely more general than just 'linguistic categories and syntax', for it is actually a full-fledged *theory of rationality*, and in particular, a *pragmatist* explanation of some fundamental *semantic* categories, i.e., an explanation of what people *say* in terms of what they *do*. A Brandomian view, hence, is as far from the (Carnapian?) 'received-view of scientific theories' of the positivist age as any of the other semantic-plus-mediating-models approaches may be.

[4]I would call these inferences from-target-to-target 'material' if the term were not already associated to another very precise meaning in philosophy of language and philosophy of logic.

but what needs a 'pedigree' is the *whole cycle* of inferences, not only the ones from model to target. In fact, some of the content of Khalifa *et al.*'s 'inferential pedigree' (for example, measurement) necessarily consists in fact in inferences *from the 'real' world to the model* (in this example, transforming empirical observations into numbers that can be expressed in the model's language). Khalifa *et al.*'s way of expressing it seems to present the role of measurement, and of other related arguments, as something that merely serves to 'justify', 'entitle', or 'support' the 'final' inference from model to target, but I tend to see measurement as simply one *part* of the whole process of scientific inference, and hence, as in need of an 'inferential pedigree' as any other part of the process.

3 A short interlude: do we learn from models?

The idea according to which the fundamental question of a theory of scientific models is that of what 'justifies' the inferences from models to targets seems to be equivalent to another assumption I find regrettably common in the relevant literature: the opinion that the main philosophical problem in this field is "how we can learn from models" (e.g., Morgan 1999). Actually, I think the answer cannot be simpler: *we just do not learn (about the world) from models*. What we learn about the world is *that* some models work and others do not (or which models work better and which models work worse), but *this* is something that we obviously do not learn *from the models themselves*, but that is learnt *from the world*, i.e., from empirical observations, or, more exactly, from repeated applications of the DDI cycle. *That* one model will work is simply a *conjecture* (at least at the beginning), and it is only *after* this conjecture gets enough empirical support that we can use the model as a 'sufficiently enough good representation' of its target. Obviously, *I myself* can learn a lot about chemical elements 'from' the model we call 'the periodic table', but this is because generations of chemists before myself learnt that the *empirical facts* support very strongly the hypotheses on which the table is grounded, and this is not something they could have learnt 'from the table itself'.[5] It is also true that models can *suggest* 'connections and order' *in the target* that we would not have envisaged without their help; after all this is the main reason why (at least according to an inferentialist viewpoint) we wanted models *for* to begin with: to draw consequences not easy to derive without the models. But these new consequences are in principle *as conjectural* as the conjecture that the model will be a good enough representation of its target (in fact, they are simply a

---

[5]There can be cases in which a model gets its support by the fact that it naturally derives from other models of theories *already well confirmed*, but this does not go against the general claim that *it is experience* what help us to ultimately learn *whether* models work better or worse.

part of *this* conjecture), and we need empirical knowledge *to learn whether* those inferences are materially correct or not, or to what extent they are.

In summary, we learn *about the world* from scientific models simply in the same way and in the same sense in which we 'learn' *from any other scientific hypothesis*: by applying the good-old-fashioned hypothetico-deductive method in any of its many variants. We do not learn *from the model* that the model is a useful representation of its target: we learn *this* from the experience about the target, even if that experience has been obtained in big part by following the specific conjectures suggested by the model. Stated otherwise: one model might be very fruitful in 'teaching' us lots of new interesting consequences from its internal structure, but if empirical data strongly *falsify* these consequences once they are applied to the real target systems (even if those consequences are stated in some loose approximate way), we would not say that this model 'teaches' us something *about the world*, except the possibly interesting fact that the world is *not* well represented by it.

4 Sketch of an inferential theory of scientific representation

As I said a few pages before, the most important test for an inferentialist theory of scientific (models as) representations would be to show whether and how it answers the main problems of a general theory of scientific representation. To avoid much speculation from my part, I will directly make use of Frigg and Nguyen own list of such fundamental problems for a theory of scientific representation:[6]

1. The representation problem: what makes of something a representation of something else.

2. The demarcation problem: what makes of something an epistemic/scientific representation.

3. The accuracy problem: under what conditions is scientific representation accurate.

4. The problem of carriers: what kinds of objects carriers are, and how are they handled.

5. The problem of targetless representations.

I think that our view of models as inferential prostheses allows to illuminate all these questions in a rather straightforward way. As for the first problem, this is just what 'surrogate inference' consists in, to begin with: the model is used to perform *indirectly* inferences about the target

---
[6]Frigg and Nguyen (2020), ch. 1.

system. The model's *being* a representation of the target just consists in its being *used* as a surrogate inference mechanism. There is no need of any substantive philosophical general explanation of how is this possible (our explanation is, hence, deflationary in Suarez's sense), for different models will work (better or worse) thanks to different 'physical', 'mathematical' or 'logical' reasons, and not because of some universal property like 'correspondence', 'isomorphism', etc. Furthermore, as I explained above, *that* a model 'rightly represents' its target is not a philosophical presupposition, but just a scientific conjecture that may end being corroborated or contradicted by the empirical facts.

A similarly so simple (or even simplistic) answer can be given to the second problem: what makes of a representation a *scientific* representation is just that it is used as such in the scientific process. There is no bigger mystery in this case than in the question of what is what makes of a laboratory, a measuring instrument, or a journal, a 'scientific' one. Of course, what is far from easy is to state what is the general difference (if there is one) between 'science' and 'non-science'. Generations of schollars have dismayed about trying to solve this old 'demarcation problem', or trying to determine if there is a solution at all, and it will not be me who pretends to have an answer to any of those questions. But, assuming that we have at least a minimal *pragmatic* understanding of when it is appropriate to use the adjective 'scientific' in numerous everyday contexts, I do not think we need more than this 'ordinary speaker' lexical knowledge to answer Frigg and Nguyen's second question.

The answer to the third problem comes also implicit with our answer to the first one: there is no general philosophical explication of what an 'accurate scientific representation' is, but, instead, how good one specific model is will depend on the contingent reasons that specific scientists will have for using that model in particular. The most general answer an inferentialist account can give is that a fundamental criterion to determine the value of a model will be how well it works in allowing to make numerous, useful and successful inferences about its targets. Donato and I summarised these types of reasons into what we considered the two most general categories applicable to the evaluation of models: *credibility* (or 'realisticness': how well scientists consider in the end that the model 'describes' the target) and *enlightening* (or 'understanding': how 'fluent' the process of inference-making is made, cognitively speaking, thanks to the model); but we doubt that there is something like a universal algorithm that can transform these two rather vague and context-dependent values into a precise philosophical theory of epistemic virtues.[7]

---

[7]Some may rightly point to a possible inconsistency between what I have just said in this paragraph and my own extended work on verisimilitude as a mathematical function of

As for the carriers problem, our approach sympathizes with Knuutila's artifactualism, as I already said. Models are inferential prostheses, and there are no limits as to the kinds of 'stuff' those prostheses can be 'made of', as long as they allow to make appropriate inferences in the way desired by their users. Models can be fully material (as plastic-and-wire models of organic molecules, or as Phillips hydraulic model of the British economy), or they can be totally abstract (at least, as abstract as mathematical equations can be, like in the case of Lotka-Volterra prey-predator model, or like the first cosmological relativistic models), or they can contain any mix of material-plus-computing machinery (as in the innumerable cases of mathematical models aided by graphic diagrams, or as the equally countless models that combine the use of computer programmes and of diverse hardware-processing and interface-devices). It is not even necessary that the model-'makers' know in detail how *it* performs the inferences it is supposed to make; this is clearly the case in the use of organism models in biology, but also in the case of deep-learning models in computer science: in these examples, the inferences the models make are not anything like 'mental' or 'abstract' operations, but are really physical *causal* processes whose *physical effects* are taken as the *consequences* of the relevant inferences.

Lastly, the problem of targetless representations is answered in the surrogate inference view just by 'switching-off' the target-model and model-target links (the first and third steps of the DDI-account), leaving them 'open' to possible future applications. Targetless models are just inferential prostheses that have not (yet) been 'attached' to a 'real system'. Their denotation-interpretation is just an open function that can be filled with a real system if and when appropriate. We can 'play' with them just to test their inferential capacities, with a pedagogical function (like 'finger exercises'), or as a representation of a non-existent by somehow 'possible' entity (like the discarded scale model of a building project, or the map of an imaginary land).

The account of models as inferential prostheses allows to understand, hence, the function of scientific models as representations in a way which is non-problematic from the philosophical point of view, and is even quasi-trivial in the sense that it shows that 'representation' is not an obscure and deep ontological relation between models and the world, but just a name for an important part of what model users *do* when they use the models: employing some elements of the model, and their formal configuration, in

---

the epistemic value of scientific theories (e.g., Zamora Bonilla 2013). The answer to that concern is that my work is not intended to be taken as a metaphysical speculation on the essential goal of scientific knowledge (or something like that), but only as a (quasi-)scientific *model* of scientists' epistemic preferences. Viewed this way, the model has to be assessed as a simplified, idealized, approximate, limited, and conjectural explanation of a small set of stylized empirical facts about how scientists evaluate their own hypotheses.

order to carry out surrogate reasonings about some real systems. This can be read as a *deflationary* theory of representation, both in the more general sense of not needing a *substantive definition* of what a representation is (beyond the fact that something is *used* to represent—i.e., to facilitate surrogate reasoning about—something else), and in the Brandomian sense of offering a merely pragmatical explication of the use of *representational vocabulary* in ordinary language (like Brandom did with the semantic concepts of truth and reference).

The near triviality with which an inferentialist theory of scientific representation permits to understand the use of representational vocabulary in the context of science makes me being more surprised of attempts aimed, not to offer an alternative theory of representation, but to dispense with all representational concepts whatsoever, like in the case of what Sanches de Oliveira calls 'radical artifactualism',[8] i.e., the project of explaining the use of scientific models as artifacts without any kind of representational function (that is, without assuming that models are models *of* something, or *about* something), but limiting ourselves to a purely 'enactive' description of the *material use* the agents make of models. I do not deny that there are lots of interesting things we can learn from the study of scientific activities from the point of view of enactivist approaches, and even from the study of the innumerable scientific practices that clearly are 'operational-but-not-representational', but I simply fail to see the point of a philosophical project that forces itself to interpret the pervasiveness (or rampantness) of representational vocabulary in science as just a misleading 'way of speaking' the poor scientists are led to use by the confounding influence of some nefarious philosophical dogmas. For me, this is as unintelligible as an attempt of explaining in enactive terms the material practices of luthiers and musicians avoiding all possible use of musical vocabulary, and interpreting the own musicians' use of that vocabulary as just the careless adoption of unsound metaphysical concepts. After all, the fact that pianos are most often made and used in order to play music with them is (at least for me) something as blatant and straightforward as the fact that the Crick-Watson model of DNA was a (better or worse) representation of the real DNA molecules of real cells, that Kepler's drawing of the elliptical orbits of the planets was a representation of their real trajectories around the sun, or that the periodic table is a representation of the types and mutual relations between the real types of chemical elements. If some *philosophical theory* of scientific representation leads its supporters to commit themselves to some outrageous or implausible metaphysical claims when interpreting this type of trivial facts, that would be a reason to doubt of the soundness of *that* theory, but not to react with the *still more implausible* opinion like that 'the Rutherford's

---

[8]Sanches de Oliveira (2022).

model of the atom was not a model *of the atom*, because nothing is a model *of anything'*. And I think that the view of scientific models and representations as instruments for surrogate reasoning allows to make philosophical sense of those trivial facts without forcing us to choose between any kind of controversial philosophical explication (either 'ontological' like Frigg and Nguyen's, or 'nihilist' like Sanches de Oliveira's) about the 'ultimate nature' of scientific representation.

5 Idealization and truth

In this last section I turn to what is perhaps the most philosophically controversial issue regarding scientific models and representations: their relation to the idea of truth. This is particularly problematic because of the also obvious fact that scientific models tend to *clearly deviate from being an accurate description* of the real systems we try to represent with them. Hence, they are in most many cases *literally false and distorted* descriptions of the world, or what we can call, following Angela Potochnik recent work on this question, 'rampant and unchecked' *idealizations*.[9] In fact, I think that one of the reasons why in the last decades both scientists and philosophers of science speak much more of 'models', rather than of 'theories' and 'laws' as their grandparents used to do, is because we have become much more aware of the fact that scientific representations tend to be ephemeral caricatures much more often than marble-engraved decrees. "Of course the real-world target systems", every scientist worth her salt would unhesitantly acknowledge, "are not *literally* like our models say they are; models are most often *extremely distorted* and *very partial* representations of their targets!". The question is, can we derive from this platitudinous fact the conclusion that, as Potochnik claims, "science isn't after truth" at all? According to her, the prevalence of un-truth in science would immediately prove that "science is not in a lockstep pursuit of truth. Instead, there are a variety of scientific aims that are in tension with one another, and the ultimate epistemic aim of science is not truth but understanding".[10]

I cannot enter here into a full discussion of the very detailed and interesting work Potochnik does on the presence in science of different types of idealizations, and of the roles of most of the 'epistemic aims' she mentions, and so my comments will probably be much more abstract, limited and general than what an exhaustive criticism of her work would demand. My main argument is that neither the widespread presence (and use) of blatant falsities in science, nor the existence of other goals different from 'literal truth', entail in any way that the pursuit of truth has to be discarded as one essential goal of the kind of practice we call 'scientific research', and

---

[9]Potochnik (2017).
[10]See esp. Potochnik (2017), pp. 90–91.

more seriously, that forcing ourselves to see science as an endeavour totally disconnected from the pursuit of true knowledge about the world prevents us to rightly understand the methods and the accomplishments of science. First of all, the inference from the premise that 'most scientific models contain radically false assumptions' to the conclusion that 'being in some relevant sense closer to the truth is not an important goal of science' is prima facie as doubtful as the inference from 'almost all human beings through history have lived in misery' to 'the pursuit of economic wealth is not an important goal for humans'. Perhaps most scientific models are indeed very far from the truth, but this does not mean that scientists would not often be happier if they knew how to replace them with some models that were substantially closer to the relevant truths. It is even conceivable that in some cases scientists may consider that the passing from some old model to a new one that is recognisably 'less true' *in all the relevant aspects* is a case of scientific progress, because other values different from 'truth' are better exemplified in the second model; but in order to show that this makes truth an *irrelevant* value in science one should have to demonstrate that this type of examples are not something occasional, but systematic, or at least, that we cannot just explain them as cases in which one of the multiples values is given preference over another value without entailing that this second value is 'unimportant'. Let's illustrate this argument with a different goal in mind, one that (though non-epistemic in nature) is obviously very important in scientific practice: *cheapness*. A research team may opt for using a calculator that is known to commit more mistakes than another one, if the second is extraordinarily more expensive than the first. From this we should not infer that exactitude in the calculations is 'not relevant at all as a scientific goal', only that, as most kind of goals human beings have, there may be trade-offs between them. Hence, we may also say that truth and understanding (or, in the terms employed a few pages above: credibility and enlightening) can be in a trade-off relation, without this entailing that some of the two goals is *irrelevant* just because the other happens to have more weight in some, or even in most cases.

Second, and more importantly, it is not even that the pursuit of (closeness to the) truth can in principle be taken as an important *goal* of science even in spite of most scientific models containing blatant falsities: I think that we can argue for the much stronger thesis that science has actually been considerably (and often spectacularly) *successful* in providing us with knowledge of the world that is substantially close to the truth, and that history shows, without the need of any kind of whiggism, that in many areas we have made a lot of progress in getting more and more detailed knowledge of the furniture and working of the world. In some cases, this may have been done even at the cost of having *less* understanding as we (thought we) had before: often what happens is that we transit from a vision of some segment of nature that provides both a neat small collection of elements and a simple explanation of its mutual interconnections, to a view that recognises the existence of a plethora of very different entities but simultaneously a much messier and less intelligible causal or taxonomic network between them (think, for example, in the evolution of the catalogues of astronomical entities, or of the groups of living beings at different levels). In cases like this, it is absurd to require scientists that they renounce to the big amounts of new mundane truths they have discovered, just because the previous vision of the field gave them a stronger feeling of 'understanding'. But, of course, in many other cases the progress in truth has fortunately gone hand in hand with a parallel progress in understanding, and we end both knowing much more things about the world, and understanding them in a more efficient way.

In the third place, I think that the (for me, rather bizarre) anti-veritist attempt of dispensing with the basically trivial claim that science has very often been considerably successful in the pursuit of truth has a similar explanation to the one I have just offered of Sanches de Oliveira anti-representationism: the confusion of the possible shortcomings of some *philosophical theories* about the nature of truth or representation, with failures in the run-of-the-mill understanding that *ordinary scientists* may have of the properties and virtues of their models *when they themselves use representational or veritistic language* to discuss a lot of things about those models and their connection with the world. In the case of Potochnik, the confusion probably derives from the supposition that the concept of 'truth' must refer to something like an absolute point-by-point metaphysical correspondence between our statements and an absolutely precise ontological scaffolding of the world in itself, or something like that, and hence, that the scientific acceptance of anything that fails to be exactly identical to such a 'literal, absolute, and eternally unchanging truth' should be considered as a refutation of the idea that scientists pursue in some interesting sense 'true knowledge about the world'. But if we understand the concept of truth *and the concept of approximate truth* in a deflationary sense,[11] as just expressive tools of ordinary scientific language (rather than as a philosophical relation—whatever that could mean—between language and the world), we can easily see that a scientific model *being successful* in the sense of being approximately true (or 'close enough to the truth' for the relevant purposes) is not something requiring an ontological analysis (probably doomed to be engulfed by conceptual paradoxes), but just one of the things real scientists *say of their models* when they evaluate them: employing a model usually consists (as we

---

[11]The simplest deflationary definition of 'approximate truth' is given by Smith (1998): *a proposition 'X' is approximately true if and only if approximately X*. Of course, it is not the philosopher, but the practicing scientist, who has to decide in each case what senses and degrees of 'approximation' are relevant.

saw above) in the *conjecture* that the causal structure of the target system is 'close enough' to the inference-permitting structure of the model, so that the inferences made with the help of the model will be 'accurate enough' when applied to the target, and the model *being successful* usually consists in the fact that this conjecture (i.e., *the conjecture that the world is 'approximately like' the model in some relevant aspects*) being 'confirmed enough' by the empirical data. Once this success has been established strongly enough in the course of empirical research, the fact that some aspects of the model are not exactly, nor even remotely, 'like' their possible 'analogues' in the target systems is in many cases no argument against the conclusion, for the original conjecture did not affirm that the world had to be *literally or exactly* like the model system in all respects, only that it was 'similar enough in the relevant ways'. Changing the discussion from whether science tries to discover a true description of the world, to whether it tries to understand real causal patterns (as Potochnik defends) does not move a millimetre the argument in favour of Potochnik's anti-veritism, for our deflationary view of truth helps us to be agnostic about the 'right transcendental stuff' the world may be made of, inviting us to concentrate just on scientists' assertions or claims, taking 'truth' as just another expressive tool with which to formulate those same assertions: if scientists *claim* that one model captures better the causal patterns of a target system than another model, then what a deflationist infers from this is that scientists consider that *it is true* that the first model captures better those causal patterns than the second, and *that's all the truth that is relevant* in the discussion about whether scientists pursue the truth or not.[12]

Hence, scientific models and scientific theories being filled with idealizations 'that radically depart from the truth' is no reason at all to put into doubt science's capacity of getting an increasingly approximate knowledge of the truth about the systems it studies, for many of these idealizations are, on the one hand, not 'mere falsities', but approximately accurate descriptions of some real things (like point-masses in astronomy may be 'accurate enough' for many purposes), and on the other hand, because even if some idealizations are not justifiable as 'approximations' in this loose sense, this does not go against the fact that the models containing them can succeed in *saying many right things about the world* thanks in part to the working of those fictional elements. Paraphrasing Teresa of Ávila, we can say that very often *science discovers the truth by means of false idealizations*.[13]

---

[12] For a more detailed argument between the connection between scientific realism and deflationism, see Zamora Bonilla (2019).

[13] I cannot finish these comments on Potochnik's book without mentioning the surprise it caused me to realize that she failed to even mention the author that has been probably most influential in promoting the idea that all interesting scientific hypotheses are basically false (and in introducing the debate on whether this fact can be nevertheless coherent

Acknowledgement. Research for this paper has benefited from the Ministerio de Ciencia e Innovación (España) research projects PID2021-123938NB-I00, PID2021-125936NB-I00 and PRX22/00154.

References

Brandom, R., 1994, *Making It Explicit: Reasoning, Representing, and Discursive Commitment.* Harvard University Press.

Brzeziński, J., et al., 1990, *Idealization I: General Problems*, Rodopi.

Donato Rodríguez, X, and J. Zamora Bonilla, 2009, "Credibility, Idealization, and Model Building: An Inferential Approach", *Erkenntnis*, 70:101–118.

Donato Rodríguez, X, and J. Zamora Bonilla, 2011, "Explanation and Modelization in a Comprehensive Inferential Account", in H. W. de Regt et al., *EPSA Philosophy of Science: Amsterdam 2009*, Springer, pp. 33–42.

Frigg, R., 2023, *Models and Theories: A Philosophical Inquiry*, Routledge.

Frigg, R., and J. Nguyen, 2020, *Modelling Nature: An Opinionated Introduction to Scientific Representation*, Springer.

Hertz, H., 1894, *Die Prinzipien der Mechanik in neuem Zusammenhange dargestellt*, Johann Ambrosius Barth.

Hughes, R. I. G., 1997, 'Models and Representation', *Philosophy of Science*, 64:325–336.

Khalifa, K., J. Millson, and M. Risjord, 2022, "Scientific Representation: An Inferentialist-Expressivist Manifesto", *Philosophical Topics*, 50:263–291

Knuuttila, T., 2011, "Modelling and representing: An artefactual approach to model-based representation", *Studies in History and Philosophy of Science, Part A*, 42: 262–271.

---

with the idea that scientists try to discover theories that are closer and closer to the truth). I'm referring, of course, to Karl Popper. Potochnik did not also refer at all to the philosophical literature on truthlikeness or verisimilitude stemming from Popper, probably disdaining it by assuming that, for those philosophers, scientific progress is "a lockstep pursuit of the truth" (which of course *it is not* what they assume). Lastly, it is equally shocking for me Potochnik's failure to even recognize the existence of the large philosophical literature on idealization elaborated from a formal point of view (see, e.g., Brzeziński et al. (1990), and all the subsequent series of volumes on idealization in the *Poznan Studies on Philosophy of Science*). It seems as if Potochnik were denying to philosophers of science what she acknowledges that scientist constantly do in a "rampant and unchecked" way: using idealized models to understand their object of study.

Morgan, M., 1999, "Learning from Models", in M. Morgan and M. Morrison (eds.), *Models as Mediators: Perspectives on Natural and Social Science*, Cambridge University Press, pp. 347–388.

Potochnik, A., 2017, *Idealization and the Aims of Science*, The University of Chicago Press.

Sanches de Oliveira, G., 2022, "Radical Artifactualism", *European Journal for Philosophy of Science*, 12:1–33.

Sellars, W., 1963, *Science, Perception and Reality*, Routledge & Kegan Paul Ltd.

Smith, P., 1998, "Approximate Truth and Dynamical Theories", *The British Journal for the Philosophy of Science*, 49:253–277.

Suárez, M., 2015, "Deflationary representation, inference, and practice", *Studies in History and Philosophy of Science, Part A*, 49:36–47.

Suárez, M., 2024, *Inference and Representation: A Study in Modelling Science*, The University of Chicago Press.

Zamora Bonilla, J., 2013, "Why are good theories good? Reflections on epistemic values, confirmation, and formal epistemology", *Synthese*, 190:1533–1553.

Zamora Bonilla, J., 2019, "Realism versus anti-realism: philosophical problem or scientific concern?", *Synthese*, 196:3961–3977.

www.ingramcontent.com/pod-product-compliance
Lightning Source LLC
Chambersburg PA
CBHW050135170426
43197CB00011B/1840